Migration Law in Serbia

Migration Law in Serbia

Second Edition

Vladimir Grečić
Vatroslav Vekarić
&
Dragoljub Todić

This book was originally published as a monograph in the International Encyclopaedia of Laws/Migration Law.

General Editors: Roger Blanpain, Frank Hendrickx
Volume Editor: Dirk Vanheule

Wolters Kluwer

Published by:
Kluwer Law International B.V.
PO Box 316
2400 AH Alphen aan den Rijn
The Netherlands
Website: www.wklawbusiness.com

Sold and distributed in North, Central and South America by:
Wolters Kluwer Legal & Regulatory U.S.
7201 McKinney Circle
Frederick, MD 21704
United States of America
Email: customer.service@wolterskluwer.com

Sold and distributed in all other countries by:
Turpin Distribution Services Ltd.
Stratton Business Park
Pegasus Drive, Biggleswade
Bedfordshire SG18 8TQ
United Kingdom
Email: kluwerlaw@turpin-distribution.com

Printed on acid-free paper

ISBN 978-90-411-8267-8

e-Book: ISBN 978-90-411-8296-8
web-PDF: ISBN 978-90-411-8312-5

This title is available on www.kluwerlawonline.com

Printed and Bound by CPI Group (UK) Ltd, Croydon, CR0 4YY.

The Authors

Prof. Vladimir Grečić, Ph.D. was born in Laznica (Serbia) in 1938. He received his Ph.D. in the field of international migration from the University of Belgrade in 1972. He had been working at the Institute of International Politics and Economics in Belgrade since 1968, as a researcher and as Assistant Director (1984–1988), and Deputy Director of the Institute (1990–1997 and 2001–2006). From 1992 to 2003, he taught Economics of Labour at the School of Economics, University of Belgrade; he was also teaching at other universities in the country and abroad. His field of interest included labour economics and labour relations, international economic relations and international law. He has published over 180 papers, studies, chapters and books in the country and abroad. He is a member of the Academy of Economic Sciences in Serbia since 2009. During his career, he was doing research abroad at several institutions in historical and other material in the field of research: in the United States (1978, 1980 in 1991, and the user Fulbright Scholarship, 1985–1986), the Russian Federation, Poland, Hungary, the Netherlands, Mexico, Great Britain, Switzerland and Australia. He also attended over hundred scientific conferences at home and over eighty abroad.

Prof. Vatroslav Vekarić, Ph.D. born 4 March 1944 in Dubrovnik (Croatia); until retirement he was Director of the Institute of International Politics and Economics, the leading Serbian research institute in the field of international law and international relations (2000–2005). He graduated from the School of Law, Belgrade University (1967), where he also obtained his master's (1973) and doctoral (1979) degrees in law. He is author of numerous books and articles in the field of international law and international relations covering various issues of international private law, international public law and human rights. Although his professional work mainly focused on research, he was also visiting lecturer in International Law and International Relations at many universities in Serbia and abroad. His professional engagements include, among others, membership in the National Bar Examination Board of Ministry of Justice – examiner in International Private Law (2008–2012), membership in the National Foreign Policy Council of the Ministry of Foreign Affairs (2008–2012), lecturing at the Diplomatic Academy of the Serbian Ministry of Foreign Affairs, managing projects and writing legal studies for UNDP, membership in the International Law Association, attending diplomatic and scientific conferences, etc.

Prof. Dragoljub Todić, Ph.D. was born in 1958 in Lopare (Bosnia and Herzegovina). He received his Doctorate and Master's Degree at the Faculty of Law of Belgrade University and the Diploma of the School of Political Sciences from Belgrade University. Currently he is employed at the Institute of International Politics and Economics, Belgrade. He was professor at the Faculty of Public Administration and Management, and Faculty of International Economics in Belgrade (2001–2012). Before that, he was engaged in the former federal state administration and was working on competent for environmental issues. His fields of interest include Environmental Law and Policy, EU Environmental Policy and Law, EU Integration, Sustainable Development, International Law, Human Rights, and Migration Law. He is a member of the Serbian International Law Association, the Serbian Association of Lawyers and several non-governmental organizations active in the environmental and European integration fields. Authored and co-authored of twelve books, two guidance publications, two dictionaries, one collection of laws and more than hundred articles and other shorter works. He has participated in a number of conferences in Serbia and abroad and in several domestic and international projects.

Table of Contents

List of Abbreviations

AFIS	Automatic Fingerprint Identification System
CoE	Council of Europe
EC	European Commission
EEA	European Economic Area
EULEX	EU Rule of Law Mission (Kosovo)
EUR	Euro
EUROPOL	European Police Office
FIIS	Facial Image Identification System
FPRY	Federal People's Republic of Yugoslavia
Frontex	European Agency for the Management of Operational Cooperation at the External Borders of the Member States of the European Union
FRY	Federal Republic of Yugoslavia
HHC	Hungarian Helsinki Committee
IBM	Integrated Border Management
ICAO	International Civil Aviation Organization
ID	Identity Document
IDP	Internally Displaced Persons
ILO	International Labour Organization
INTERPOL	International Criminal Police Organization
KFOR	Kosovo Force
NES	National Employment Service
NGO	Non-governmental organization
OSCE	Organisation of Security and Cooperation in Europe
RSD	Serbian Dinar
RSDP	Refugee Status Determination Procedure
SAA	Stabilization and Association Agreement (EU)

List of Abbreviations

SaM	Serbia and Montenegro
SFRY	Socialist Federal Republic of Yugoslavia
UNHCR	United Nations High Commissioner for Refugees
UNMIK	United Nations Interim Administration Mission in Kosovo
WHO	World Health Organization

Preface

Although Serbia has rich a history of migrations, its migration law is still in the early stages of shaping. Suffice it to say that today in Serbia legal provisions of four countries are applied: three of them were federal states in which Serbia was one of the entities and which no longer exist: (Socialist Federal Republic of Yugoslavia – SFRY, Federal Republic of Yugoslavia – FRY, State Community Serbia and Montenegro – SaM), and the Republic of Serbia. The process of European integration of Serbia and its intention to become member of the European family of nations integrated in the European Union, directed Serbia towards more emphasis upon this important branch of law. This became particularly important in view of the fact that in the recent decades an increasing number of refugees and asylum seekers were coming to Serbia – first of all those coming from the former Yugoslav republics, and more recently also from other world regions. In the recent years, Serbia has been intensively working on relevant legislation based on the theoretical and practical foundations of European law and the *acquis communautaire*. Customizing the Serbian migration law with demands of the modern times in which interstate borders should cease to be insurmountable barriers and become links and points of cooperation is one of the priorities of the modernization of the whole legal system of Serbia.

The authors' intention was to make an informative manual that would fully and accurately explain all relevant provision of Serbian migration law and, at least, indicate its theoretical benchmarks. This volume addresses the applicable legal rules relating to both immigration and emigration; however, emphasis is on immigration law. Where they have found necessary, in addition to the descriptive presentation of the applicable laws, authors have pointed out the challenges, weaknesses and shortcomings of this law. They did not hesitate to apply a critical approach and to point at certain deficiencies in the legislation in force. By doing so, they wanted to confirm the need for a more rapid harmonization of Serbian migration law with demands imposed by developments in real life of Serbia in its European surrounding. They are very much aware that it is a branch of law that is changing very dynamically and quickly. The presentation of changes in Serbian legislation takes into account the period until 1 June 2014.

General Introduction

§1. Immigration History and Statistical Information

1. Serbia is a country with a long history of emigration and immigration. Due to a turbulent history filled with wars and ethnic conflicts in the Balkan area, migration has been predominantly forced and 'irregular'. Serbia reached its territorial, political and economic apogee during the medieval reign of Emperor Dušan in the fourteenth century when the country was attractive for neighbouring ethnic groups and was predominantly a country of immigration. Emperor Dušan enacted the known *Dušan's Code*, considered an early constitution, containing an advanced set of laws, which regulated all social spheres. The Code was based on Roman-Byzantine law. The legal transplanting is notable in Articles 171 and 172 of Dušan's Code, which regulated juridical independence. Among other things, the Code granted special status to foreign communities residing in Serbia in this time (Saxons working in silver mines, merchants from Dubrovnik – Ragusa, etc.).

2. After Serbia was defeated by Turks in the Battle of Kosovo in 1389, the Balkan region found itself in between two great empires, the Ottoman and the Austro-Hungarian one. For several hundred years the boundary between these two shifted back and forth numerous times, putting the smaller regions under control of one ruler or another – and the shifting borders have led to numerous migrations and multi-ethnic grouping of people everywhere.

3. From the fourteenth century onward, due to Ottoman occupation, an increasing number of Serbs began migrating to the north to the region today known as Vojvodina, which was under the rule of the Kingdom of Hungary in that time. The Hungarian kings encouraged the immigration of Serbs to the Kingdom, and hired many of them as soldiers and border guards. Another wave of refugees from Serbia moved to the Adriatic coast.[1]

4. The Great Serb Migrations also known as the '*Great Exodus*', refers mainly to two large migrations of Serbs from the Ottoman Empire to the Habsburg Monarchy. The First Serbian Migration (1689–1692) occurred during the Great Turkish War under Patriarch Arsenije III Čarnojević, and came as a result of the Austrian retreat from Ottoman territories in the Balkans, which were temporarily held by the

1. Dragoljub Dragojlović, *Migrations of the Serbs in the Middle Ages*, in *Migrations in Balkan History* 64 (Ivan Ninić ed., Serbian Academy of Sciences and Arts 1989).

Austrians between 1689 and 1692.[2] The Second Serbian Migration took place in 1737–1739 under the Patriarch of Peć, Arsenije IV Jovanović, also in parallel with the Habsburg withdrawal from territories that they held in the Balkans, which between 1718 and 1739 were known as the Kingdom of Serbia and Banat of Temeswar. The great migrations from 1689 to 1692 and 1737–1739 brought a great number of Serbs to Habsburg territories; due to their number, the Austrian and Hungarian rulers granted them privileges to improve the status of Serbs within the Habsburg Monarchy. The Serbs that in these migrations settled in the then Austrian provinces Vojvodina and Slavonia increased the existing Serb population in these regions and made over time the Serbs an important political factor in the Habsburg Monarchy.

5. After several uprisings against the Ottoman rule, first of all those in 1804 and 1815, Serbia became autonomous within the Ottoman Empire in 1830. It became a fully independent state after the Congress of Berlin in 1878, and was declared a Kingdom in 1882. For most of the nineteenth century, Serbia was a land of immigration as many Serbs and Montenegrins, as well as other Balkan nationalities, from both the Ottoman and Habsburg lands were lured to Serbia by the prospect of land ownership. By the 1890s, however, this process was gradually reversed, so that in the twentieth-century Serbia became a country of emigration. Wars played a major role in this process.[3] However, the nineteenth century migrations were not as massive as those of two previous centuries, when huge masses of the Serbian population moved from the south to the north reaching the suburbs of Budapest. Still, the migrations of the nineteenth century, which were taking place in several waves, finally drew the ethnographic map of Serbia, although the Balkans remained an area of instability and continual change until nowadays.[4]

6. The main massive immigration flows into Serbia can be divided into several periods. First of all, during the First Insurrection (1804–1813), and Second Insurrection (1815–1830) against the Turks; then, after the Serbian-Turkish wars in 1876–1878; after the First World War; during the World War II; and during the Yugoslav crisis in the 1990s when Serbian population was forced to leave Bosnia and Herzegovina, Croatia and other republics of the former Yugoslavia.

7. In 1804, Serbia had about 368,000 inhabitants. Already in 1808, the estimates assumed that Serbia had about 600,000 inhabitants.[5] During that same period (1806–1807), a number of wealthier Serbs from Austrian areas (Srem and Slavonia), Bosnia, Southwestern Macedonia and western parts of Bulgaria moved to Serbia.

---

2. Radovan Samardžić, *Migrations in Serbian History*, in *Migrations in Balkan History* 84 (Ivan Ninić ed., Serbian Academy of Sciences and Arts 1989).
3. Serbia experienced virtual exoduses in the periods from 1912 to 1918, 1941 to 1945 and 1991 through 1995, *see* Vladimir Grečić, *The Serbian Academic Diaspora* 35 (Institute of International Politics and Economics 2013).
4. Milan St. Protić, *Migrations Resulting from Peasant Upheavals in Serbia During the 19th Century*, in *Migrations in Balkan History* 91 (Ivan Ninić ed., Serbian Academy of Sciences and Arts 1989).
5. *Ibid.* at 92.

They inhabited mostly cities and smaller towns and formed a new layer of elementary urban class: businessmen, merchants, teachers, administrators and students (First High School was founded in 1808). Massive migration has occurred from Eastern Bosnia, regions of river Lim, Novi Pazar, Niš, Leskovac and Vidin in the 1807–1813 period. However, as a result of the final breakdown of the Insurrection in 1813, about 100,000 Serbs moved to Austrian territory.

8. The process of migration of Christian population to Serbia continued during the Second Insurrection (1815–1830). In that period, Serbia numbered 43,527 persons who paid taxes (*harach*) in 1815. That number augmented to 115,885 in 1818 and by 1819 it reached 119,854. Finally, 177,427 Serbs paid dues to the Turks in 1833. Therefore, the Serbian population doubled in the 1815–1833 period.[6] Three major ethnic groups came to Serbia during that period: Christians from Bosnia, Rumeli, Macedonia, Epirus, Thessaly and Bulgaria; Tsintsars and Greeks from Turkish regions; and Vlachs and Gypsies (Roma) from Wallachia. The causes of those migrations were essentially related to the fact that Serbia of this time was a region of favourable natural and economic conditions where Prince Miloš Obrenović distributed land to all those who took Serbian citizenship. For those reasons, during the period 1815–1830, the Serbian village made substantial progress becoming the major cornerstone of Serbian economic strength. After the breakdown of the rebellion against the Ottoman rule in the city of Niš region several hundred families from Niš and surrounding areas moved to Serbia. In fact, the Serbian population grew from 678,133 in 1833 to 849,236 in 1844.[7] Another wave of migration to Serbia from the North came after revolutionary movements in Hungary which resulted in severe reprisals in the spring of 1849, when substantial number of Serbs from Vojvodina escaped to Serbia (between 20,000 and 25,000 people). The growth of the overall population in Serbia continued and reached 1,350,000 in 1874.[8]

9. The Serbian-Turkish wars 1876–1878 caused the most massive migration process in the Balkans. About 200,000 Serbs escaped from Kosovo to Serbia. After the uprising in Herzegovina in 1875, another 200,000 Serbs migrated to Serbia.[9] Migrations to and out of Serbia in the course of the nineteenth century had at least three major aspects. First, they were caused by political turmoil and upheavals. Second, those migrations were religiously coloured. Third, these population movements caused by socio-economic changes enabled the build-up of the urban class and modern society in general.[10]

10. In the second half of the nineteenth century, Serbia strengthened its statehood as the Kingdom of Serbia. It thus became part of the constellation of European states and the first political parties were founded, thus giving new momentum to political life. The 'May Overthrow' in 1903, bringing to the throne King Petar I,

6. *Ibid.* at 93.
7. *Ibid.* at 94.
8. *Ibid.*
9. *Ibid.*
10. *Ibid.* at 95.

opened the way for parliamentary democracy in Serbia. The Balkan wars 1912–1913, terminated the Turkish domination in the Balkans and that contributed to slowing down of migration movements.

11. The First World War had disastrous consequences for population and economy of the Kingdom of Serbia. Serbia in World War I had 1,264,000 casualties – 28% of its total population (4,529,000) which also represented 58% of its male population – a loss it never fully recuperated from.[11] With the end of World War I and the collapse of both the Austro-Hungarian and Ottoman Empires the conditions were met for proclaiming the Kingdom of Serbs, Croats and Slovenes in December 1918. (The name was changed to Kingdom of Yugoslavia in 1929).

12. A specific phenomenon of Serbian migration history was the mass immigration of Russians (so-called *white émigrés*) in Serbia in the wake of the Russian Revolution. The first refugees' wave from Russia due to its civil war began to appear in Serbia in late 1919 after the French evacuation of Odessa. Refugees from the Crimea and Novorossiya were taken by sea, primarily to Istanbul, Varna and Constanza. A significant portion of these people ended up settling in the Kingdom of Serbs, Croats and Slovenes.[12] According to Vladimir Maevsky, an historian of the Russian emigration and a contemporary to those events:

> Russians moved to Serbia, unhampered by quotas, visas, restrictions, passports or anything similar. A friendly country let the Russians in, not feeling constrained by the formalities that existed upon entry into other countries in Europe or America.[13]

Russian refugees opened schools in Serbia and by mid-1925; there were seventeen Russian schools with 2,820 students in the Kingdom. Russian refugees, according to the standards of the time, were very well educated and professionally trained. According to the 1922 census, the number of Russian *émigrés* in the Kingdom of Serbs, Croats and Slovenes with a higher and middle-level education was 72%. The educational level of Russian émigré group was highly unusual for Serbia, given that 50% of her entire population in 1921 over the age of twelve was illiterate.[14] The number of Russians who settled in Yugoslavia reached 70,000 in the 1920s.[15] Many engineers, lawyers, doctors, teachers, architects, scientists and other specialists were able to obtain work commensurate with their skills. Certificates of education and diplomas received before the Revolution were officially recognized. From 1920 to 1941, more than seventy Russian professors taught in six faculties at the University

---

11. Embassy of the Republic of Serbia in the USA, http://www.serbiaembusa.org/serbiatext.php?subaction=showfull&id=1197024341&archive=&start_from=&ucat=21& (accessed 9 Nov. 2013).
12. Nikita Bondarev, *Russia and Russians in Serbian History*, Part 3 (20 Jul. 2009), http://illyria.proboards.com/thread/35925 (accessed 7 August 2016).
13. *Ibid.*
14. *Ibid.*
15. Yury Azarov, *From the History of Russian Belgrade* (28 Dec. 2009), http://russkiymir.ru/en/publications/139488/ (accessed 7 August 2016).

of Belgrade and eleven of them became full members and corresponding members of the Serbian Academy of Sciences and Arts.[16]

13. The end of the Russian Diaspora in Yugoslavia began with the Second World War and the simultaneous civil war in Serbia, and later entry of Soviet troops into Yugoslav territory (1944). During the Germans' occupation of Serbia, a great number of the 'White émigrés' was interned. These factors, as well as the natural decline and the outflow of wealthy Russian émigrés from Yugoslavia in the pre-war years led to the fact that by 1945–1946, only 7,000 Russian émigrés remained.[17]

14. On 6 April 1941 the Axis powers led by Germany invaded the Kingdom of Yugoslavia and afterward divided the country. The western parts of the country together with Bosnia and Herzegovina were turned into a quisling so-called Independent State of Croatia (NDH). Most of the territory of modern Serbia was occupied by the German army and was governed by the German Military Administration in Serbia. The northern territories were annexed by Hungary, and eastern and southern territories by Bulgaria. Kosovo was mostly annexed by Albania which was under the sponsorship of fascist Italy. Yugoslavia was among the countries that had the greatest losses in World War II: 10.8% of the population. During the war many Serbs from the western parts of the former Kingdom of Yugoslavia were forced to escape to Serbia.

15. After the Second World War and the establishment of the Federal People's Republic of Yugoslavia (FPRY) (with the constitution coming into force in 1946)[18] there was an organized influx of settlers-colonists in the Serbian Autonomous Province of Vojvodina. The colonists, in fact internally displaced persons (IDPs), came from the poorest parts of Montenegro, Bosnia and Herzegovina, and Croatia. The first measure of Yugoslavia's Temporary People's Assembly was enacting the Law on Agrarian Reform on 23 August 1945.[19] Under the slogan 'land belongs to the person who works on it', the authorities seized without compensation the land of great estate owners (private owners and Churches). As a result of those measures, the state agricultural land fund of 1,611,867 hectares had been created, of which 407,037 hectares were allocated to 263,000 poor families; 336,047 hectares to 67,000 colonized families; remaining 868,783 hectares served to create the state agricultural sector.[20]

16. The Republic of Serbia in the past two decades also faced stormy and turbulent migration flows. First of all, arrival of refugees from the former Yugoslavia

---

16. *Ibid.*
17. Nikita Bondarev, *ibid.*
18. The state became the Socialist Federal Republic of Yugoslavia (SFR Yugoslavia, SFRY) in 1963.
19. Law on Agrarian Reform and Colonization, Official Journal of Federal People's Republic of Yugoslavia, No. 64/1945.
20. *Ekonomska enciklopedija* (Economic Encyclopedia), Part Two, p. 154 (Savremena administracija, Beograd, 1984); Nikola Gaćeša, *Agrarna refarma i kolonizacija u Jugoslaviji 1945-1948* (Agrarian Reform and Colonization in Yugoslavia 1945–1948), Matica Srpska (Novi Sad 1984).

and IDPs from Kosovo and the departure of a large number of citizens who emigrated to the countries of Western Europe and North America are the trends of the nineties. Besides, Serbia has also faced asylum seekers from countries in Asia and Africa, illegal migrants and returnees under the Readmission Agreement. The largest wave of immigration to and emigration from Serbia was caused by the wars in the nineties, first in Croatia, than in Bosnia and Herzegovina, in the period from 1991 to 1995.[21] Since 1991 Serbia has received the largest number of refugees and IDPs within Europe. The main arrival of refugees from Croatia, Bosnia and Herzegovina and Slovenia occurred between 1991/1992 and 1995/1996, due to war and ethnic conflicts. In 1995, after the intensive military operations in Croatia, more than 200,000 Serbs were forced to leave the areas in which they had lived since the fifteenth century, and have come to Serbia. The same process occurred from Bosnia and Herzegovina before the Dayton Peace Accords were signed by the leaders of Bosnia, Croatia and Serbia, and thus ending the four-year wars. In 1999, due to political unrest, which resulted in the territory of the Serbian Autonomous Province of Kosovo, over 200,000 persons left the Province and came to Serbia proper.

17. The first census on refugees and war-affected population in Serbia was conducted in 1996 by the United Nations High Commissioner for Refugees (UNHCR). According to data from the first census of refugees of 1996, the Republic of Serbia hosted 537,937 refugees (44% from Bosnia and Herzegovina, 54% from Croatia) and 79,791 war-affected people.[22] The number of refugees fell by more than 80% in the period between 1996 and 2010. According to data of the Serbian Commissariat for Refugees and Migrations, on 1 November 2010, there were 86,155 persons with the formal status of refugees, of which 72% were from Croatia and 28% from Bosnia and Herzegovina. The reduction in the number of refugees is largely the result of their integration in the Republic of Serbia. About 300,000 refugees have acquired the citizenship of the Republic of Serbia.[23] With 86,155 refugees and 210,148 IDPs, Serbia was the first country in Europe as regards the extent of forced migration in 2010.

18. Serbia[24] ranks alongside other small countries of immigration in the region, such as Bulgaria and Hungary. However, the number of aliens has been on the rise

21. The Socialist Federal Republic of Yugoslavia broke up in 1991/1992 in a series of wars following the independence declarations of Slovenia and Croatia on 25 Jun. 1991, and Bosnia and Herzegovina on 5 Mar. 1992. Macedonia left the federation peacefully on 25 Sep. 1991.
22. Danilo Rakić (ed.), *Challenges of Forced Migration in: Serbia: Position of Refugees, Internally Displaced Persons, Returnees and Asylum Seekers*, 11 (Group 484, Belgrade 2011).
23. *Ibid.*
24. According to the 2011 census, the population of Serbia is 7,186,862. Serbs make up to 83.32% of the population, Hungarians 3.53%, Roma 2.05%, Bosniaks 2.02%, Croats 0.81%, Slovaks 0.73%, Montenegrins 0.54%, Vlachs 0.49%, Romanians 0.41%, Macedonians 0.32, Yugoslavs 0.32%, Muslims 0.31% and other 5.16% (RSO), http://media.popis2011.stat.rs/2013/publikacije/Saopstenje29novembarKnjiga1_engl.pdf) (accessed 12 Nov. 2013).

in recent years. Serbia's anti-discrimination legislation has contributed the most to integration, as is the case in other Central European countries with similar laws.[25]

19. According to data obtained from the Serbian Ministry of Interior, a total of 7,710 aliens were permanently residing in 2012 (compared with 7,272 in the 2011), predominantly citizens from Romania (21.2%), Russian Federation (10.5%), Albania (8.9%) and Macedonia (6.6%).[26]

20. The most common ground for permanent residence in both years was marriage, and the share of other grounds was extremely small. When considering the category of aliens staying on the basis of temporary residence in the Republic of Serbia and holding temporary residence permits valid at the end of 2012, the total number of persons temporarily residing amounted to 19,912. The structure by citizenship was dominated by persons from China, followed by Russian Federation, Macedonia and Libya.

Table 1 Aliens Permanently Residing in the Republic of Serbia, According to Grounds of Settlement, in 2011 and 2012

Ground of Settlement	*2011*		*2012*	
	Number of Persons	*%*	*Number of Persons*	*%*
Stay of ten years	35	0.5	105	1.4
Stay of five years	411	5.7	472	6.1
Marriage	6,599	90.8	6,093	79.0
Humanitarian grounds	202	2.8	840	10.9
Originating from the territory of Serbia	20	0.2	200	2.6
Total	**7,267**	**100.0**	**7,710**	**100.0**

Source: Vlada Republike Srbije, *Migracioni profil Republike Srbije za 2012. godinu* (Government of the Republic of Serbia, Migration Profile of the Republic of Serbia 2012), p. 16, (Belgrade, 2013).

21. The image does not change significantly as regards the basis for stay in the Republic of Serbia as well, since the most represented permits are based on family reunification followed by work, while the number of aliens with valid residence permits on the basis of education and other reasons is rather small.

25. Thomas Huddleston, Migration Policy Group, *Serbia: a MIPEX assessment* (Grupa 484 December 2012), http://www.grupa484.org.rs/sites/default/files/Serbia%20MIPEX%20Assessment,%202013.pdf (accessed 9 Nov. 2013).
26. Vlada Republike Srbije, *Migracioni profil Republike Srbije za 2012. godinu* (Government of the Republic of Serbia, Migration Profile of the Republic of Serbia 2012) 16 (Belgrade, 2013).

Table 2 Temporary Residence Permits Valid at the End of 2012, by Citizenship

Citizenship	*Number of Persons*	*%*
Republic of China	5,763	28.94
Russian Federation	1,743	8.75
Macedonia	1,396	7.01
Libya	1,147	5.76
Romania	955	4.79
Croatia	601	3.01
Ukraine	537	2.69
Italy	535	2.68
Germany	531	2.67
Bosnia and Herzegovina	468	2.35
Greece	421	2.11
Bulgaria	405	2.03
Montenegro	356	1.78
Turkey	317	1.65
Other	4,737	23.78
Total	**19,912**	**100.00**

Source: Vlada Republike Srbije, *Migracioni profil Republike Srbije za 2012. godinu* (Government of the Republic of Serbia, Migration Profile of the Republic of Serbia 2012), p. 16 (Belgrade, 2013).

22. The National Employment Service (NES) issued a total of 2,958 work permits to foreigners in 2012, of which 98.2% to aliens with temporary residence and 1.8% to foreign nationals with permanent residence.[27] According to data obtained from the NES, the number of issued work permits indicates their steady increase since 2006 (1,699 issued permits at that period). If analysed by citizenship, among aliens with temporary residence Turkish citizens were most represented (381), followed by citizens of the Russian Federation (290). Macedonia (255), Greece (203), Bosnia and Herzegovina (199), China (194), Croatia (120) and Italy (108), while among those with permanent residence the most represented were Macedonian citizens followed by citizens of the Russian Federation, Ukraine and Romania. Most work permits to aliens were issued in Belgrade (68%), followed by Novi Sad (16%).[28] Work permits were mostly issued to skilled professionals working in foreign representative offices, banks, construction, trade, etc.

27. Vlada Republike Srbije, *Migracioni profil Republike Srbije za 2012. godinu* (Government of the Republic of Serbia, Migration Profile of the Republic of Serbia 2012) 19 (Belgrade, 2013).
28. *Ibid.* at 20.

Table 3 Temporary Residence Permits Valid at the End of 2012, According to Grounds for Approval

Ground for Approval	*Number of Persons*	*%*
Family reunification	10,248	51.46
Work	8,095	40.65
Education	1,041	5.23
Other	528	2.66
Total	**19,912**	**100.00**

Source: Vlada Republike Srbije, *Migracioni profil Republike Srbije za 2012. godinu* (Government of the Republic of Serbia, Migration Profile of the Republic of Serbia 2012), p. 16 (Belgrade, 2013).

23. Unemployed foreigners recorded by the NES are holders of temporary or permanent residence permits (approved by the Ministry of Interior). At the end of 2012, some 800 aliens were recorded by the NES, of which 18.9% were from Romania, followed by citizens from Macedonia (17.1%), the Russian Federation (11.5%), Bosnia and Herzegovina, and Montenegro (7.6%).[29] These are mostly women who married Serbian citizens. Among the unemployed aliens, 55.2% were long-term unemployed persons as they were registered as unemployed for more than twelve months. If analysed by age, most of these persons were middle aged, between 30 and 49 year old (65.6%).[30]

23.1. Over the past two years (2014 and 2015), Serbia has experienced a rapid increase in the number of migrants attempting to reach northern Europe through Serbia and in asylum seekers. According to official statistics, 5,066 people registered to seek asylum in 2013. A very large number of people sought asylum in Serbia in 2014 – 16,490, or three times more than in 2013.[31] However, only some 1,400 people were effectively registered for asylum and 400 submitted an application. Only eighteen interviews were conducted and fourteen decisions taken, resulting in eight rejections, one person granted recognition of refugee status and five people granted other forms of protection.[32]

From January 2015 to September 2015, 169,156 migrants were registered when transiting through the territory of the Republic of Serbia. Only 546 applied for asylum. In the same period, sixteen persons got asylum and fourteen subsidiary protection. Twenty-eight received a negative decision.[33] Finally, as of 11 November 2015, 404,022 migrants and refugees had entered into Serbia, most from FYR of Macedonia. The main point of registration is the *Preševo One Stop Centre*, just

29. Vlada Republike Srbije, *Migracioni profil Republike Srbije za 2012. godinu* (Government of the Republic of Serbia, Migration Profile of the Republic of Serbia 2012) 21 (Belgrade, 2013).
30. *Ibid.* at 22.
31. Lena Petrović (ed.), *Right to Asylum in the Republic of Serbia 2014* 14 (Belgrade: Belgrade Centre for Human Rights, 2015).
32. European Commission, Serbia 2015 Report, Brussels, 10, 11, 2015. SWD (2015) 211 final, p. 60.
33. European Commission, Serbia 2015 Report, Brussels, 10, 11, 2015. SWD (2015) 211 final, p. 60.

north of the border with FYROM. Average daily arrivals for the first two weeks of November were 6,343 per day.[34]

23.2. In September 2015, the Serbian government adopted a 'Response plan in the case of mass influx of migrants', which aims at managing flows of third country nationals who intend to seek asylum in the EU or in Serbia. Serbia's current accommodation capacity stands at 810 beds and through the implementation of the plan could be extended substantially. In January 2015 the Asylum Office was set up as a separate civilian unit within the border police directorate. It will be responsible for determining refugee status in the first instance. Up to twenty-nine staff are planned with nineteen positions occupied.[35]

23.3. The Ministry of Interior in 2013 formed a Project Group, mandated with reviewing and analysing the legislation and the situation in the field of asylum and issuing proposals based on which a new asylum law would be drafted. The Project Group invited the civil sector and international organizations to actively involve themselves in addressing the problems in the asylum system. It, unfortunately, stopped working after the March 2014 parliamentary elections. One still cannot qualify the asylum system in Serbia as efficient or the situation in this area as satisfactory. Although the number of asylum seekers has been growing continuously, the capacities of the relevant authorities have not been raised. The Asylum Act remains unchanged, despite the endeavours to improve it by entrusting the Ministry of Interior Project Group with amending it. Practice has shown that there are many legal lacunae and ambiguities additionally hindering the procedure for obtaining international protection because the circumstances have changed significantly since the Asylum Act was adopted. Of the 28,295 people, who have expressed the intention to seek asylum in Serbia since 2008 (when the Asylum Act came into force), only six have been granted refugee status and twelve subsidiary protection.[36] A total of 9,536 people stayed in the asylum centres from 2008 to early 2014. The asylum centres accommodated 11,118 people in 2014 alone, i.e., more than over the previous five years together.[37]

§2. Overview of National Legal Instruments

I. Historical Overview

24. History of Serbia's migration legislation is marked by the fact that the country was facing turbulent migration flows in the past two decades – both as a constituent member of a federal state (up to 2006), and as an independent state (since

34. Briefing Note Update – 17 Nov. 2015, The Balkans: Asylum Seekers, Migrants, and Refugees in Transit, http://reliefweb.int/sites/reliefweb.int/files/resources/b-acaps-start-bn-the-balkans-asylum-seekers-migrants-and-refugees-in-transit-17-nov-2015.pdf.
35. European Commission, Serbia 2015 Report, Brussels, 10, 11, 2015. SWD (2015) 211 final, p. 60.
36. Lena Petrović, *Right to Asylum in the Republic of Serbia 2014* 14 (Belgrade: Belgrade Centre for Human Rights 2015).
37. Lena Petrović, *Right to Asylum in the Republic of Serbia 2014* 20 (Belgrade: Belgrade Centre for Human Rights/Dosije studio, 2015).

2006). Following the dissolution of the SFRY, the FRY was established in 1992. It consisted of only two republics of SFRY, SaM, and its Constitution came into effect in April 1992.[38]

25. As regards issues relevant for migration legislation, the Constitution stipulated federal jurisdiction and judicial protection and common policies in matters concerning, among others, basic human rights, citizenship, border crossing and control of the circulation of goods, services and passengers across the border and the status of aliens.[39] The Constitution also stipulated that all citizens shall be guaranteed freedom of movement and residence and the right to leave and return to the FRY. The freedom of movement and residence, however, could be restricted by federal statute, if 'so required for criminal proceedings, to prevent the spread of contagious diseases, or for the defence of the FRY'.[40] According to the Constitution, aliens in the FRY may be extradited to another state only in cases provided for under international treaties which are binding on the FRY. The right of asylum was also guaranteed to foreign citizens and stateless persons.[41] An alien may acquire property rights and the right to engage in business on terms of reciprocity, in accordance with the federal statute.[42] Like SFRY legislation, the Constitution stipulated a double level of citizenship: first, basic citizenship belonging to citizens at the level of the constituent republic (Serbia or Montenegro) and, second, the 'federal' one, i.e., 'Yugoslav citizenship' belonging automatically and simultaneously to the citizens of each of its member republics.[43]

26. On 14 March 2002, the Belgrade Agreement was signed, by which the FRY would become a loose state union through the adoption of the Constitutional Charter of the State Union of SaM (*Ustavna povelja državne zajednice Srbije i Crne Gore*) replacing the FRY Constitution. The Constitutional Charter came into force on 4 February 2003 and stipulated that immigration policy, granting of asylum, the visa regime and integrated border management (IBM) – that should be in line with the standards of the European Union – remain under common jurisdiction. However, responsibility for implementation of basic international legal instruments – i.e., regulating, ensuring and protecting human rights – was transferred to the Member States in their respective territories. Simultaneously, SaM Assembly adopted the Charter on Human and Minority Rights and Civil Freedoms[44] as an integral part of the Constitutional Charter, containing more detailed regulations regarding migration matters. Thus, this Charter stipulated that every citizen shall have the right to free movement and residence anywhere in the territory of the State Union, as well

38. Constitution of the Federal Republic of Yugoslavia (*Ustav Savezne Republike Jugoslavije*), Official Gazette of the Federal Republic of Yugoslavia, No. 1/1992.
39. Article 77 of the Constitution of the Federal Republic of Yugoslavia.
40. Article 30 of the Constitution of the Federal Republic of Yugoslavia.
41. Article 66 of the Constitution of the Federal Republic of Yugoslavia.
42. Article 70 of the Constitution of the Federal Republic of Yugoslavia.
43. Article 17 of the Constitution of the Federal Republic of Yugoslavia.
44. *Povelja o ljudskim i manjinskim pravima i građanskim slobodama*, Official Gazette of the State Union of Serbia and Montenegro, No. 6/2003.

as the right to depart therefrom and return thereto. The right of asylum was confirmed. Any forcibly displaced person shall be entitled to an effective protection and assistance in the territory of SaM in accordance with SaM laws and international obligations. The State Union came to an end after Montenegro's independence referendum and the subsequent formal declaration of independence on 3 June 2006, and the Serbian parliament formally ascertained independence on 5 June. After the dissolution, Serbia was declared to be the legal successor of SaM, while Montenegro (re)applied for membership in international organizations.

27. Due to the war and the undemocratic regime, in the last decade of the twentieth century, in the period from the dissolution of Yugoslavia to the democratic changes in 2000, legislative activity in Serbia pertaining to migration was very poor. FRY and SaM applied (admittedly, slightly modified or just technically corrected) SFRY laws relating to the rights of aliens, border regime, etc. This legislation was largely restrictive and not fully adjusted to democratic principles and modern standards. While within the FRY (1992–2003) and SaM (2003–2006), Serbia applied the following laws:

- Permanent and Temporary Residence of Citizens Act.[45]
- Movement and Stay of Foreigners Act.[46]
- Crossing the State Border and Movement in the Border Area Act.[47]
- Conditions for Foreign Citizens Employment Act[48] (amended in 1994 and 1996).[49]

28. From 1992 until 2000 the only new laws related to the migration/aliens rights were:

- Refugees Act.[50]
- Yugoslav Citizenship Act.[51]
- Travel Documents of Yugoslav Citizens Act.[52]

29. Serbia's modern legal history, including her migration legislation, actually began after democratic changes in 2000 when migration management issues were

45. *Zakon o prebivalištu i boravištu građana*, Official Gazette of the Socialist Republic of Serbia, No. 42/1977.
46. *Zakon o kretanju i boravištu stranaca*, Official Journal of the Socialist Federal Republic of Yugoslavia, No. 56/1980.
47. *Zakon o prelaženju državne granice i kretanju u graničnom pojasu*, Official Journal of the Socialist Federal Republic of Yugoslavia, Nos 34/1979, 56/1980 and 53/1985.
48. *Zakon o uslovima za zasnivanje radnog odnosa sa stranim državljanima*, Official Journal of the Socialist Federal Republic of Yugoslavia, Nos 11/1978 and 64/1989.
49. Official Gazette of the Federal Republic of Yugoslavia, Nos 42/1992, 24/1994 and 28/1996.
50. *Zakon o izbeglicama*, Official Gazette of the Republic of Serbia, No. 18/1992.
51. *Zakon o jugoslovenskom državljanstvu*, Official Gazette of the Federal Republic of Yugoslavia, Nos 33/1996, 9/2001.
52. *Zakon o putnim ispravama jugoslovenskih državljana*, Official Gazette of the Republic of Serbia, No. 18/1992.

vividly debated in Serbia. It was obvious that in almost all aspects the FRY legislation did not meet international standards, which was also due to the rapidly changing forms of immigration and increasing number of refugees and IDPs. In October 2006 the citizens of the Republic of Serbia endorsed by referendum the new Constitution of Serbia (the first one after disintegration of the State Union), which constitutes the backbone for subsequent Serbian legislation regarding human rights and migration issues and relevant applicable legislation.

II. Current Applicable Legislation

30. Current applicable legislation concerning migration management in Serbia is based, first of all, on the 2006 Constitution.[53] Provisions protecting human rights – some of which refer to the rights and status of aliens and/or immigrants – are defined in Chapter II of the Constitution. Namely, Article 18 states that human and minority rights guaranteed by the Constitution should be implemented directly. The Constitution shall guarantee, and as such, directly implement human and minority rights guaranteed by the generally accepted rules of international law, ratified international treaties and domestic laws. The law may prescribe the manner in which these rights shall be exercised only if explicitly so stipulated in the Constitution, or if necessary to exercise a specific right due to its nature, whereby the law may not under any circumstances influence the substance of the relevant guaranteed right. Provisions on human and minority rights should be 'interpreted to the benefit of promoting the values of a democratic society, pursuant to valid international standards in human and minority rights, as well as the practice of international institutions which supervise their implementation'.[54]

31. Regarding the status of aliens, the Constitution states in Article 17 that foreign nationals in Serbia shall have all rights guaranteed by the Constitution and law with the exception of rights to which only the citizens of Serbia are entitled under the Constitution and law. (This refers primarily to the right of citizens to participate in political elections and the prohibition to deprive them of citizenship or expel them). The Constitution guarantees the right to free movement and residence in the Republic of Serbia, as well as the right to leave and return. Freedom of movement and residence, as well as the right to leave the Republic of Serbia, may be restricted only by law, if that is necessary for the purpose of conducting criminal proceedings, protecting public order, preventing the spread of contagious diseases or for the defence of the Republic of Serbia. Entry and stay of foreign nationals in the Republic of Serbia should be regulated by special law. A foreign national may be expelled only upon the decision of the competent body, in a procedure stipulated by the law and if time to appeal has been provided for him/her and only when there is no threat of persecution based on his/her race, sex, religion, national origin, citizenship, association with a social group, political opinions or when there is no threat of serious violation of rights guaranteed by this Constitution (Article 39). The right to asylum

53. *Ustav Republike Srbije*, Official Gazette of the Republic of Serbia, No. 98/2006.
54. *Ibid.*

is also guaranteed. Article 57 stipulates that any alien with reasonable fear of prosecution based on his/her race, gender, language, religion, national origin or association with any other group, or on his/her political opinions, has the right to asylum in Serbia. Besides, foreign natural and legal entities may obtain real estate property, in accordance with the law or international contract. They may obtain a concession right for natural resources and goods, as well as other rights stipulated by the Act (Article 85). At the legislative level, the above-mentioned aliens' rights are elaborated in the Aliens Act (2008),[55] Migration Management Act (2012),[56] Refugees Act (1992, amended 2002)[57] and the Asylum Act (2007)[58] and other laws or bylaws that will be presented below.

32. The European Union accession process has been a priority of the Republic of Serbia in the last decade. In that context the Government has elaborated a number of sectorial strategies and policies whose aim is to facilitate the harmonization of Serbian legal regulations with regulations applicable in the European Union. The most important strategic document is the National Programme for Integration of the Republic of Serbia into the European Union, containing, among other, an overview of legislative and other activities pertaining to migration management, visa policy and asylum. Strategies of the Republic of Serbia directly or indirectly concerning the field of migration management include the following:

- Migration Management Strategy.[59]
- Strategy for the Suppression of Illegal Migration in the Republic of Serbia for the Period 2009–2014.[60]
- Strategy for the Reintegration of Returnees under the Readmission Agreement Strategy.[61]
- National Strategy on Resolving the Problems of Refugees and IDPs for the Period 2011–2014.[62]
- Strategy for IBM in the Republic of Serbia.[63]
- Strategy for Combating Human Trafficking in the Republic of Serbia.[64]
- National Strategy for Improvement of the Status of Roma in the Republic of Serbia.[65]
- Strategy for the Sustainable Subsistence and Return to Kosovo and Metohija.[66]
- Strategy for Preserving and Strengthening the Relations between the Homeland and the Diaspora and the Homeland and the Serbs in the Region.[67]

55. *Zakon o strancima*, Official Gazette of the Republic of Serbia, No. 97/2008.
56. *Zakon o upravljanju migracijama*, Official Gazette of the Republic of Serbia, No. 107/2012.
57. *Zakon o izbeglicama*, Official Gazette of the Republic of Serbia, Nos 18/1992, 45/2002.
58. *Zakon o azilu*, Official Gazette of the Republic of Serbia, No. 109/2007.
59. Official Gazette of the Republic of Serbia No. 59/2009.
60. Official Gazette of the Republic of Serbia No. 25/2009.
61. Official Gazette of the Republic of Serbia No. 15/2009.
62. Official Gazette of the Republic of Serbia No. 17/2011.
63. Official Gazette of the Republic of Serbia No. 11/2006.
64. Official Gazette of the Republic of Serbia No. 111/2006.
65. Official Gazette of the Republic of Serbia No. 27/2009.
66. Official Gazette of the Republic of Serbia No. 32/2010.
67. Official Gazette of the Republic of Serbia Nos 4/2011 and 14/2011.

33. The Migration Management Strategy (2009) stipulates that the Republic of Serbia shall manage migrations in a comprehensive manner, observing the European standards in the field of migration and appreciating its own specificities. According to this document, values that are fundamental to migration management are based on the:

> safeguarding of state borders and all the citizens; respect of human rights of all groups of migrants; facilitation of integration of vulnerable migrant groups into the society; international cooperation with the countries in the region and beyond, in particular with the countries of origin; prohibition of discrimination; facilitation of family reunification; and respect of the needs of all stakeholders.

34. The adoption of the Migration Management Act (2012)[68] established a coordinated system for migration management and defined the basic concepts of migration. This Act is considered as the 'umbrella-law' expressing the basic approach of Serbia to migration issues and it was drafted in close cooperation with EU experts. The concept of migration management defined by the Migration Management Act includes the following processes: (a) Gathering and analysis of data relevant to migration management; (b) Establishing a uniform system for collecting, organizing and sharing information; (c) Identifying and proposing objectives and priorities of migration policy; (d) Proposing and taking measures for the implementation of migration policy, and (e) Coordination of state bodies, which perform tasks related to migration management. The Act also establishes new responsibilities of the Commissariat for Refugees and Migrations in the field of migration management. The Commissariat for Refugees and Migrations, which was established by the 1992 Refugees Act continued to work as the Commissariat for Refugees and Migration in accordance with the scope determined by this Act and other laws. Finally, the Migration Management Act obliges local authorities to create local councils for migration as a body which will locally conduct migration policies. A total number of 128 local governments have established local councils for migration composed of representatives of various institutions at the local level relevant to the realization of the rights of migrants, with the goal to coordinate activities of the local administration, police, employment service, school administration, local trustee, health centre, the centre for social work, the Red Cross and civil society organizations.

35. The Migration Management Act transformed the central institution for dealing with refugee and IDPs issues, the Commissariat for Refugees, into the Commissariat for Refugees and Migrations, in order to include into its competences also the care for, and integration of, asylum seekers and reintegration of returnees on the basis of readmission agreements (pertaining to Serbian citizens unlawfully residing in various European countries). The Act stipulates that the Commissariat will keep a unique register of missing persons from the time of the armed conflicts in the territory of former Yugoslavia (1991–1995) and in the territory of Kosovo in the period up to 2000, as well as the register of exhumed, identified and non-identified remains

---

68. *Zakon o upravljanju migracijama*, Official Gazette of the Republic of Serbia, No. 107/2012.

from individual and mass graves. In 2012 the Serbian Parliament ratified the Convention on the Reduction of Statelessness, which was an important symbolic step, given that Serbian legislation already had envisaged avoidance of statelessness. In March 2012 the Government of Serbia also decided to remove the administrative fee for citizens from the region (Slovenia, Croatia, Bosnia and Herzegovina, Montenegro, Macedonia, Romania, Hungary and Albania) who wish to apply either for the acquisition or termination of Serbian citizenship. This move makes it even easier for a wide group of people to acquire Serbian citizenship under less strict conditions.

36. In November 2011, the new Permanent and Temporary Residence of Citizens Act was adopted.[69] It governs the registration of permanent and temporary residence and notification of a temporary stay abroad of citizens and their return to the country. The major contribution of the Law is the possibility to register the permanent residence on a wide range of bases (property ownership/rent, spouse's address, etc.) and even to register at the addresses of a local social security centre. This is an important step towards the resolution of a pressing problem of 'legally invisible people' in Serbia who mostly belong to the Roma community, who are either not listed or not properly enlisted in registers of birth and citizens, and lack ID and travel documents. With this legislative solution, the legally invisible will now be able to be enlisted in birth registers and in citizenship registers, to obtain documents and enjoy all the rights envisaged for the citizens. This change will hopefully provide for their better protection and make the population less prone to becoming victims of organized crime, namely human trafficking.

37. The Aliens Act (2008) constitutes a basic law regulating the conditions for entry, movement and stay of foreigners, as well as the competence and activities of the public administration bodies in the Republic of Serbia in this matter. This Act is not applicable to foreigners who have applied for asylum, or have been granted asylum in Serbia, who have been granted the status of refugee and who enjoy privileges and immunities pursuant to international law. Stateless persons could be subject to the provisions of this Act only if the Convention Relating to the Status of Stateless Persons is not more favourable to them. The Act introduced important changes to the rights and status of foreigners in Serbia and related administrative rules, replacing the anachronistic and restrictive Movement and Residence of Foreigners Act (1980) from the times of the former Yugoslavia. That can be seen from the structure of the Aliens Act containing the following sections: I. Basic provisions; II. Entry of foreigners into and exit from the Republic of Serbia; III. Visas; IV. Stay of foreigners; V. Unlawful stay; VI. Forced removal; VII. Foreigner's travel documents; VIII. Identity documents (IDs); IX. Foreigner's temporary and permanent residence and personal data collection; X. Special provisions on the movement of foreigners in uniforms; XI. Registers and central database; XII. Supervision; and, XIII. Penalty provisions. The Aliens Act has been harmonized with EU standards contained in the Schengen Agreement of 14 June 1985.

---

69. *Zakon o prebivalištu i boravištu gradjana*, Official Gazette of the Republic of Serbia, No. 87/2011.

38. The manner in which certain provisions of the Aliens Act have to be implemented has been further regulated by various subsequent implementing acts. The most important among them are the following:

- Decree on More Specific Conditions for Refusal of Entry of Foreigners into the Republic of Serbia.[70]
- Rules on Visas.[71]
- Decree on More Specific Conditions and Procedure for Issuing Visas at the Border Crossing Point.[72]
- Rules on More Specific Conditions, Request Form and Manner of Extending the Visa Validity Period.[73]
- Rules on the Manner of Registering the Domicile, Residence and Change of Address and Deregistration of Foreigner from their Residence.[74]
- Rules on Meeting the Requirements for Permitting the Temporary Residence to Foreigner for the Purpose of Family Reunification.[75]
- Rules on Meeting the Requirements for Permitting the Temporary Residence to Foreigner Concerning Health Insurance.[76]
- Rules on Meeting the Requirements for Permitting the Temporary Residence to Foreigner for the Purpose of School Education, Studying or Specialization, Scientific and Research Work, Practical Training, Participation in International Exchange Programmes for School and University Students and/or Other Scientific and Education Activities.[77]
- Rules on the Manner of Entering the Compulsory Residence into the Travel Document and the Layout of Form of the Temporary Identity Card.[78]

39. The Asylum Act (2007)[79] stipulates the principles, conditions and procedure for granting and cessation of asylum, as well as the status, rights and obligations of asylum seekers and persons granted the right to asylum in Serbia. Persons submitting a valid explanation for their unlawful entry and residence to an authorized

70. *Uredba o bližim uslovima za odbijanje ulaska stranca u Republiku Srbiju*, Official Gazette of the Republic of Serbia, No. 75/2009.
71. *Pravilnik o vizama*, Official Gazette of the Republic of Serbia, No. 27/2010.
72. *Uredba o bližim uslovima i načinu izdavanja vize na graničnom prelazu*, Official Gazette of the Republic of Serbia, No. 59/2009.
73. *Pravilnik o bližim uslovima, obrascu zahteva i načinu produžavanja roka važenja vize*, Official Gazette of the Republic of Serbia, No. 59/2009.
74. *Pravilnik o načinu prijavljivanja boravišta, prebivališta i promene adrese i odjave prebivališta stranca*, Official Gazette of the Republic of Serbia, No. 59/2009.
75. *Pravilnik o ispunjenosti uslova za odobravanje privremenog boravka stranca radi spajanja porodice*, Official Gazette of the Republic of Serbia, No. 59/2009.
76. *Pravilnik o ispunjenosti uslova za odobrenje privremenog boravka stranaca u pogledu zdravstvenog osiguranja*, Official Gazette of the Republic of Serbia, No. 59/2009.
77. *Pravilnik o ispunjenosti uslova za odobravanje privremenog boravka stranca radi školovanja, studiranja ili specijalizacije, naučno-istraživačkog rada, praktične obuke, učestvovanja u programima međunarodne razmene učenika ili studenata, odnosno drugim naučno-obrazovnim aktivnostima*, Official Gazette of the Republic of Serbia, No. 59/2009.
78. *Pravilnik o načinu unošenja obaveznog boravka u putnu ispravu i izgledu obrasca privremene lične karte*, Official Gazette of the Republic of Serbia, No. 66/2009.
79. *Zakon o azilu*, Official Gazette of the Republic of Serbia, No. 109/2007.

police officer of the Ministry of Interior and filing a request for asylum without delay are exempt from misdemeanour liability for violating the legal entry regime and residing in the country. This Act was harmonized with the relevant EU Council legislation on minimum requirements for admission of asylum-seekers in state members, status of third-country citizens or stateless persons for acquisition of refugee status, i.e., persons in need of international protection and guaranteed protection services, and for provision of temporary assistance in cases of mass inflows of displaced persons.

40. Some of the most important accompanying regulations of the Asylum Act are as follows:

- Rules on Conditions for Accommodation and Provision of Basic Living Conditions in the Asylum Centre.[80]
- Rules on the Manner of Record Keeping and Contents of Registry of Persons Accommodated at the Asylum Centre.[81]
- Rules on Social Assistance for Asylum Seekers or Persons who Have Been Granted Asylum.[82]
- Rules on Contents and Layout of Asylum Application Form and Documents which May Be Issued to Asylum Seekers and Persons who Have Been Granted Asylum or Temporary Protection.[83]
- Rules on Medical Examinations of Asylum Seekers during the Admission to the Asylum Centre.[84]
- Decree on Establishing a List of Safe Countries of Origin and Safe Third Countries.[85]

41. The 1992 Refugees Act regulates the status, position and rights specifically for refugees coming from the territory of one of the republics of the former SFRY. This Act regulates the reception of refugees, their temporary accommodation and support in nutrition adequate health care and certain rights to social protection. Until the adoption of the Asylum Act in 2007 the status of refugees other than ex-Yugoslav nationals was regulated by the obsolete 1980 Movement and Residence of Foreigners Act. The 1992 Refugees Act has defined refugees as persons who have escaped from former Yugoslav republics to the territory of the Republic of Serbia due to events from 1991 to 1998 and consequences thereof, and who are unable or unwilling, due to their fear of persecution or discrimination, to return to

---

80. *Pravilnik o uslovima smeštaja i obezbeđivanju osnovnih životnih uslova u Centru za azil*, Official Gazette of the Republic of Serbia, No. 31/2008.
81. *Pravilnik o načinu vođenja i sadržini evidencija o licima smeštenim u Centru za azil*, Official Gazette of the Republic of Serbia, No. 31/2008.
82. *Pravilnik o socijalnoj pomoći tražiocima azila i osobama kojima je odobren azil*, Official Gazette of the Republic of Serbia, No. 44/2008.
83. *Pravilnik o sadržini i formi dokumenta koji se izdaje tražiocima azila i osobama kojima je odobren azil ili privremena zaštita*, Official Gazette of the Republic of Serbia, No. 53/2008.
84. *Pravilnik o lekarskim pregledima tražilaca azila za vreme boravka u Centru za azil*, Official Gazette of the Republic of Serbia, No. 93/2008.
85. *Uredba o utvrđivanju liste sigurnih zemalja porekla i sigurnih trećih država*, Official Gazette of the Republic of Serbia, No. 67/2009.

the territory they have fled; included are persons who have chosen to be integrated (namely, a person who has applied for the citizenship of Serbia).

42. Matters of citizenship have been regulated by the Citizenship Act of the Republic of Serbia (2004) and the Act on Amendments to this Act (2007).[86] The Act has introduced new rules that imply an easier and faster obtaining of Serbian citizenship. The procedure is particularly simplified and facilitated for refugees from the former SFRY republics. The 2007 amendments gave to ethnic Serbs residing outside Serbia the right to citizenship, including also Montenegrin citizens living in Serbia after Montenegro's independence in 2006. This Act and amendments thereto are based primarily on the principle of *ius sanguinis*. The law stipulates that any foreign national with Serbian descent has the right to acquire Serbian citizenship by written request. The law also tolerates dual citizenship, allowing an individual the right to retain his/her current citizenship and receive Serbian citizenship.

43. The impact of the unilateral Declaration of Independence proclaimed by the Kosovo Assembly in February 2008 remains controversial for Serbia in regard to the issue of citizenship in the territory of Kosovo. Namely, although Kosovo has been under UN protectorate since 1999, Serbia still considers Kosovo as its Autonomous Province of Kosovo and Metohija and, consequently, considers residents who meet the criteria stipulated in Serbia's Citizenship Act to be Serbian citizens. In the meantime, the Kosovo Authorities have adopted the Citizenship Act in 2008, which provides transitional provisions for the acquisition of citizenship for two groups of people. Article 28 confers citizenship on those registered as 'habitual residents' in Kosovo pursuant to UNMIK Regulation No. 2000/13. Article 29 provides citizenship to former citizens of the FRY who resided in Kosovo prior to 1 January 1998, 'irrespective of their current residence or citizenship'.

44. The State Border Protection Act of the Republic of Serbia (2008)[87] was drafted in close cooperation with EU experts and stipulates a modern system for managing the state border. Protection of the border was demilitarized, given that until then the border was monitored and controlled by military units. This Act ensures an enhanced free flow of people and goods by introducing 'integrated border management', which includes regulated cooperation of all services present at border crossings (intra- and inter-service cooperation and international cooperation) as well as other public authorities and institutions, for the purpose of 'achieving the state border that is open for movement of persons and trade and closed for any criminal or other activities jeopardizing the stability in the region' (Article 2).

45. The Criminal Code of the Republic of Serbia (2005)[88] recognizes a number of criminal offences that are relevant to different aspects of migration management.

---

86. *Zakon o državljanstvu Republike Srbije*, Official Gazette of the Republic of Serbia, Nos 135/2004 and 90/2007.
87. *Zakon o zaštiti državne granice*, Official Gazette of the Republic of Serbia, No. 97/2008.
88. *Krivični zakonik Republike Srbije*, Official Gazette of the Republic of Serbia, Nos 85/2005, 88/2005 and 107/2005.

In the group of criminal offences against the freedoms and rights of man and citizen, the following criminal offences may be relevant for migrants: *'Violation of equality'* (Article 128), *'Violation of the right to use a language or script'* (Article 129), *'Violation of the right to expression of national or ethnic affiliation'* (Article 130) and *'Violation of the freedom of religion and performing religious service'* (Article 131). As regards criminal offences against the constitutional order and security of the State, the criminal offence that should be emphasized is '*Instigating national, racial and religious hatred and intolerance*' (Article 317) among the nations and ethnic communities living in Serbia. In migration management of specific importance is the criminal offence of '*Illegal crossing of the state border and people smuggling*' (Article 350), belonging to the group of offences against public order and peace. The criminal offence of '*Human trafficking*' (Article 388) has been separated from the criminal offence of people smuggling and belongs to the group of offences against humanity and other values protected by international law. In addition to the criminal offence of human trafficking, in the group of criminal offences against humanity and other values protected by the international law the following criminal offences should be noted: '*Racial and other discrimination*' (Article 387), *'Trafficking in children for adoption'* (Article 389) and *'Holding in slavery and transportation of enslaved persons'* (Article 390). Among criminal offences against honour and reputation, the most relevant is '*Ruining the reputation due to racial, religious, ethnic or other affiliation*' (Article 174).

46. Criminal legislation did not include 'hate crime' as a separate criminal offence, but it did include a number of other offences that indirectly relate to such offence. Amendments to the Criminal Code in 2012 provided that – when a criminal offence was committed on the grounds of the victim's race or religion, national or ethnic affiliation, gender, sexual orientation – the court was to consider this as an obligatory aggravating circumstance, relevant for determining the sanction. Besides, amendments to the Criminal Code (2009) have introduced stricter penalties for human trafficking, especially when committed against minors.

47. Laws of interest, particularly in the field of migration matters, are also: Conditions for Foreign Citizens Employment Act (1978),[89] and Aliens Employment Act (2014);[90] General Administrative Procedure Act;[91] Police Act (2005);[92] Permanent and Temporary Residence of Citizens Act (2011);[93] and, Travel Documents Act (2007).[94] For issues regarding the human rights of migrants relevant are the Discrimination Prohibition Act (2009)[95] and the Ombudsman Act (2005).[96]

---

89. *Zakon o uslovima zasnivanja radnog odnosa sa stranim državljanima*, Official Journal of the SFR Yugoslavia, Nos 11/1978 and 64/1989, Official Gazette of the Federal Republic of Yugoslavia, Nos 42/1992, 24/1994 and 28/1996, and Official Gazette of the Republic of Serbia, No. 101/2005.
90. *Zakon o zapošljavanju stranaca*, Official Gazette of the Republic of Serbia, No. 128/2014.
91. *Zakon o opštem upravnom postupku*, Official Gazette of the Republic of Serbia, No. 111/2009.
92. *Zakon o policiji*, Official Gazette of the Republic of Serbia, No. 101/2005.
93. *Zakon o prebivalištu i boravištu građana*, Official Gazette of the Republic of Serbia, No. 87/2011.
94. *Zakon o putnim ispravama*, Official Gazette of the Republic of Serbia, No. 90/2007.
95. *Zakon o zabrani diskriminacije*, Official Gazette of the Republic of Serbia, No. 22/2009.
96. *Zakon o zaštitniku gradjana*, Official Gazette of the Republic of Serbia, No. 79/2005.

48. In order to assess the quality and the weaknesses of Serbia's currently applicable immigration law it is helpful to look at the National plan for adoption of the *acquis communautaire*, which has been harmonized with the suggestions of the EU Commission and the Council of Europe's (CoE's) Venice Commission in the context of the forthcoming opening of negotiation on Serbia's membership in the European Union. According to the *National plan for the adoption of the acquis (2013–2016)*,[97] one of the most important priorities in the field of immigration law is drafting amendments to the Serbian immigration legislation in order that the following regulations of the European Union are transposed into national legislation to the greatest possible extent:

- Council Directive 2003/86/EC on the right to family reunification.
- Council Directive 2003/109/EC concerning the status of third-country nationals who are long-term residents.
- Council Directive 2005/71/EC on a specific procedure for admitting third-country nationals for the purpose of scientific research.
- Council Directive 2004/114/EC on the conditions of admission of third-country nationals for the purposes of studies, pupil exchange, unremunerated training or voluntary service.
- Council Directive 2009/50/EC on the conditions of entry and residence of third-country nationals for the purposes of highly qualified employment.
- Council Directive 2002/90/EC defining the facilitation of unauthorized entry, transit and residence.
- Directive 2009/52/EC of the European Parliament and of the Council providing for minimum standards on sanctions and measures against employers of illegally staying third-country nationals.[98]

III. Administrative and Judicial Authorities

49. As the field of migration management is multisectoral in character, and the competences in this field are, therefore, divided between several authorities within public administration. The relevant institutional framework is defined in line with the competences of the respective public administration authorities, pursuant to the Law on Ministries, Migration Management Act, Aliens Act, Asylum Act, Refugees Act and corresponding bylaws. They include different ministries and state bodies responsible for particular issues or groups of migrants, whose competences are described below.

50. The Ministry of Interior (*Ministarstvo unutrašnjih poslova*) is responsible for: security of the state border and control of border crossing; movement and stay within the border zone; stay of foreigners; citizenship; residence and domicile of citizens; identity cards and travel documents; international assistance and other

97. European Integration Office of the Government of the Republic of Serbia, *National Plan for the Adoption of the Acquis 2013-2016* (Belgrade, February 2013).
98. *Ibid.* at 441–442.

forms of international cooperation in the field of internal affairs, including readmission; illegal migration; asylum and administrative proceedings in the second instance pursuant to regulations on refugees.

51. Ministry of Foreign Affairs (*Ministarstvo spoljnih poslova*) is responsible for: protection of rights and interests of the Republic of Serbia, its citizens and legal entities abroad; issuance of visas through the diplomatic-consular network, providing the adequate consent previously obtained from the Ministry of Interior; keeping electronic an database of the issued and denied visas; and issuance of travel documents free of charge to Serbian citizens, victims of human trafficking, who have been rescued abroad.

52. The Ministry of Labour, Employment and Social Policy (*Ministarstvo rada, zapošljavanja i socijalne politike*) is competent for the protection of citizens employed abroad; conclusion of agreements on referring the employees to work abroad and referring the employed to temporary employment abroad; keeping records in the field of labour and employment; anti-discrimination policy; exercise of rights and integration of refugees and displaced persons, returnees under the readmission agreements, Roma population and other socially vulnerable groups; taking part in preparation, conclusion and enforcement of international treaties on social insurance; employment in the country and abroad; conclusion of employment contracts with foreign employers and other contracts related to employment; and harmonization with the European legislation and standards in the field of employment and monitoring of enforcement of international conventions.

53. The Ministry of Health (*Ministarstvo zdravlja*) is responsible for taking part in preparation and implementation of international treaties on mandatory social insurance and health care of foreigners.

54. The Commissariat for Refugees and Migrations (*Komesarijat za izbeglice i migracije*), is of particular importance, being responsible for: carrying out the expert and other tasks related to providing care, return and integration of persons who were granted the status of refugees; establishing the status of a refugee and keeping records of refugees and IDPs; providing care to refugees; harmonizing the assistance efforts by other entities and organizations in the country and abroad; provision of accommodation and distribution of refugees across the area of local units; provision of assistance to refugees in the process of refugee return and reintegration; resolving the housing needs of refugees; provision of accommodation to asylum seekers in the asylum centre and the asylum centre management; provision of primary accommodation in redesigned collective centres to returnees under the Readmission Agreement; providing care to IDPs and protection of their rights, etc.

55. The Office of Human and Minority Rights (*Kancelarija za ljudska i manjinska prava*) is the governmental body responsible for performance of expert tasks for the Government and competent ministries related to: protection of human rights and providing assistance to vulnerable migrant groups, such as refugees and displaced persons, returnees under readmission agreements and asylum seekers; monitoring harmonization of the national legal framework with international treaties and EU standards and initiating changes in the national legal framework; providing assistance to vulnerable migrant groups, particularly when it comes to returnees returning to the country under the readmission agreements.

56. The Council for Integration of Returnees under the Readmission Agreements (*Savet za integraciju povratnika po osnovu sporazuma o readmisiji*) is responsible for: considering and proposing the measures and activities for the implementation of admittance, provision of care and integration of returnees; providing support in establishing and implementation of measures at the local self-government level aimed at offering assistance to returnees; proposing the framework for a dialogue between countries concerning the issues of protection and exercise of the rights of migrants and problems associated with the illegal migration, etc.

57. The Council for Combating Human Trafficking (*Savet za borbu protiv trgovine ljudima*) is responsible for: coordination of national and regional activities in combating human trafficking; considering the reports of relevant international bodies on human trafficking; taking stands and proposing measures for implementation of recommendations by international bodies in combating human trafficking.

58. The Commission for Monitoring the Visa-Free Travel Regime with the European Union (*Komisija za praćenje bezviznog putnog režima sa Evropskom unijom*) is responsible for considering the issues related to the increase in the number of false asylum seekers in the countries of the European Union coming from the territory of Serbia and proposing considerations and decision-making to the Government as regards the measures focused on reducing the number of false asylum requests.

59. All decisions of the ministries and governmental bodies are subject to judicial review by the Administrative Court of the Republic of Serbia (*Upravni sud*). Appeals or other legal remedies filed against the decisions of the Administrative Court are dealt with by the Supreme Court of Cassation of the Republic of Serbia (*Vrhovni kasacioni sud*) who decides on regular and extraordinary legal remedies instituted against decisions of all courts in Serbia. If the procedure violated constitutional rights of the individual, a constitutional appeal may be filed to the Constitutional Court (*Ustavni sud*). According to Article 170 of the Constitution of Serbia, a constitutional appeal may be lodged against individual general acts or actions performed by state bodies or organizations exercising delegated public powers which violate or deny human or minority rights and freedoms guaranteed by the Constitution, if other legal remedies for their protection have already been applied or not specified. Migration legislation frequently refers to the jurisdiction of misdemeanour courts. There are forty-five Misdemeanour Courts (*Prekršajni sudovi*) in Serbia having a broad jurisdiction over various administrative offences and less serious criminal cases.

60. The Ombudsman as an independent state institution was introduced into the Serbian legal system by the Ombudsman Act in 2005.[99] Its status was confirmed by the 2006 Constitution – Article 138 lays down that the Ombudsman is an independent administrative body which safeguards the rights of citizens and controls the activities of the bodies of government administration and organizations, companies and institutions entrusted with the exercise of public powers. Anyone who believes that his/her right has been violated by unlawful or irregular acts or the lack of acts by administrative authorities or public services, may address the Ombudsman, including aliens and stateless persons.

§3. Overview of International Legal Instruments

61. Serbia is signatory to most UN and CoE's legal instruments relating to immigration, free movement and human rights. Many of them were ratified already by SFR Yugoslavia (1945–1992) and/or Kingdom of Yugoslavia (1918–1943), and Serbia acceded to them by succession. When over viewing currently applicable international agreements in Serbian legal practice one should observe that on 28 June 2013 the European Council endorsed the Council of Ministers' conclusions and recommendations to open accession negotiations with Serbia, and announced that they would commence by January 2014 at the latest. At the moment of this writing Serbia was close to opening negotiations with the EU within which the harmonization of Serbian legislation to the *acquis communautaire* is of particular importance; this process will have a crucial impact on Serbian migration management. It should be said that Serbia has already adopted parts of *acquis* pertaining to migration management during negotiations with the European Union on visa liberalization until 2009. According the Serbian Constitution, generally accepted rules of international law and ratified international treaties are considered an integral part of the legal system in the Republic of Serbia and are applied directly.[100] Consistently, the courts are applying the above-mentioned legal instruments directly perceiving them as Serbian internal law.

I. United Nations/League of Nations

62. Serbia ratified the following United Nations and/or the League of Nations conventions and protocols with relevance to the status and fundamental rights of migrants:

- Convention to Suppress the Slave Trade and Slavery (League of Nations, entered into force 1927).

99. *Zakon o zaštitniku gradjana*, Official Gazette of the Republic of Serbia, Nos 79/2005 and 54/2007.
100. Article 16 of the Constitution of the Republic of Serbia, Official Gazette of the Republic of Serbia, No. 116/2007.

- International Convention for the Suppression of the Traffic in Women and Children (League of Nations, ratification date: 28 February 1929).
- International Convention for the Suppression of the 'White Slave Traffic' (League of Nations, entered into force: 1929).
- Convention for the Suppression of the Traffic in Persons and of the Exploitation of the Prostitution of Others (UN, ratification date: 28 December 1950).
- Supplementary Convention on the Abolition of Slavery, the Slave Trade, and Institutions and Practices Similar to Slavery (UN, ratification date: 14 January 1958).
- Convention Relating to the Status of Refugees (UN, ratification date: 29 September 1959).
- Convention Related to the Status of Stateless Persons (UN, entered into force: 6 June 1960).
- International Convention on the Elimination of All Forms of Racial Discrimination (UN, entered into force: 1 June 1967).
- Additional Protocol on the Status of Refugees of 1967 – 'New York Protocol' (UN, ratification date: 11 October 1967).
- Convention on the Elimination of All Forms of Discrimination against Women (UN, entered into force: 11 November 1967).
- UN International Covenant on Civil and Political Rights (UN, ratification date: 30 January 1971).
- Convention on the Rights of the Child (UN, ratification date: 18 December 1990).
- Convention against Torture and Other Cruel, Inhuman or Degrading Treatment or Punishment (UN, ratification date: 20 June 1991).
- Amendment to Article 43, paragraph 2, of the Convention on the Rights of the Child (UN, ratification date: 26 June 1997).
- Optional Protocol to the International Covenant on Civil and Political Rights (UN, ratification date: 22 June 2001).
- Second Optional Protocol to the International Covenant on Civil and Political Rights, Aiming at the Abolition of the Death Penalty (UN, ratification date: 22 June, 2001).
- Protocol against the Smuggling of Migrants by Land, Sea and Air, supplementing the United Nations Convention against Transnational Organized Crime (UN, ratification date: 6 September 2001).
- Optional Protocol to the Convention on the Rights of the Child on the Sale of Children, Child Prostitution and Child Pornography (UN, ratification date: 2 July 2002).
- Protocol to Prevent, Suppress and Punish Trafficking in Persons, especially Women and Children, supplementing the United Nations Convention against Transnational Organized Crime (UN, entered into force 25 December 2003).
- Convention on the Protection on the Rights of All Migrant Workers and Members of Their Families (UN, signed: 11 November 2004).
- Optional Protocol to the Convention against Torture and other Cruel, Inhuman or Degrading Treatment or Punishment – OPCAT (UN, ratification date: 1 December 2005).
- Convention on the Reduction of Statelessness (UN, signed: 7 December 2011).

II. Council of Europe

63. Serbia joined the CoE on 3 April 2003, but even before joining had signed and ratified a number of CoE conventions and protocols related to the status and fundamental rights of migrants. Ratification of remaining CoE's legal instruments relevant for migration management followed afterward. Following is the list of all ratified documents:

- European Convention on Extradition (date of ratification: 30 September 2002; entered into force: 29 December 2002).
- Additional Protocol to the European Convention on Extradition (date of ratification: 30 September 2002; entered into force: 29 December 2002).
- European Convention on Mutual Legal Assistance in Criminal Matters (date of ratification: 30 September 2002; entered into force: 29 December 2002).
- Convention on the Transfer of Sentenced Persons (date of ratification: 30 September 2002; entered into force: 1 January 2003).
- First Additional Protocol to the European Convention on Mutual Legal Assistance in Criminal Matters (date of ratification: 23 June 2003; entered into force: 21 September 2003).
- Additional Protocol to the Convention on the Transfer of Sentenced Persons (date of ratification: 30 September 2002; entered into force: 1 January 2003).
- European Convention for the Protection of Human Rights and Fundamental Freedoms (date of ratification: 3 March 2004).
- Protocol No. 2 to the Convention for the Protection of Human Rights and Fundamental Freedoms concerning the possibility of the European Court of Human Rights to provide advisory opinions (date of ratification: 3 March 2004).
- Protocol No. 3 to the Convention for the Protection of Human Rights and Fundamental Freedoms which are changed on 29, 30 and 34 Convention Article (date of ratification: 3 March 2004).
- Protocol No. 4 to the Convention for the Protection of Human Rights and Fundamental Freedoms, securing certain rights and freedoms other than those already included in the Convention and in the first Protocol thereto (date of ratification: 3 March 2004; entered into force: 3 March 2004).
- Protocol No. 5 to the Convention for the Protection of Human Rights and Fundamental Freedoms which are changed 22nd and 24 Convention Article (date of ratification: 3 March, 2004).
- Protocol No. 6 to the Convention for the Protection of Human Rights and Fundamental Freedoms, concerning the abolition of the death penalty (date of ratification: 3 March 2004).
- Protocol No. 7 to the Convention for the Protection of Human Rights and Fundamental Freedoms (date of ratification: 3 March 2004; entered into force: 6 January 2004).
- Protocol No. 8 to the Convention for the Protection of Human Rights and Fundamental Freedoms (date of ratification: 3 March 2004; entered into force: 3 March 2004).

- Protocol No. 11 to the Convention for the Protection of Human Rights and Freedoms, amending the control system established by the Convention (date of ratification: 3 March 2004; entered into force: 3 March 2004).
- Protocol No. 12 to the Convention on the Protection of Human Rights and Fundamental Freedoms (date of ratification: 3 March 2004; entered into force: 1 April 2005).
- Protocol No. 13 to the Convention on the Protection of Human Rights and Fundamental Freedoms, concerning the abolition of the death penalty in all circumstances (date of ratification: 3 March 2004; entered into force: 1 July 2004).
- Protocol No. 14 to the Convention on Human Rights and Fundamental Freedoms, amending the control system established by the Convention (date of ratification: 9 June 2005; entered into force: 9 June 2005).
- Convention for the Protection of Individuals with regard to Automatic Processing of Personal Data regarding supervisory authorities and trans-border data flows (date of ratification: 9 June 2005; entered into force: 1 January 2006).
- Additional Protocol to the Convention for the Protection of Individuals with regard to Automatic Processing of Personal Data regarding supervisory authorities and trans-border data flows (date of ratification: 9 June 2005; entered into force: 1 January 2006).
- Second Additional Protocol to the European Convention on Mutual Legal Assistance in Criminal Matters (date of ratification: 26 April 2007; entered into force: 1 August 2007).

64. The Republic of Serbia has signed, but not ratified, the following Conventions and Protocols of the CoE:

- Convention on Action against Trafficking in Human Beings (signed: 16 May 2005).
- Convention on the Protection of Children against Sexual Exploitation and Sexual Abuse (signed 25 October 2007).
- First Additional Protocol to the Convention on the Protection of Individuals with regard to Automatic Processing of Personal Data, regarding supervisory authorities and the trans-border data flows (signed: 2 February 2008).

III. International Labour Organization (ILO)

65. As one of the successors to SFR Yugoslavia, Serbia applies also the following conventions of the ILO:

- Convention No. 97, Migration for Employment Convention (date of ratification: 5 November 1962).
- Convention No. 143, concerning Migrations in Abusive Conditions and the Promotion of Equality of Opportunity and Treatment of Migrant Workers (date of ratification: 1 December 1980).

IV. Hague Conference on Private International Law

66. Serbia applies the following conventions of the Hague Conference on Private International Law relevant to migration matters:

- Convention Abolishing the Requirement of Legalization for Foreign Public Documents of 5 October 1961.
- Convention on the Service Abroad of Judicial and Extrajudicial Documents in Civil or Commercial Matters of 15 November 1965.
- Convention on the Civil Aspects of International Child Abduction of 25 October 1980.
- Convention on International Access to Justice of 25 October 1980.

67. Serbia has access to, but has not signed, the following conventions of the Hague Conference on Private International Law:

- Convention relating to the settlement of the conflicts between the law of nationality and the law of domicile of 15 June 1955.
- Convention on the law applicable to maintenance obligations towards children of 24 October 1956.
- Convention concerning the powers of authorities and the law applicable in respect of the protection of infants of 5 October 1961.
- Convention on Protection of Children and Co-operation in Respect of Intercountry Adoption of 29 May 1993.

V. European Union

68. Serbia and the European Union signed on 18 September 2007 the Agreement on the Readmission of Persons Residing Without Authorisation (Agreement on Readmission). The Serbian Parliament ratified this Agreement on 7 November 2007, and it entered into force on 1 January 2008. This Agreement defines obligations of Serbia and the EU with respect to persons subject to readmission, either as regards readmission of their own nationals or readmission of third-country nationals and stateless persons. At the request of EU Member States, Serbia has pledged to accept – without additional formalities other than those stipulated by this Agreement – any person not meeting conditions in force for entry, temporary or permanent residence in the territory of an EU Member State which has submitted a readmission application, provided that it has been proved or it may be validly assumed, on the basis of prima facie evidence furnished, that the said person is the citizen of Serbia. The Agreement also specifies cases in which Serbia is obliged to accept readmission of a third-country national or stateless person (for instance, if that person is in possession of a valid visa or residence permit, issued by the Republic of Serbia, or if he/she directly and unlawfully entered the territory of the European Union, after having resided in or transited through the territory of Serbia). Serbia should also readmit nationals of the former SFR Yugoslavia who have acquired no other citizenship and whose place of birth and domicile, on 27 April

1992, was in the territory of Serbia. On the other hand, the EU Member State shall readmit, at the request of Serbia, any person who does not meet conditions in force for entry, temporary or permanent residence in the territory of Serbia, provided that it has been proved or it may be validly assumed, on the basis of prima facie evidence furnished, that the said person is the citizen of the respective Member State.

69. Following the conclusion of the Readmission Agreement with the EU, Serbia signed protocols on the implementation of the Agreement with several EU Member States. By the end of 2012, Serbia had signed such protocols and bilateral Readmission Agreements with Austria, Bulgaria, Croatia, Belgium, Denmark, Estonia, France, Germany, Great Britain, Hungary, Italy, Luxembourg, Malta, Netherlands, Slovakia, Slovenia, Sweden and Romania. Serbia signed readmission agreements also with the following non-EU countries: Albania, Bosnia and Herzegovina, Canada, Macedonia, Norway and Switzerland.

70. The Readmission Agreement with the European Union was a precondition for liberalization of the visa regime for Serbia's citizens travelling to the Schengen area that came into effect on 19 December 2009. The EU Commission set up a post-visa-liberalization monitoring mechanism to assess whether the implementation of reforms introduced by Serbia was consistent and sustainable. This was complemented by an alert mechanism to prevent abuses.

Part I. Border Control and Entrance

Chapter 1. Organization of Border Control

§1. General Framework

71. The Republic of Serbia borders seven states: Hungary, Romania, Bulgaria, Macedonia, Albania, Croatia, and Bosnia and Herzegovina. Total length of the state frontier of the Republic of Serbia is 2351.8 km. Length of the border with neighbouring countries is: to Hungary 174.7 km; to Romania: 547.9 km; to Bulgaria: 360.4 km; to Macedonia: 283 km; to Albania: 113.4 km; to Montenegro: 249.5 km; to Bosnia and Herzegovina: 363 km; and, to Croatia: 259 km. Border crossings and border security on the border of Kosovo with Albania and part of the border with the Republic of Macedonia are controlled performed by members of the North Atlantic Treaty Organization (NATO) military units Kosovo Force (KFOR), stationed in Kosovo in accordance with UN Security Council Resolution 1244.

72. There are seventy-one border crossings open in the territory of Serbia, out of which sixty are for international traffic (thirty-six road, eleven railway, three airports, and ten river crossings), eight for local cross-border traffic, two for interstate traffic, and one border crossing is for exceptional traffic.

73. As mentioned above, border control in Serbia is based on the Strategy for IBM in the Republic of Serbia adopted in 2006.[101] The State Border Protection Act of the Republic of Serbia (2008)[102] stipulates a modern system for IBM which ensures regulated cooperation of all agencies operating at the border crossings in order to achieve the openness of the borders for the movement of people and trade, and to close the borders for all criminal and other activities that threaten stability in the region. The concept of IBM, already functioning elsewhere, has been developed in the Western Balkans by the European Commission (EC) and is defined in the 'Guidelines for Integrated Border Management in the Western Balkans'.[103] The IBM strategy of the Republic of Serbia closely follows these guidelines and focuses on main services with responsibilities related to the border: the Ministry of Interior

101. Official Gazette of the Republic of Serbia, No. 11/2006.

102. *Zakon o zaštiti državne granice*, Official Gazette of the Republic of Serbia, No. 97/2008.

103. *Guidelines for Integrated Border Management in the Western Balkans, Updated Version*, Document of the European Commission (EC) (January 2007), http://ec.europa.eu/enlargement/pdf/financial_assistance/cards/publications/ibm_guidelines_en.pdf (accessed 12 Sep. 2013).

– border control, the Ministry of Finance and Economy – customs administration, Ministry of Agriculture, Forestry and Water Management – phytosanitary and veterinary border inspection.

74. According to the EU Commission 2013 Serbia Progress Report which assesses Serbia's achievements in the process of accession to the EU, the IBM strategy was revised in November 2013 to enhance the implementation capacity of the coordination body. Serbia has continued to improve the infrastructure and equipment at border crossing points by completing the installation of an immigration and case management system and increasing operational field equipment (special cameras, scanners, fingerprint capturing devices and detection devices). Operational biometric system solutions at borders, such as the existing Automatic Fingerprint Identification System (AFIS) and Facial Image Identification System (FIIS), have also been upgraded. Also, Serbia has been increasingly involved in joint activities with the European Agency for the Management of Operational Cooperation at the External Borders of the Member States of the European Union (Frontex) and the Western Balkans Risk Analysis network.[104]

§2. Organization

75. Border police (Border Guard) are highly centralized and hierarchically organized at the central, regional and local level. At the central level, the work of the Border Police is coordinated and managed by the Ministry of Interiors' Border Police Directorate which performs activities related to regular control of border crossing, to securing the state borders and to measures to suppress cross-border crime. It has direct responsibilities related to the movement and stay of aliens and, among other, it is participating in procedures of acknowledging asylum.

76. The internal organization of the Directorate seems to be rather 'over-institutionalized' and bureaucratized. The Directorate has the following departments:

- Department for Borders, in charge of the organization and control of border crossing and of border security; it includes the subdivisions 'Border Crossing Control', 'Border Surveillance' and 'Monitoring of Specific Aspects of International Traffic'.
- Department for Aliens, responsible for the status of foreign nationals legally entering and residing in Serbia, as well as for control of movement and status of all foreign nationals in the Republic of Serbia. The department includes subdivisions 'Acceptance and Accommodation of Aliens' and 'Asylum'.
- Department for Combating Trans-border Crime and Criminal Intelligence.
- Department for International Cooperation.

---

104. *Serbia 2013 Progress Report*, p. 49. Commission Staff Working Document SWD (2013) 412 final in *Enlargement Strategy and Main Challenges 2013–2014*, Communication from the Commission to the European Parliament and the Council COM (2013) 700 final (Brussels, 16 Oct. 2013).

– Department for Development of IBM.
– Duty Centre.

77. The Border Police Directorate is responsible for the work of eight regional centres and eighty-two border police stations. Published are phone numbers and the e-mail address to which citizens have access 24/7 to complain about malfunction and treatment by border police and/or to promptly provide any information and data related to any kind of illegal activities across the border.

Chapter 2. Right to Enter the Country

§1. Conditions for the Right to Enter

78. Basic conditions for entry into Serbia are defined in the State Border Protection Act and in the Aliens Act. Border control includes control of persons and travel documents, vehicles and objects in the zone of a border crossing point or immediately after crossing of the state border, as well as other controls of the flow of people, goods, services, vehicles, animals and plants across the state border. An alien is obliged to undergo the border control procedure for entry into or exit from Serbia. The border police should perform border protection in compliance with the competences determined by the above-mentioned legislation.[105]

79. When performing these tasks, a border police officer is authorized to check travel documents or other necessary documents required for crossing of the state border, to establish the identity of persons and perform identity checks in specified records. He/she may also take fingerprints and palm prints as well as other biometric data of entering persons if there is suspicion regarding their identity, i.e., validity of a travel document or other document required for border crossing. The border police must check whether a person fulfils entry/exit requirements regarding the Republic of Serbia; they must also verify the travel document or other document prescribed for crossing of the state border, the data on entry/exit, as well as data on denied entry into the country, data on bringing into the country weapons and ammunition and transit thereof, and perform other relevant checks regarding the person's travel purpose. If the person cannot be checked in any other way, such person may be submitted to personal examination and search.[106]

80. The border police officer is also authorized to detain a person for a period of time necessary to perform proper, unhindered and quick control. He/she may request persons who cross the state border to show items and objects which they carry with them or in the vehicle, and may examine these items and objects and also the interior and exterior of the vehicle; he/she may also perform specified record checking in the event of suspicion that the person who is crossing the state border is transporting hidden persons or banned objects and items in his/her vehicle.[107]

81. When performing state border protection tasks a police officer is obliged to use powers, measures and activities only for attaining lawful purposes. When applying these measures, a police officer must not cause damage disproportionate to the objective for which they were used. Powers, measures and activities may be applied by a police officer only until the objective for which they have been employed is achieved or until it is established that the objective cannot be achieved by means of this particular power or ordered measure.[108]

---

105. Article 5 of the State Border Protection Act.
106. Article 6 of the State Border Protection Act.
107. Article 6 of the State Border Protection Act.
108. Article 7 of the State Border Protection Act.

82. The border police may control persons, vehicles and objects, in accordance with the law, outside the zone of a border crossing point, on public roads and facilities, for the purpose of preventing and detecting illegal migration and repressing cross-border criminal activities. Such control is performed only for security reasons and is based on relevant knowledge of competent security services or other state authorities, with the aim of detecting and apprehending perpetrators of such criminal offences. Under conditions prescribed by law, border controls may be performed outside the zone of a border crossing point in trains, aircrafts and vessels and during their movement outside the zone of a border crossing point, in accordance with international agreements.[109]

83. If due to specific circumstances a border control cannot be thoroughly performed because of unacceptable waiting periods for the crossing of the border or other deviations in traffic at the border crossing, the border police may temporarily order partial suspension of border controls. In certain situations, border police may apply minimum border control measures, which include identity control and reliable validity control of persons who are crossing the state border.[110]

84. The police officer responsible for the organization and management of border controls should lay down priority objectives. These must be adapted to concrete safety conditions, in order to achieve maximum effective border control. Entry border controls have priority over exit border checks.[111]

85. Temporary border crossing points may be designated by decision of the minister responsible for internal affairs, with consent of the ministers responsible for financial and foreign affairs and the competent authority of the neighbouring state, if this is necessary for implementation of short-term events and activities: cultural, scientific, sport, religious and tourist, for performing agricultural works, economic activities and other activities in compliance with the international agreement, performing of natural disaster exercises as well as redirection of traffic across the state border.[112]

§2. Administrative Procedures and Documents

86. An alien may enter into and stay in the Republic of Serbia, under conditions stipulated by the Aliens Act.

87. Basic requirements for the entry into Serbia are:

- Valid passport/travel document.
- Valid visa in the passport, if a Serbian visa is required for passport holders of the respective country.

109. Article 9 of the State Border Protection Act.
110. Article 29 of the State Border Protection Act.
111. *Ibid.*
112. Article 15 of the State Border Protection Act.

- Proof of sufficient funds for staying in Serbia. Sufficient funds are considered to be 50 EUR per day of stay, proved by possession of the appropriate amount in cash, bank statement, traveller's cheques, credit cards or a letter of guarantee.
- Certificate of vaccination or a note that he/she has not contracted a contagious disease despite coming from an area affected by a pandemic, as defined by the information of the Ministry of Health.

88. If underage children are travelling with one of their parents, it is necessary to submit a relevant certified authorization by the other parent; or, if the child is travelling with a third person, such authorization is required from either the parents or the guardian;

89. It is recommended to have a health insurance for the period of stay in Serbia, covering possible medical costs to the amount of not less than 20,000 EUR.

90. The Aliens Act defines a valid travel document as a foreign travel document that includes the personal, family, collective, diplomatic or service passport, seaman's book containing a visa and other documents recognized by international treaties as travel documents, which may be used to reveal the identity of its holder, the term of validity of which has not expired and which has been issued in accordance with the regulations of a foreign country or an international organization. Valid travel documents are also a refugee travel document, a stateless person's travel document and the alien's laissez-passer.[113]

91. The alien using a collective travel document shall only be allowed to enter into and exit from Serbia if they travel together. Aliens listed in a collective travel document may also be required to have a document with their personal photograph. The leader of the group should have his/her ordinary personal travel document. An alien listed in the travel document of another person may enter into and exit from Serbia only if accompanied by the person in whose travel document he/she is listed.[114]

92. The Border police may, given a justified interest in compliance with the international agreement, i.e., with consent of the competent authority of the neighbouring state and in agreement with the competent customs office, at request of a group of persons or individuals, issue a cross-border permit for crossing of the state border beyond regular border crossing points, in terms of either location or operating hours. A cross-border permit is issued to certain persons and is valid up to one year. A cross-border permit shall be taken away in case of abuse or if the reasons for its issuance cease to exist.[115]

93. The crossing of the state border of Serbia is verified with stamp, as follows: to the Serbian citizens upon exiting the country, and at their request upon entering

113. Article 3 of the Aliens Act.
114. Article 9 of the Aliens Act.
115. Article 12 of the State Border Protection Act.

Serbia; and to foreign nationals only upon entering. The police officer is obliged to issue a certificate to persons who cross the state border with an identification card, at their request, as proof of entering, i.e., exiting the country.[116]

94. With the purpose of more efficiently performing the state border protection tasks, the border police are authorized to collect personal data from persons subject to exercise of powers of the border police, and to enter these data into records and process them. Recordings of personal data collected with the help of devices and means shall be destroyed within five years from the date of recording, unless they are required for persecuting a criminal offence or misdemeanour.[117]

95. Border police must keep records of the following persons:

- Persons subject to border control.
- Persons that are denied crossing of the state border.
- Persons subject to identification procedure.
- Persons issued with cross-border permits and cards for crewmembers of foreign vessel, train or aircraft, where they do not have the necessary visa, for the period in which vessel, train or aircraft are staying in the zone of a border crossing point.
- Persons whose application for permit issuance was rejected, or their permit was taken away.
- Members of foreign security services, to whom approval was issued to enter Serbia, i.e., whose entry into the Republic of Serbia was announced.
- Persons to whom identification cards were issued for movement and stopping in the zone of the border crossing point.
- Persons who violated the state border.
- Persons who had announced hunting activities, i.e., fishing activities along the border line.
- Persons with issued approval for bringing into and carrying out from the country of weapons and ammunition.

96. The Serbian government adopted on 2 June 2011 the Decree regulating the exercise of police powers by border police officers and duties of persons crossing the state border;[118] this Decree empowers the border police to ask Serbian citizens to show apart from a valid passport – if travelling to a country of the Schengen area – also the evidence of the purpose of travel and of sufficient funds for their stay in this area. Given the high number of asylum seekers from Serbia (mostly Roma population) in the countries of the Schengen zone, the purpose of this additional test is to prevent abuse of the visa-free regime for Serbian citizens in Schengen area.

116. Article 30 of the State Border Protection Act.
117. Article 61 of the State Border Protection Act.
118. *Uredba o bližem uređivanju načina vršenja policijskih ovlašćenja policijskih službenika granične policije i dužnostima lica koje prelazi državnu granicu*, Official Gazette of the Republic of Serbia, No. 39/2011.

97. Given that Serbian authorities do not administer border crossings between Kosovo and Macedonia, Kosovo and Montenegro, and Albania and Kosovo, entry stamps from these border crossings are considered null and void by the Serbian authorities. If the alien has entered Kosovo via one of these border crossings (or via the Kosovo capital Pristina airport) and intends to proceed to Serbia, he/she will be denied entry at the administrative crossing and he/she needs to leave Kosovo and enter Serbia via one of the 'regular' border crossings with Macedonia or Montenegro where Serbian border police cancels any Kosovo entry/exit stamps. However, although Serbia officially does not recognize Kosovo as an independent state, the EU-sponsored negotiations on the normalization of relations (2011–2013) led to the conclusion of the Serbia–Kosovo Agreement on the introduction of the concept of IBM. According to this Agreement, permanent border checkpoints will be established on the Kosovo/Serbia 'administrative line' (de facto border line) and Kosovo and Serbian customs and police officers will work under one roof once the agreement becomes operational. Until the full application of this Agreement, Serbian border police still applies the Government's *Decree on Control of Crossing of the Administrative Line with the Autonomous Province of Kosovo and Metohija*,[119] which regulates border-crossing, movements and stay on the borderline and administrative measures that may be taken against individuals who act contrary to this Decree. The Decree stipulated movement of persons and trade only through eleven specified checkpoints.[120] (*see more*: Part I, Chapter 2, §4)

§3. Visa Regime of Serbia

98. According to the Aliens Act, an alien may enter into and stay in the Republic of Serbia using a valid travel document containing a visa (if Serbian visa is required for passport holders of the respective country), or a permission to stay. Visa is defined as a 'permission of entry, stay or transit obtained by an alien prior to entering the territory of the Republic of Serbia'.[121] In other words, visas are required if the alien comes from a country that is not exempted from the visa-requirement and if the stay is a short one. If the stay is a long one, the alien must obtain a residence permit granted for the particular purpose of the stay.

99. Entry into and stay in the Republic of Serbia without a visa is possible only in the case that an international treaty or a Government decision establish that citizens of particular countries may enter the Republic of Serbia without a visa, provided that there are no obstacles for entry referred to in Article 11 of this Act (reasons for denial of entry are presented in the next Chapter). Citizens of such countries may enter Serbia using a valid personal identity card, and/or other document which can confirm their identity and citizenship. An alien who does not need

---

119. *Uredba o kontroli prelaska administrativne linije prema Autonomnoj pokrajini Kosovo i Metohija*, Official Gazette of the Republic of Serbia, No. 98/2011.
120. Depče, Končulj, Dobrošin, Breznica, Muhovac, Medevče, Sponce, Merdare, Rudnica, Tabalije – city of Novi Pazar and Vučja Lokva – Odojević - city of Novi Pazar.
121. Article 14 of the Aliens Act.

a visa to enter Serbia may stay in the country for a maximum period of ninety days, within a timeframe of six months starting from the day of the first entry.

100. Visa is required for holders of emergency travel documents and travel documents for refugees and aliens of all countries. Nationals from states with which the Republic of Serbia has no diplomatic relations need visas for entering the country.

101. The general rule is that a visa should be issued by a diplomatic mission or consular office of Serbia. Exceptionally, when there are serious humanitarian reasons or 'it is in the interest of the Republic of Serbia', the border police may, with consent of the Interior Ministry, issue a transit visa for a single transit, or a visa for a short stay for a single entry with the term of validity of up to fifteen days, when an alien has had no opportunity to apply for a visa via a Serbian diplomatic mission or consular office, provided he/she presents adequate proof of urgency of the trip for which he/she needs the visa.[122] According to the Decree on More Specific Conditions and Procedure for Issuing Visas at the Border Crossing Point, 'serious humanitarian reasons' and urgency of the trip exist if an 'emergency medical assistance or intervention is needed, if humanitarian aid is transported over the territory of Serbia and if immediate presence of an alien in Serbia for personal, professional or other reasons is needed'.[123]

102. Aliens Act recognizes four types of visas: airport transit visa (type A visa); transit visa (type B visa); short stay visa (type C visa) and temporary residence visa (type D visa).[124]

103. Airport transit visa (type A visa) is issued exceptionally and may be required from aliens if this is found necessary due to 'reasons related to protection of public order or safety of the Republic of Serbia and its citizens', or pursuant to an international treaty. Otherwise, an alien who does not leave the international transit area of airports or the aircraft during the intermediate stop between two legs of a flight or between connecting flights shall not need a visa.[125]

104. A transit visa (type B visa) is issued to an alien for a single or multiple transit through the territory of Serbia with the term of validity of up to six months, and the duration of stay in the country per one transit shall not exceed five days. A transit visa may be issued to an alien who has the visa for entry into the destination country or the country through which he/she is transiting if his/her obligation to have that visa is not abolished by an international treaty.[126]

---

122. *Ibid.*
123. *Uredba o bližim uslovima i načinu izdavanja vize na graničnom prelazu*, Official Gazette of the Republic of Serbia, No. 59/2009.
124. Article 15 of the Aliens Act.
125. Article 16 of the Aliens Act.
126. Article 17 of the Aliens Act.

105. A short stay visa is issued for the purpose of tourism, business and other travelling for a single or multiple entry. The duration of an uninterrupted stay, and/or the total duration of successive visits of an alien with a short stay visa must not exceed ninety days within a period of six months which starts on the day of the first entry. A short stay visa with the multiple entry option is issued with the term of validity of up to one year; however, it may also be issued with a longer term of validity.[127]

106. A temporary residence visa implies issuing of the permission for the alien to enter into and temporary reside in the Republic of Serbia. It may be issued for the purposes of work, employment, business, enrolling to a school or university, family reunification, etc. (For conditions for obtaining temporary residence in Serbia *see* Part II, Chapter 3, §1). This type of visa is necessary if an alien intends to stay more than ninety days in Serbia.[128]

107. The general rule is that a visa's term of validity is not extendable. As an exception, visa's term of validity may be extended if so required by humanitarian, professional or personal reasons and force majeure, given that elaborated conditions and the procedure for extension of the visa validity term in the mentioned circumstances are prescribed by the minister competent for interior affairs.[129]

108. According to the Aliens Act the authority competent for issuing visas shall not issue a visa if: (a) the term of validity of a foreign travel document expires in less than ninety days; (b) any of the already mentioned obstacles referred to in Article 11 of the Aliens Act exist, and (c) if an alien fails to present himself/herself when summoned by a diplomatic mission or a consular office. There is no right of appeal against the decision to refuse one's application for visa or to cancel a visa, and such a decision is not requiring a statement of grounds.[130]

109. It is possible to extend a visa expiration date (for a period of up to ninety days) in exceptional cases, namely if required by humanitarian, professional or personal reasons. Visa expiration date may be extended upon explicit foreign citizen's request submitted to a relevant authority of the Ministry of the Interior, competent for aliens' affairs according to the place of temporary residence of the foreign citizens.

110. Citizens of 28 European Union member countries and Schengen countries Switzerland, Norway and Iceland may enter and stay in Serbia without a visa for up to ninety days every six months. Moreover, they do not need to present passports at border checkpoints, but just their national ID card.[131] No visa is required to stay in Serbia up to ninety days also for citizens of the following countries: Albania,

127. Article 18 of the Aliens Act.
128. Article 19 of the Aliens Act.
129. Article 20 of the Aliens Act.
130. Article 21 of the Aliens Act.
131. Given that Denmark, Iceland, Norway, Ireland and the United Kingdom do not issue ID cards to their citizens, this rule currently does not apply to them and they enter Serbia with passports.

Andorra, Argentina, Australia, Bolivia, Bosnia and Herzegovina,[132] Brazil, Canada, Chile, Costa Rica, Cuba, Holy See, Israel, Japan, South Korea, Lichtenstein, Macau, Macedonia, Mexico, Monaco, Montenegro,[133] New Zealand, San Marino, Seychelles, Singapore, Tunisia, Turkey, United Arab Emirates, United States and Uruguay. No visa is required for a stay of up to thirty days for citizens and holders of ordinary passports of Belarus, Hong Kong,[134] Kazakhstan, Russia and Ukraine.

111. Pre-arrival visa is required for citizens of the following sovereign countries and dependent territories: Afghanistan, Algeria, Angola, Antigua and Barbuda, Armenia, Azerbaijan, Bahamas, Bahrain, Bangladesh, Barbados, Belize, Benin, Bhutan, Botswana, Brunei, Burkina Faso, Burundi, Cambodia, Cameroon, Cape Verde, Central African Republic, Chad, China, Colombia, Comoros, Democratic Republic of Congo, Congo, Djibouti, Dominica, Dominican Republic, Ecuador, Egypt, El Salvador, Equatorial Guinea, Eritrea, Fiji, Gabon, Gambia, Georgia, Ghana, Grenada, Guatemala, Guinea, Guinea-Bissau, Guyana, Haiti, Honduras, India, Indonesia, Iran, Iraq, Ivory Coast, Jamaica, Jordan, Kenya, Kiribati, North Korea, Kuwait, Kyrgyzstan, Laos, Lebanon, Lesotho, Liberia, Libya, Madagascar, Malawi, Malaysia, Maldives, Mali, Marshall Islands, Mauritania, Mauritius, Federal States of Micronesia, Moldova, Mongolia, Morocco, Mozambique, Myanmar, Namibia, Nauru, Nepal, Nicaragua, Niger, Nigeria, Oman, Pakistan, Palau, Palestine, Papua New Guinea, Paraguay, Peru, Philippines, Qatar, Rwanda, Saint Kitts and Nevis, Saint Lucia, Saint Vincent and the Grenadines, Sao Tome and Principe, Saudi Arabia, Senegal, Sierra Leone, Solomon Islands, Somalia, South Africa, South Sudan, Sri Lanka, Sudan, Suriname, Swaziland, Syria, Taiwan, Tajikistan, Tanzania, Thailand, Timor-Leste, Togo, Tonga, Trinidad and Tobago, Turkmenistan, Tuvalu, Uganda, United Kingdom overseas territories Anguilla, Bermuda, British Virgin Islands, Cayman Islands, Montserrat, Saint Helena, Turks and Caicos Islands, Uzbekistan, Vanuatu, Venezuela, Vietnam, Samoa and Yemen

112. Citizens of the following countries must have visas with the permit of stay up to thirty days, with the necessary presentation of a voucher or invitation letter at the border crossing: Armenia, Azerbaijan, China (business only), Georgia, Kyrgyzstan, Mongolia (business only), North Korea (business only), Tajikistan, Tanzania and Turkmenistan.

113. According to the EU Commission 2013 Serbia Progress Report which assesses Serbia's achievements in the process of accession to the EU, as regards Serbian visa policy, a unified visa information system which would allow a swift exchange of information among the authorities is still lacking. The list of countries for whose citizens a visa is required has yet to be fully aligned with the *acquis communautaire*.[135] Serbian Government stated, in its response to the EU Questionnaire regarding a timeline for the alignment of Serbia's visa regime with EU Regulation

132. Citizens of Bosnia and Herzegovina may enter Serbia with an ID card only.
133. Citizens of Montenegro may enter Serbia with an ID card only.
134. Up to fourteen days.
135. Serbia 2013 Progress Report, *ibid.* at 50.

539/2001,[136] that visa introduction for particular countries – those still on the EU *negative list* regarding visas – is determined by the pace of Serbia's integration into the European Union. According to the Government:

> this means that Serbia will align its legislation with EU *acquis* in phases; namely, the visa regime will be fully aligned with the above Regulation at the time of opening the issue of Serbia's membership in the EU, in the same way as it was done by other states in the process of their becoming full members of the EU.[137]

113.1. Interconnection of the integrated Serbian Visa Information System with diplomatic and consular missions and other relevant databases has yet to be completed. The list of countries for which visas are required has not been fully aligned with the *acquis*. On implementation of the visa-free regime with the EU, Serbia continued to take measures to address the phenomenon of unfounded asylum applications lodged by Serbian nationals in EU Member States and Schengen associated countries. Border controls and surveillance were stepped up and twelve criminal charges for facilitating the abuse of the right to asylum in a foreign country were filed. The high number of unfounded asylum applications filed by Serbian citizens in EU Member States and Schengen-associated countries continues to be a problem as the total share of applications from Serbian citizens to the top five targeted destinations in 2014 is close to 44% (around 18 847 out of the total 42 840).[138]

§4. Boundary/Border Regime between Serbia and Kosovo and Related Issues

114. Residents of Kosovo who meet the requirements according to Serbia's Citizenship Act, may apply for the Serbian passport, which is issued by the Serbian Coordination Directorate, the authority responsible for issuing Serbian passports to citizens residing in Kosovo. The UN administration of the province (UNMIK) is issuing its own travel document which is recognized by a number of countries. Serbian authorities do not recognize the validity of the UN issued document, or the passport of Kosovo.

115. In the framework of normalization talks mediated by the European Union, governments of Serbia and Kosovo reached on 24 March 2012 in Brussels the Agreement on IBM provided that Kosovo recognizes the border line as a 'border' and Serbia as an 'administrative boundary'. The two parties agreed, in line with the

136. Council Regulation (EC) No. 539/2001 of 15 Mar. 2001 listing the third countries whose nationals must be in possession of visas when crossing the external borders and those whose nationals are exempt from that requirement, Official Journal of the European Communities L 81/1, Brussels, 21 Mar. 2001.
137. *Responses of the Government of Serbia to the EU Questionnaire*,. http:/www. responses_to_the_eu_commission_questionnaire2011.zip – ZIP archive, unpacked size 33.247.408 bytes (accessed 17 Oct. 2013).
138. European Commission, Serbia 2015 Report, Brussels, 10, 11, 2015. SWD (2015) 211 final, p. 61.

Lisbon Treaty and relevant EU legislation[139] (and given that both parties are part of the EU's Western Balkans agenda), to gradually harmonize their legislation with the *acquis communautaire*, and in particular to apply the concept of IBM.

116. Basic provisions of this Agreement are as follows:

- The parties intend gradually to set up joint integrated posts at all their common IBM crossing points. This cooperation will follow the best European practice as it is progressively further developed by the EC. The work will be given a high priority; the projects will be identified jointly and will be implemented as soon as practically possible.
- The joint, integrated, single and secure posts will be located within a 'common area of IBM crossing points', jointly delineated, where officials of each party carry out relevant controls. Exceptionally, and limited to the common IBM areas, the parties will not display symbols of their respective jurisdictions.
- The arrangements will include a balanced presence, in line with requirements, from both parties of all related services such as customs, police, etc. and will cover matters such as the location of the crossing points, the nature of the facility, opening hours, etc. In line with, and for the duration of its mandate[140] at the crossing points will be present EU Rule of Law Mission (Kosovo) (EULEX)[141] officials.
- At the core of the arrangement there will be a clear assignment of applicable legal responsibilities and liabilities to each party's jurisdiction.[142]

117. The fact that Serbian authorities do not recognize IBM as border crossings poses a problem for foreign citizens who travel from Kosovo to Serbia. They are only allowed to cross into Serbia from Kosovo if their first point of arrival was through official crossings with Serbia. This rule excludes citizens of Bosnia and Herzegovina, Montenegro, FYR Macedonia and all EU countries since those countries have agreements with the Government of Serbia to freely travel in Serbia only with the ID cards. Citizens of other countries have ninety days to re-enter Serbia from Kosovo as long as they have entered Kosovo via Serbia and have not left and re-entered Kosovo from any other country.

118. Previously, within the same normalization process, Serbia and Kosovo reached on 2 July 2011 in Brussels an Agreement on Freedom of Movement. The most important provisions of this Agreement are the follows:

- Residents of each party should be able to travel freely within or through the territory of the other.

139. As defined especially in the Schengen Borders Code, Frontex Regulation, Local Border Traffic Regulation, VIS Regulation and Community Code on Visas.
140. As defined by Council Joint Action 2008/124 CEFSP, Art. 3, s. a.
141. EU Rule of Law Mission (Kosovo).
142. Serbian Government, The Agreements reached in Belgrade-Pristina Dialogue with EU Mediation (Vlada Republike Srbije, Sporazumi postignuti u dijalogu sa Prištinom uz posredovanje EU), http://www.srbija.gov.rs/kosovo-metohija/index.php?id=82315 (accessed 16 Nov. 2013).

- Each party will apply, as soon as operationally feasible, an ID card system for cross border/boundary travel of residents from the other party.
- Each party may apply a system whereby ID cards will be accompanied by written 'entry/exit' documents (travel waiver) for persons from the other party who wish to transit to a third country.
- As an interim solution, each party will enable residents of the other to purchase border/boundary insurance. Under the auspices of the EU, the parties will continue to work for a commercial arrangement on mutual vehicle insurance cover so that all vehicles are covered on both sides of the border/boundary as soon as possible.
- Each party will take all necessary measures to enable residents of the other party to travel freely within or through the territory of the other using driving licenses issued by their own authorities.
- As an interim measure, the authorities in Kosovo will extend the validity of Kosovo vehicle license plates for an initial period of five years at the end of which the issue will be reviewed by the two parties (with the facilitation by the EU if required).
- As an interim measure, the authorities in Belgrade will enable vehicles from Kosovo bearing Kosovo vehicle license plates to travel freely in or through its territory.
- As an interim measure, for every car owner who so wishes, temporary vehicle license plates will be made available at the relevant border/boundary crossings.
- With regard to readmission, and taking account of Kosovo's obligations in this area, the arrangements agreed above will not create new obligations for Serbia to accept readmission requests for persons holding Kosovo documents within the context of the existing readmission agreement between Serbia and the EU.[143]

119. The Freedom of Movement agreement became fully operational in May 2013. It was especially important for Kosovo residents who got the opportunity to travel to or through Serbia with ID cards issued by the Government of Kosovo, which was not the case before.

120. The Government of Serbia on 15 September 2009 adopted the Decree on Procedure for Determining Fulfilment of the Requirements for the Issuance of Passports to Citizens of Serbia from the territory of Kosovo and Metohija.[144] According this Decree, citizens of Serbia who have registered permanent residence in the territory of Kosovo and the citizens possessing the citizenship certificate issued by the competent authorities of Serbia for Kosovo can obtain a new Serbian biometric passport[145] in the Special Coordination Directorate of Serbian Interior Ministry, based in Belgrade. However, for these people, EU Council Decision 1244/2009 on

---

143. *Ibid.*

144. *Uredba o postupku utvrdjivanja ispunjenosti propisanih uslova za izdavanje pasoša za lica sa područja AP Kosovo i Metohija*, Official Gazette of the Republic of Serbia, No. 76/2009.

145. Serbian Travel Documents Act, which came into force on 9 Oct. 2007, adopted standards imposed by European regulations and standards of the International Civil Aviation Organization (ICAO), requiring introduction of biometric travel documents with the integrated photo and 'read-only zone'. Use of new biometric passports began on 7 Jul. 2008.

visa liberalization for Serbia[146] is not applicable and for travelling to EU countries they must possess an appropriate valid visa.

146. Council Regulation (EC) No. 1244/2009 of 30 Nov. 2009 amending Regulation (EC) No. 539/2001 listing the third countries whose nationals must be in possession of visas when crossing the EU external borders and those whose nationals are exempt from that requirement, Official Journal of the European Communities L 336 18 Dec. 2009.

Chapter 3. Refusal of Entry

§1. Reasons for Refusal of Entry

121. Possession of a visa and a valid passport, or residence permit, does not automatically mean that an alien will be allowed entry into Serbia. Even if an alien is fulfilling these requirements, his/her entry may be refused. Reasons for denying entry into Serbia to an alien are regulated by the Aliens Act and elaborated in more detail in the Decree on More Specific Conditions for Refusal of Entry of Foreigners into the Republic of Serbia.[147]

122. According to the Aliens Act, the first reason why an alien may be refused entry into the Republic of Serbia is the case when he/she does not possess a valid travelling document or visa (if necessary). Moreover, not possessing a document prescribed for crossing the state border is considered as a misdemeanour that may be fined from RSD 5,000 to 50,000 or up to thirty days' imprisonment.[148] Attempt of entry by use of someone else's or a false travelling or other document is considered unlawful (illegal) entry in Serbia[149] that may be treated as a misdemeanour or criminal offence, depending on the circumstances.

123. Entry into Serbia may be refused to an alien if he/she does not have sufficient funds to support themselves during their stay in Serbia, or to return to their country of origin or transit to a third country, or have no other way to ensure subsistence during their stay. This requirement is fulfilled if an alien offers proof to the competent authority of having the means of subsistence in the amount of EUR 50 per day of stay. Proof of sufficient funds can be the cash in an appropriate amount, bank statement, traveller's checks, credit cards and a letter of guarantee. These rules are not applicable to aliens who are invited by foreign diplomatic missions or international organizations to provide economic, humanitarian and other assistance to the Republic of Serbia.[150]

124. Further reason for denial of entry to an alien is the situation when the alien is in transit but he/she does not meet the requirements for entry into the third country. What occurs most often is that aliens in transit have no regular visa to enter their country of destination. Border officer will refuse entry also to an alien when a protective measure of expulsion or security measure of deportation is in force against him/her, or his/her residence permit was cancelled, or if 'another measure was recognized in internal or international law that includes a prohibition to cross the state border – for the duration of such measure'.[151]

---

147. *Uredba o bližim uslovima za odbijanje ulaska stranca u Republiku Srbiju*, Official Gazette of the Republic of Serbia, No. 75/2009.
148. Article 65 of the Protection of the State Border Act of the Republic of Serbia.
149. Article 10 of the 2009 Alien Act.
150. *Uredba o bližim uslovima za odbijanje ulaska stranca u Republiku Srbiju*, Official Gazette of the Republic of Serbia, No. 75/2009.
151. Article 11 of the Aliens Act.

125. Specific reasons for denial of entry to an alien are related to health issues. Namely, entry will be refused if an alien coming from the area affected by an epidemic of infectious disease and does not have a certificate of vaccination or other evidence of good health, in accordance with the regulations on the protection of the population against contagious diseases. Such a situation will be determined by the data available to the ministry responsible for health, based on the report of the World Health Organization (WHO). Moreover, an alien coming from countries affected by an epidemic of contagious disease, or from gatherings of high epidemiological risk, although having needed certificates, may be placed under medical supervision if any of these diseases may threaten the health of the population.[152]

126. An alien may be refused entry into Serbia for reasons pertaining to protection of public order or security of the state and its citizens.[153] According to the interpretation offered in the Decree on More Specific Conditions for Refusal of Entry of Foreigners into the Republic of Serbia, the competent authority may refuse the entry to an alien if it finds that his/her stay could violate public order or security. Such a decision should be based on data obtained from security services which suggest that the entry and stay of the alien could represent an unacceptable security risk. Entry may be rejected if an alien is a member of associations whose objectives and activities are prohibited by the Constitution and laws of Serbia, ratified international agreements and generally accepted rules of international law; if there is a reasonable suspicion that the alien is a member of an association or a person in touch with associations in other countries whose activities are illegal and/or subversive and are directed against the interests of the Republic of Serbia, or if he/she participates in, or is a member of, paramilitary organizations. Based on data from the records of the security services, the competent authority also may refuse an alien to enter Serbia – in accordance with ratified international legal instruments – where the alien is participating in financing, planning, preparing, executing or supporting terrorist activities against other States or their citizens or in such activities of organized cross-border crime, or is part of a group or network that deals with this type of crime.[154] Entry of an alien may be refused also if he/she is indicated in the relevant records (International Criminal Police Organization (INTERPOL), European Police Office (EUROPOL) and others) as an international felon.[155]

127. Finally, a specific reason for denying an alien to enter Serbia as stipulated by the Aliens Act is a 'reasonable doubt that he/she shall not use his/her stay for the intended purpose'.[156] In other words, border police may refuse entry to an alien if they get the impression that the purpose of the aliens' trip was not the one that was

---

152. *Ibid.*
153. *Ibid.*
154. Article 5 of the Decree on More Specific Conditions for Refusal of Entry of Foreigners into the Republic of Serbia (*Uredba o bližim uslovima za odbijanje ulaska stranca u Republiku Srbiju*), Official Gazette of the Republic of Serbia, No. 75/2009.
155. Article 11 of the Aliens Act.
156. *Ibid.*

declared, or if they have reasonable doubts that the alien is simulating a legitimate stay and intends to use it for undeclared or unclear purposes. The meaning of this provision was the subject of lively discussions and different interpretations among legal experts at the time of drafting of the Aliens Act. The main objection of some of the experts was that the term 'reasonable doubt' is not enough precise and that such a provision gives excessive powers to the border police. Finally, it was concluded that the proposed provision exists in the laws of the majority of other states, and has survived as such. In the Decree on More Specific Conditions for Refusal of Entry of Aliens into the Republic of Serbia there were no additional explanations or interpretations of this provision.

128. The refusal of entry should be marked in the alien's passport and recorded in the relevant register. If an alien manages to enter the country in spite of this measure, his/her entry is considered unlawful. Other instances of unlawful entry regulated by the Aliens Act are:

- entry beyond the place and time determined for crossing of the state border;
- entry by avoiding border control;
- entry by use of someone else's, unlawful, i.e., false travelling or other document;
- entry by giving false data to border police;
- entry in the course of duration of protective measure of expulsion.

129. A foreign national who has unlawfully entered or unlawfully resides in Serbia, or who does not leave the country within the specified deadline, may be forcibly removed from the country by the competent authority. However, it is forbidden to forcibly remove an alien to a territory where there is a fear of his/her persecution on the grounds of race, gender, language, religion, nationality, membership in a particular social group or his/her political opinion. An alien also must not be forcibly removed to a territory where there is a risk that he/she would be subjected to torture, inhuman or degrading treatment or punishment.[157]

§2. Temporary Refusal of Exit from Serbia

130. An alien is free to exit Serbia respecting usual procedure of identity control at the border checkpoint. As an exception to this general rule, the border police are entitled to temporarily deny exit of Serbia to an alien in three cases:

- if he/she is in possession of another person's, invalid, and/or forged travel or other document;
- if he/she does not have the visa required to enter the next country;

157. Article 10 of the Aliens Act.

– if there is justified suspicion that, by exiting the Republic of Serbia, the person may escape legal prosecution with respect to a criminal act or misdemeanour, avoid serving the sentence of imprisonment or execution of a court order, avoid being arrested or be subject to execution of a due liability imposed by a competent authority.[158]

After the reasons have ceased to exist, an alien is allowed to exit Serbia.

158. Article 13 of the Aliens Act.

Part II. Right of Residence

Chapter 1. General Provisions

131. The Serbian legal framework regarding the aliens' right of residence in Serbia is stipulated mostly by the Aliens Act. According to this Act, an alien may enter into and stay in Serbia using a valid travel document containing a visa, or a permission to stay, unless provided otherwise by the law or an international agreement. In other words, an alien who has entered Serbia lawfully, and who meets the general preconditions for entry and residence as defined in the Aliens Act, may freely stay in the country in accordance with the declared purposes of stay, observing the regulations and decisions of the public authorities during his/her movement and stay in the country. A specific exception to this general rule can be found in Article 5 of the Aliens Act which stipulates that movement and stay of aliens may be limited or prohibited in a 'specific territory' in Serbia if this is necessary due to reasons related to protection of public order or safety of the Republic of Serbia and its citizens, or pursuant to an international convention.[159] This provision is related mainly to restricted entry of aliens to areas with military infrastructure (which is most often imposed also to the local citizens) or to the protection of public order in case of 'high risk gatherings'.[160]

132. Basic preconditions for legal stay in Serbia are lawful entry into the country and possession of valid documents. The Aliens Act defines lawful entry of foreigners into Serbian territory as such entry which is approved by the competent public authority, i.e., crossing the state border at an official checkpoint at which border control is performed. The stay of foreigners in the transit area of airports or harbours and port anchorage through which international transport is conducted is not, in the context of this Act, regarded as entry into the Republic of Serbia.[161]

133. A valid travel document, as a necessary precondition for lawful entry into and stay in Serbia, according to the Aliens Act, means an ordinary personal, family, collective, diplomatic or service passport, seaman's book containing a visa and other documents recognized by international agreements as travel documents, which

159. Article 5 of the Aliens Act.

160. A recent example of the application of this section of the Aliens Act was the ban for Croatian fans to attend a football match with Serbia in Belgrade in September 2013, because – according to common assessment of both Serbian and Croatian police – there was a threat of uncontrollable incidents.

161. Article 3 of the Aliens Act.

can be used to reveal identity of its holder, the term of validity of which has not expired and which has been issued in accordance with the regulations of a foreign country or by a relevant act of an international organization. Valid aliens' travel documents are also the refugee's travel document, a stateless person's travel document and foreigner's laissez-passer.[162]

134. One of the general preconditions for entry and residence that an alien has to meet in order to be entitled to stay in Serbia for a short term, is possession of a passport or other travel document that is issued by the authorities of the foreigner's country of citizenship or permit for permanent residence that is valid throughout her/his entire period of stay in Serbia. Although a possession of appropriate visa is also considered a basic element of valid travel documents, as elaborated before, an international agreement or a Government decision may establish that citizens of particular countries may enter Serbia without a visa, provided that there are no obstacles referred to in Article 11 related to the grounds for denial of entry. Namely, the Government is competent to decide that citizens of particular countries may enter using just a valid personal identity card or other document which can confirm their identity and citizenship.[163] Such governmental decision was made in regard of citizens of EU member countries, as well as citizens from a number of other countries – they may enter without a visa, but must have a personal passport (*see* Part I, Chapter 2, §3). Regardless of their citizenship, individuals holding a refugee travel document are not required to hold a visa, as well asylum seekers who may stay in Serbia without a visa while their asylum application is being considered.

135. The Aliens Act specifies three types of aliens' stay in Serbia:

- Short stay (Stay of up to ninety days).
- Temporary residence.
- Permanent residence.

162. *Ibid.*
163. Article 12 of the Aliens Act.

Chapter 2. Short Stay

§1. Conditions for Short Stay

136. The Aliens Act defines short stay of aliens as a 'stay of up to ninety days either without a visa or on the grounds of a visa, unless otherwise stipulated by this Act or an international agreement.'[164] A short stay visa shall be issued for the purpose of tourism, business and other travelling for a single, double or multiple entries into Serbia. The duration of an uninterrupted stay, and/or the total duration of successive visits of a foreigner with a short stay visa must not exceed ninety days within a period of six months which starts on the day of the first entry.

137. A short stay visa with the multiple entry option is issued with the term of validity of up to one year. However, it may also be issued with a longer term of validity to the staff of a foreign diplomatic mission or a consular office on condition of reciprocity.

138. A short stay visa with the term of validity of up to thirty days may also be issued to an organized group (established for the purpose of joint travelling) of at least five and at most fifty persons, provided that the members of that group are entering the territory of Serbia together, staying in Serbia and exiting as a group, where the leader of the group shall be obliged to have a separate visa, if required.

139. It is important to point out that a visa is a title for entry that should be distinguished from residence titles, such as residence permits, although a visa also has a function of allowing an alien to stay in the country for the period for which a visa is issued. Namely, a visa allows the alien to come to the Serbian border crossing and request for entry and stay in the country (or for transit) but it does not automatically allow entry and short stay because it could still be refused if any of the reasons for entry denial exist.

§2. Administrative Procedure and Documents

140. Basic administrative requirements for getting short stay are common for all types of aliens' residence in Serbia. General visa administrative requirements include:

- Valid passport (passport must be valid at least ninety days after the visa had been issued);
- Letter of invitation: for a private visit – invitation letter certified by the relevant authority of the Republic of Serbia; for a business visit – invitation letter by a company in Serbia; for a tourist trip – a proof of payment for the trip issued by a travel agency (voucher or other type of payment receipt);

164. Article 25 of the Aliens Act.

- Completed visa application form;
- Photo;
- Return ticket or Itinerary (copy of Driving License and Insurance if travelling by car);
- Proof of sufficient funds for staying in Serbia (EUR 50 per one day stay);
- Proof of health insurance; and
- Visa fee (around EUR 70).

141. Visa applications should be submitted to the Embassy or Consulate General of the Republic of Serbia abroad. Before issuing a visa, the relevant diplomatic mission or consular office of the Republic of Serbia is obliged to obtain prior consent of the Ministry competent for interior affairs. As said before, exceptionally, when there are serious humanitarian reasons, the border police may, again with consent of the Interior Ministry, issue a transit visa (type B visa) for a single transit, or a visa for short stay (type C visa) for a single entry with the term of validity of up to fifteen days, when a foreigner has had no opportunity to apply for a visa via a diplomatic mission or a consular office of Serbia, provided he/she presents adequate proof of urgency of the trip for which he/she needs the visa.[165]

142. A legal or natural person that provided a foreigner with a letter of guarantee whereby the guarantor accepts the responsibility to cover any costs of the foreigner's stay and forced expulsion (if these costs cannot be charged to the foreigner), shall be obliged to submit a certified copy of the letter of guarantee to the competent authority in accordance with the place of foreigner's temporary residence.[166]

143. The general rule is that an alien who intends to reside in Serbia for a short time does not have to undergo any administrative procedures apart from the regular border formalities. He/she will be requested to present at the border his/her passport or other travel document, and a visa unless they are exempted from the visa-requirement. Sometimes (i.e., not necessarily, and not always) aliens may be asked to present documents that indicate the purpose of their intended stay and to prove that they meet the requirements for entry and short stay, most often that they have sufficient funds to finance their entire stay. However, Serbian legislation on aliens' rights includes a specific requirement related to the mandatory registration of residence of an alien (even when residing in Serbia under short stay conditions) as well the change of his/her address in Serbia and termination of residence. Namely, according to the Aliens Act, legal and natural persons providing accommodation services to foreigners against payment (hotels and other types of accommodation services), as well as private persons receiving visits from foreigners, are obliged to notify the competent authority of the alien's stay within twenty-four hours of the provision of service to the foreigner or of the moment of foreigner's arrival for a visit. Moreover, an alien who does not use accommodation services is obliged to notify the competent authority (the nearest police station) of his/her stay and change

165. Article 14 of the Aliens Act.
166. Article 23 of the Aliens Act.

of address within twenty-four hours of the arrival in the place of temporary residence, or of the day of change of address in the place of temporary residence.[167] This provision was a subject of debate among legal experts in the Aliens Act drafting process. Some of them emphasized that this provision seems not to be necessary given that border police is by law obliged to keep records of arrivals. Probably under the influence of such suggestions, in the Ministry of Interior's implementation acts was added the provision that the mandatory registration of an alien when arriving within short stay conditions may be completed also by electronic means (e-mail).

§3. Legal Position of Short Stay Resident

144. All persons residing in Serbia, including those who entered with a short stay visa, are entitled to the protection of basic rights guaranteed in the Serbian Constitution and in the international conventions to which Serbia is a party. To these conventions belong, among others, the International Covenant on Civil and Political Rights; the International Covenant on Economic, Social and Cultural Rights; the Convention on the Elimination of all Forms of Discrimination against Women; the Convention on the Rights of the Child; as well as the European Convention on Human Rights. There are, however, certain exceptions as to the reach of human rights protection: for example, full range of economic rights as well as political rights, such as the right to vote, right to be elected as a judge or prosecutor, etc. are reserved only for Serbian citizens.

145. Aliens who reside in Serbia as short stay visitors are mostly excluded from public services and benefits. They are entitled to emergency health care but should pay for it. Namely, aliens should bear the costs of emergency health assistance, as well as for other types of health services that are provided at their request. For the use of health services an alien pays a fee according to the price list of the medical institution. Costs of alien's urgent medical care can be covered by the local institutions just in the case that the financial compensation could not be recovered from an alien because he/she does not possess the necessary funds. Citizens of countries that have a bilateral agreement on social insurance with Serbia are not exempted of paying costs of medical care, but these costs are rather lower.

146. Refugees from the territory of the former Yugoslavia or the asylum seekers are entitled to limited free of charge health care in accordance with the regulations governing refugees and asylum seekers.

147. Aliens with short stay residence cannot work and be employed without a work permit and permit for temporary residence. However, they can carry out temporary and occasional jobs if arriving in the country on the basis of invitation or contract related to professional or intellectual services (experts, interpreters, artists, athletes, etc.). If they want to work in agricultural activities, Serbian citizens who

167. Article 75 of the Aliens Act.

employ them should present to the police appropriate proofs of their ownership over rural property which represents his/her only income source.

§4. Position of Family Members

148. Alien's family members should meet individually all the above-mentioned requirements for a short stay. Accordingly, each family member must hold a passport and a visa unless he/she has one of the categories (citizenship) that are exempted from the requirements of holding these documents. Although Serbia's Travel Documents Act does not no longer allows familial passports (minors must have an individual passport, too), aliens from countries where this type of passports exist are accepted on the border checkpoints. Also, the family must have sufficient funds to cover the expenses of each family member's short residence in Serbia.

Chapter 3. Temporary Residence

§1. Conditions for Temporary Residence

I. General Conditions

149. Temporary residence may be permitted to an alien whose intention is to stay in the Republic of Serbia longer than ninety days for the purposes of:

- Work, employment, performance of economic or other professional activities.
- Enrolling for school, university or advanced education course, scientific research, practical training, participation in the programmes of international exchange of pupils and students or other scientific/education activities.
- Family reunification.
- Other reasonable reasons in accordance with the law or an international treaty.[168]

150. An alien to whom temporary residence has been permitted on grounds of the above listed reasons is obliged to stay in Serbia in accordance with the purpose for which the stay has been approved. In other words, it is not allowed to change the purpose of residence during the permitted temporary stay.

151. The general rule is that an alien may be granted the permission for temporary residence:

- if he/she furnishes the proof that he/she possesses sufficient financial means to sustain him/her;
- that he/she has got health insurance; and
- that his/her reasons for temporary residence are justified and in compliance with the allowed purposes of temporary residence as stipulated in the Aliens Act.

152. Temporary residence may be approved for a period of up to one year and may be extended for the same period, unless otherwise provided for in the Aliens Act or an international agreement. The staff of a diplomatic mission or a consular office may be given the permission for temporary residence with the term of validity longer than one year, provided that the principle of reciprocity is applied. Again, an alien who is a victim of human trafficking will be allowed to temporary reside for a period corresponding with the time necessary for his/her participation in the criminal proceedings.[169]

153. The permit for temporary residence may be extended provided that the alien has filed the application for extension of the temporary residence period to the competent authority at least thirty days prior to the expiry of visa. Temporary stay is usually authorized for up to one year and may be extended for the same period.

168. Article 26 of the Aliens Act.
169. Article 29 of the Aliens Act.

To an alien who is a close family member of the citizen of the Republic of Serbia, temporary stay may be extended for the period of up to three years or until conditions are fulfilled to authorize a permanent stay. To an alien who is a close family member of the citizen of the Republic of Serbia, temporary stay may be extended even in the case when that citizen died, as well as if the marriage with a citizen of Serbia terminates, provided that it had lasted at least three years in the Republic of Serbia.

154. An alien may be denied permission for temporary residence if any of the obstacles referred to in Article 11 of the Aliens Act as reasons for denial of entry exist. That means that beside 'regular' reasons for denial of temporary residence (lack of financial means and health certificate, final ruling on expulsion, security reasons),[170] the relevant Serbian authority has the discretionary power to deny the permit for residence if it has reasonable doubt that an alien will take advantage of the stay for purposes other than those declared.

155. The Aliens Act lists reasons for which a visa application may be rejected or visa cancelled. The authority competent for issuing visas, i.e., the Ministry of Interior, shall not issue a visa if the term of validity of a foreign travel document expires in less than ninety days; it shall deny it also if any of the obstacles referred to as reasons for which an alien shall be denied entry into Serbia pursuant to Article 11 of the Aliens Act, and if he/she fails to present himself/herself when summoned by a diplomatic mission or a consular office of the Republic of Serbia. Exceptionally, a visa may be issued to an applicant – in spite of the fact that above-mentioned reasons for refusal of visa applications exist – if the competent authority finds that a visa should be issued for humanitarian reasons, if this is in the interest of the Republic of Serbia, or if accepted international obligations so require. In the case that a visa is rejected due to the expiring term of validity of a foreign travel document, the Ministry may prescribe that a foreigner shall only be allowed to enter the country at a particular border crossing.

156. Equally, the competent authority may cancel the permit for temporary residence to an alien if any of the obstacles referred to in Article 11 of the Aliens Act (denial of entry) occur, or are detected at a later stage (as said before, the same applies to a short stay of up to ninety days). In the process of cancellation, the competent authority may prescribe a deadline of maximum thirty days within which an alien will be obliged to leave the Republic of Serbia and the period during which he/she will be prohibited to re-enter Serbia. The cancellation of stay and the prohibition of entry will be entered in the aliens' travel document. Stay in the Republic of Serbia shall be cancelled to a alien who has been granted temporary residence also if changes occur regarding basic requirements for issuing temporary stay, i.e., if he/she loses the necessary means of subsistence, health insurance or place of residence.

---

170. *See* Art. 11 of the Aliens Act.

II. Specific Conditions

157. In relation to the listed specific purposes of residence in Serbia, the applicant for temporary residence also needs to meet conditions which depend on the declared purpose of residence, in addition to the general conditions (valid travel document, health insurance and means of subsistence).

158. Temporary residence for the purpose of work, employment, economic or other professional activity, according to the Aliens Act, may be permitted to an alien 'who has been granted the right to work, or the permission for temporary residence is a precondition for exercising that right, in accordance with the regulations governing the work of aliens in Serbia'.[171] In this case temporary residence shall be permitted to a foreigner until the expiry of the term of approved labour contract in Serbia, i.e., if necessary with longer term of validity than one year. The temporary permit will also be approved to an alien who intends to stay in Serbia longer than ninety days, provided that he/she has fulfilled all other conditions stipulated by this Act, and does not require a work permit in terms of regulations governing the work of aliens in Serbia.

159. Applicants for the permit for temporary residence for the purpose of enrolling to a school or university, or participating in scientific or educational activities must present the proof of fulfilment of conditions related to 'possessing sufficient financial means'.[172] The Ministry of Education and Science stipulates more specifically how to prove requested condition. (*See* Part II, Chapter 3, §1). However, the temporary residence for the above-mentioned purpose may be extended to a maximum two years after the expiry of the period prescribed for attending a school, university, advanced education or practical training course.

160. According to the Aliens Act, the application for obtaining the permission for temporary residence for the purpose of reunification the family should be submitted only by an alien who is a 'nuclear family' member of a citizen of Serbia, or a 'nuclear family' member of an alien who has been given the permit for permanent residence or temporary residence. For the purpose of this Act, the members of a 'nuclear family' include: spouses, their underage children born in or out of wedlock, underage adopted children or underage stepchildren. Exceptionally, other relatives may also be considered as members of the nuclear family, provided that there are especially important personal or humanitarian reasons for family reunification in Serbia.[173]

161. As an exception to the general rule that applicants for temporary residence should meet all general requirements (valid travel document, health insurance and means of subsistence), temporary residence without meeting above-mentioned basic requirements, may be permitted to an alien who is victim of the criminal act of

171. Article 30 of the Aliens Act.
172. Article 28 of the Aliens Act.
173. Article 32 of the Aliens Act.

human trafficking, and if this 'is in the interest of court proceedings regarding this criminal act'.[174] (*See* Part IV, Chapter 4, §3) Moreover, during the temporary residence of such an alien if he/she does not have sufficient financial means to sustain himself/herself, he/she should be provided with appropriate accommodation, meals and elementary living conditions.

§2. Administrative Procedure and Documents

162. Procedure for applying for Serbian temporary residence depends, first of all, upon the declared ground for residence, but also on the applicant's current residence. If an alien residing outside of Serbia intends to stay more than ninety days in Serbia, he/she must apply for the temporary residence visa (visa type D) to a Serbian diplomatic or consular mission. An alien who is already resident in the Republic of Serbia on other grounds (short stay, for example) must address his/her application to the 'competent authority', i.e., to the Police office nearest to his/her registered Serbian address. In both cases he/she is obliged to submit a valid foreign travel document, as well as other proof justifying the reasons on account of which he/she is requesting the approval of temporary residence. Along with the request, the applicant must enclose appropriate proofs that he/she has enough means to support himself/herself and that he/she has health insurance.

163. Depending upon the declared ground for temporary residence, it is required to enclose the following documentation as proof of request justification:

- For *foundation of company, branch or bank*, for persons who are named in the respective business's Registration Act should be submitted: (a) Registration Decision and (b) Certificate from the commercial bank of account turnover.
- For *foundation i.e., ownership of independent business* (commercial, handcraft, catering industry, etc.) or agency should be submitted: (a) Registration Decision.
- For *Agreements on Consignation, Agreement on Business Cooperation, Agreement on Business-Technical Cooperation and/or Transfer of Technologies* should be submitted: (a) Registration Decision of domestic companies, (b) Agreement on Cooperation between a foreign and domestic legal person and (c) Referral or delegation of the company that sends an alien (original document and translation by the authorized sworn-in-court interpreter).
- For *establishing employment*: (a) Registration Decision of the company or other legal person where foreign citizen sets up employment, (b) Employment Contract or Service Contract, (c) Opinion of NES when the employment is being set up for the first time or Ruling of the NES that authorizes employment setting up.
- For *citizens of former SFR Yugoslavia republics that previously set up employment as domestic citizens* should be submitted: (a) Photocopy of record book accompanied by the original for inspection, (b) Employment Certificate, (c) Registration Decision of the company, unless foreign citizen is employed at public utility services company.

174. Article 28 of the Aliens Act.

- For *carrying out of temporary and occasional jobs* (up to ninety days) should be submitted: (a) Employment or Service Contract with person that owns rural property which represents his/her only income source, (b) Registration Decision of a legal person, or in case of Agreement for agricultural works, certificate that agriculture is basic activity of that legal person.
- For *temporary residence of foreign athletes* should be submitted: (a) Ruling on club registration and (b) Agreement on hiring, verified at competent sports federation.
- For the *marriage with citizen of the Republic of Serbia* should be submitted: (a) Marriage certificate, not older than six months (b) Certificate on employment or other proof of means of support and (c) Proof of citizenship status of Serbian citizen.
- For the *Common-law marriage with citizen of the Republic of Serbia* should be submitted: (a) Certificate on free marital status for both persons (for the citizen of Serbia, Birth Certificate not older than six months is sufficient), (b) Verified statement of two witnesses that Serbian citizen an alien are in common-law marriage relationship, or if they have any children together, their Birth Certificates, (c) Certificate on employment or other proof of means of support and (d) Proof of citizenship status of Serbian citizen.
- For the *kinship with the citizen of the Republic of Serbia* should be submitted (a) Proof of kinship with Serbian citizen (Birth Certificate, Marriage Certificate, etc.) and (b) Proof of citizenship status of Serbian citizen.
- For *private visit* should be submitted: (a) Proof of citizenship status of Serbian citizen and (b) Guarantee of Serbian citizen and proof of possession of means for supporting aliens stay or proof of personal supporting means if the guarantee is not provided by Serbian citizen.
- For *family member of foreign citizen with temporary residence* in Serbia should be submitted: (a) Proof of kinship with foreign citizen with temporary residence in Serbia (Birth Certificate, Marriage Certificate, Certificate of the Embassy, etc. with translation by sworn-in court interpreter. In this case, as family members are considered spouses, their children and, under some circumstances, parents).
- For the *accreditation of journalists* should be submitted: (a) Accreditation of the Ministry of Culture.
- For the *engagement with non-governmental organizations* (NGO) should be submitted: (a) Letter by the Ministry of Foreign Affairs confirming to be familiar with NGO's activity and (b) Service or Employment Contract or NGO letter that the foreign citizen is engaged as volunteer.
- For *foreign priests' services* should be submitted: (a) Proof of church registration or letter of support of the Ministry of Religion, as well as of NGO, if priests' religious community has not been registered and (b) Employment contract or letter from church that the foreign citizen has been engaged in religious activities or for the purpose of religious service.
- For *education-studying-language* should be submitted (a) Certificate of the university or school attended by the foreign citizen.
- For *students'/researchers' training and practice* should be submitted: (a) Ruling on registration of the company where training, i.e., practice is to be carried out, (b) Certificate of the institution that organizes training or practice, with accurate

initiation and termination dates, and (c) Agreement or certificate on carrying out training and practice.

- For *highly professional specialization* should be submitted: (a) Certificate of the competent institution or organization on specialist studies with a stated duration of specialization.
- For the *employment of a Reader and Professor* at the University should be submitted: (a) Employment Contract and (b) Letter from the University.
- For *work at foreign diplomatic missions and consular offices* and for private visits to diplomatic and consular personnel should be submitted: (a) Letter of the Embassy with precisely stated data on working post at which foreign citizen is engaged and on duration of his/her engagement, signed by the Head of diplomatic mission or consular office, in which the reason and duration of private visit is explained.
- For *medical treatment in Serbia* should be submitted: (a) Proof of means for medical treatment and support, if the medical costs are not settled in advance, (b) Letter of the medical institution with personal data of the foreign citizen, predicted duration of medical treatment and way of settlement of mutual financial obligations.
- For *officers of international institutions* (UN, World Bank, IMF, etc.) and consultant companies engaged in cooperation with the Serbian state bodies should be submitted: Letter of the competent ministry with reference number and date of Agreement on Cooperation or other agreement with explanation of needs regarding engagement of foreign citizen and duration of his/her stay.
- For *property of residential or business structure* should be submitted: Proof of property possession.[175]

164. Rules on the Requirements for Aliens' Temporary Residence Permit Regarding the Health Insurance (*Pravilnik o ispunjenosti uslova za odobrenje privremenog boravka stranca u pogledu zdravstvenog osiguranja*) stipulates precise conditions on types of health insurance which are satisfying for granting a permit of residence. Namely, the competent authority shall accept as sufficient proof for authorization one of the following proofs: (a) document on international insurance, (b) health insurance document issued in accordance with bilateral agreements on social security proofing applicant's rights; (c) document on voluntary health insurance issued in the Republic of Serbia; or (d) certificate of health insurance issued in the Republic of Serbia in accordance with the regulations that apply in the area of health insurance. If the alien submits no evidence of possessing one of the above listed documents he/she will be obliged to prove that he/she possesses sufficient funds to cover necessary medical expenses that may be incurred during his/her stay Serbia.[176]

---

175. E-Government Portal of the Republic of Serbia, www.euprava.gov.rs/en/individuals/temporary_stay_terms (accessed 7 August 2016).
176. *Pravilnik o ispunjenosti uslova za odobrenje privremenog boravka stranca u pogledu zdravstvenog osiguranja*, Official Gazette of the Republic of Serbia, No. 59/2009.

165. The decision on the application is taken by the Police office with prior consent of the public authority competent to verify the justification of the reasons for temporary residence (Ministry of Interior – Department for Aliens) which is obliged by law to respond to the request for consent within fifteen days.

166. The fee for a temporary residence permit is Serbian Dinar (RSD) 8,030 (around EUR 70). This fee is 50% lower for applicants seeking a permit on the basis of marriage to a citizen of Serbia. Students and research fellows with scholarships/ sponsorship of the Serbian government, priests and church officials do not pay the fee for temporary residence, as well citizens of Cyprus, Macedonia and Mongolia.

167. A critical review of the procedure of issuing temporary residence should note that the process of obtaining and renewing temporary stay is extremely demanding. For example, the documentation that must be submitted for the extension of the residence permit is the same as for its initial acquisition, although all the relevant documents are already deposited at the Ministry of Interior. Although the basic legislative ground is harmonized according to European Union standards, the implementing acts (decrees, rulebooks, etc.) of the Ministry of Interior are oversized and confusing. The list of requested documents in some police departments sometimes is larger than the list published on the Ministry of Interior's website which contains around forty different documents. Some of these additional requested documents do not meet acceptable legal standards and even elementary logics. Thus, for example, an alien who is a volunteer at a NGO is requested to submit a 'letter of the Ministry of Foreign Affairs' that should confirm that this Ministry is 'familiar with the activities of the NGO' in which the applicant is engaged. Given that NGOs and associations usually do not have any business or any other relationship with the Ministry of Foreign Affairs, this request is rather senseless. Additionally, the number and the format of requested documents seem to depend often on the arbitrary interpretation of the police departments, without established standard procedures. In practice, some police departments incline to complicate the already oversized procedure; for instance, some of them request the CV of applicants (although nowhere mentioned in implementing acts). It seems necessary and urgent to simplify and standardize the process of issuing a temporary residence permit by defining uniform procedures regarding documentation and prescribing a smaller volume of documentation.

§3. Legal Position of Residents

168. All public authorities are obliged to treat aliens residing in Serbia in accordance with international standards in the sphere of human rights protection. Foreign nationals shall be entitled to almost all rights in the sphere of human rights protection that are guaranteed by the Serbian Constitution, including the right to address the judiciary and ombudsman in the case of violations or denial of their rights. On the other hand, an alien is obliged, during his/her stay in Serbia, to comply with regulations and decisions of the state authorities. Aliens who are issued a temporary residence permit for a specific purpose may reside in Serbia only in accordance with the purpose for which the permit was issued.

169. A temporary residence permit provides the legal basis for an alien to reside in Serbia, to move freely and to choose his/her place of residence. Also, an alien with temporary residence has the right to work in the private and public sector if he/she meets the requirements stipulated by the law, general act or collective contract. The Conditions for Foreign Citizens Employment Act[177] stipulates two conditions that an alien has to fulfil in order to be employed: (1) he/she should have a permit for permanent or temporary residence, and (2) he/she should have approval for employment (work permit). Moreover, an alien with a temporary residence permit may be employed without a work permit when employment is based on the pursuit of professional duties laid down by the agreements on business and technical cooperation, long-term cooperation, transfer of technology or foreign investment. The Employment and Insurance Against Unemployment Act stipulates that the foreign national or the stateless person may be registered as an unemployed person with the NES should he/she hold a permanent or temporary residence permit and a valid work permit. If the foreign national was insured against unemployment in the territory of Serbia and if, upon the expiry of the insurance was registered in the NES, he/she shall be entitled to the unemployment benefits in the manner and under the same conditions as the nationals of Serbia.[178] (*See more* in Part VII)

170. The Health Insurance Act regulates requirements for bearers of temporary residence permits to get the status of persons covered by mandatory health insurance. According to this Act, foreign citizens and stateless persons employed in Serbia by foreign legal or private persons, are entitled to mandatory health insurance: (a) foreign citizen employed in Serbia by local organizations, i.e., private employers on the basis of special agreements on exchanging experts or agreements on international technical cooperation; (b) foreign citizens during the schooling or professional training in Serbia; and (c) foreign citizens with whose countries a bilateral agreement on social insurance has been concluded. Health care expenses relating to these foreign citizens are paid by Serbian institutions which should reimburse such expenses from the foreign health insurance carrier.[179]

171. The Foundations of the Education System Act stipulates that foreign nationals and stateless persons shall enrol for pre-school institutions, primary and secondary schools and shall exercise the right to education under the same conditions and manner as stipulated by the law for Serbia's nationals.[180]

---

177. *Zakon o uslovima za zasnivanje radnog odnosa sa stranim državljanima*, Official Journal of SFRY Nos 11/1978 and 64/1989, and Official Gazette of FRY Nos 42/1992, 24/1994, 28/1996 and Official Gazette of the Republic of Serbia, No. 101/2005.
178. Article 85 of the Conditions for Foreign Citizens Employment Act.
179. *Zakon o zdravstvenom osiguranju*, Official Gazette of the Republic of Serbia, Nos 107/2005 and 109/2005, Arts 2 and 17.
180. *Zakon o osnovama sistema obrazovanja i vaspitanja*, Official Gazette of the Republic of Serbia, Nos 72/2009, 52/2011 and 55/2013.

172. There are, unfortunately, some unjustified examples on inequality in rights that should be changed in the process of harmonization of Serbia's legislations with *acquis communautaire*. For instance, Article 48 of the Rules on Conditions and Ways of Realisation of Rights and Obligations of Individuals Seeking Employment regulates that when the NES has in its records a person who is a citizen of Serbia and an alien with temporary residence, and they equally meet criteria established by an employer, the branch office will refuse the work permit to the alien and offer the employment to the Serbian citizen.[181] Besides, one can observe that student accommodation facilities funded by the government are not available for foreign students and, finally, costs and terms under which foreign degrees are recognized are less favourable for aliens.

§4. Position of Family Members

173. The Aliens Act stipulates that one of the purposes of applying for a temporary residence permit is family reunification. An alien residing in Serbia under a temporary residence permit has the right to family reunification with his/her close family members or – as defined in the Aliens Act – 'member of the nuclear family'. As said before, according to the Aliens Act as close family members are considered spouses, their underage children born in or out of wedlock, underage adopted children or underage stepchildren. Exceptionally, other relatives (most often parents) may also be considered as close family members, provided that there are especially important personal or humanitarian reasons for family reunification in Serbia.[182]

174. To an alien, close family member of the citizen of Serbia, temporary residence may be extended for the period of up to three years or until conditions for issuance of a permit for permanent residence are fulfilled. Moreover, to a foreign citizen, close family member of the citizen of the Republic of Serbia, temporary stay may be extended even in the case when that Serbian citizen died, as well as in the case of termination of marriage with a Serbian citizen under the condition that the marriage lasted at least three years in the Republic of Serbia. The Aliens Act also regulates that an underage alien born in the territory of Serbia shall be granted an extension of the temporary residence for the period specified for the temporary residence of one of his/her parents or guardians.

175. One thing should be added: beside above-mentioned rights related to reunification the family, employment and health insurance – for children of aliens with temporary residence in Serbia who do not speak the language used in educational or other specific curricular activities significant for the continuation of education, the school is obliged to organize Serbian language lessons, i.e., preparatory and

---

181. *Pravilnik o uslovima i načinu ostvarivanja prava nezaposlenih lica*, Official Gazette of the Republic of Serbia, Nos 35/1997, 52/1997, 22/1998, 8/2000, 29/2000, 49/2001 and 28/2002, Arts 28 and 48.
182. Article 32 of the Aliens Act.

remedial classes, in accordance with special guidelines and pursuant to the regulation adopted by the Ministry of Education. Children and students who are citizens of any of the EU countries, during their stay in Serbia are entitled to attend native language and culture classes free of charge under reciprocity conditions or at their parents' expense in the premises of the institution to be decided by the local self-government unit.[183]

183. The Foundations of the Education System Act (*Zakon o osnovama sistema obrazovanja i vaspitanja*), Official Gazette of the Republic of Serbia, Nos 72/2009, 52/2011 and 55/2013.

Chapter 4. Permanent Residence

§1. Conditions for Long Term Residence

176. Serbian legislation deals quite comprehensively with requirements which an alien must meet in order to get permanent residence in Serbia. The Aliens Act specifies conditions for granting permanent residence to foreign nationals. Permanent residence may be granted to an alien who has stayed with no interruptions in Serbia for at least five years on account of the permission for temporary residence before applying for a permanent residence permit. For permanent residence may apply also an alien who has been married for at least three years to a citizen of Serbia or to a foreign national with a permanent resident status. The Aliens Act regulates that a permanent residence permit may be granted to an underage person in temporary residence in Serbia if one of his/her parents is a Serbian citizen or an alien with permanent residence, with the consent of the other parent. Besides, granting of permanent residence is facilitated for Serbian Diaspora, i.e., for persons who have 'ancestral links to the territory of the Republic of Serbia'. Exceptionally, permanent residence may be granted to other foreigners who have been granted a temporary resident status, if so required by humanitarian reasons or if this is in the interest of the Republic of Serbia.[184]

177. The Aliens Act precisely defines the meaning of the term 'uninterrupted stay' that is a precondition for acquiring permanent residency. Namely, for granting permanent residence, the authorities shall recognize only one half of the time spent in Serbia to an alien who has been granted the temporary residence for the purposes of work, employment or enrolling for school/university. According to the Aliens Act, 'the uninterrupted stay' shall also mean the stay with multiple periods of absence from Serbia, totalling to a maximum of ten months of absence, or a single period of absence of up to six months, over a period of five years. 'Marriage', in terms of this Act, means the 'matrimonial community for the purposes of living together in the territory of Serbia', leaving unclear whether it includes common-law relationships (*sui juris* marriage) and, perhaps, even same-sex marriage although the latter one is not regulated by Serbian laws. 'Parent' means any person who is in legal terms equal to a parent, i.e., stepparents are also included. Besides, the time served in prison by a foreigner who has been granted the permission for temporary residence shall not be recognized as the time accrued for eligibility for permanent residence.[185]

178. In certain cases, an application for a permanent residence permit may be rejected and the Aliens Act lists the reasons for such decision. Permanent residence shall not be granted to an alien:

184. Article 37 of the Aliens Act.
185. *Ibid.*

- who fails to fulfil the above-mentioned basic requirements;
- who has been convicted of a criminal offence for which the perpetrator is prosecuted ex officio, or in case that proceedings have been instituted for such an offence;
- who does not have any means of subsistence;
- who does not have health insurance;
- who does not have a place of residence;
- for reasons of safeguarding public order or security of the Republic of Serbia and its citizens.

179. A foreigner who has not been granted permanent residence due to reasons related to means of subsistence, health insurance and place of residence will receive a cancellation of permit also for his/her temporary residence.[186]

180. Stay in the Republic of Serbia may be cancelled to an alien who has been granted permanent residence in the Republic of Serbia in the following cases:

- if he/she fails to fulfil the requirements pertaining to his/her obligation in regard to means of subsistence, health insurance and place of residence;
- upon release from prison, if he/she has received the final unconditional sentence to imprisonment of more than six months for a criminal offence for which perpetrators are prosecuted ex officio;
- if the protective measure of removal or security measure of deportation has been imposed on him/her;
- if this is required for reasons of safeguarding public order or security of the Republic of Serbia and its citizens;
- if he/she has provided false data regarding his/her identity or has concealed circumstances relevant for issuing the permit.

181. In the process of cancellation, the competent authority will prescribe a deadline of maximum thirty days within which an alien shall be obliged to leave the country and the period during which he/she shall be prohibited to re-enter Serbia. As an exception, the time limit within which the foreigner is obliged to leave Serbia may be extended, for humanitarian reasons, for up to six months. The cancellation of stay and the prohibition of entry shall be entered in the aliens' travel document.[187]

182. An alien's right to permanent residence may be terminated in the following cases:

- It has been ascertained that an alien has moved out of Serbia or that he/she has stayed abroad in continuity for longer than one year and has failed to notify this fact to the competent authority in Serbia.

186. Article 39 of the Aliens Act.
187. Article 40 of the Aliens Act.

– The aliens' stay has been cancelled.
– The alien has renounced his/her right to permanent residence.[188]

183. Permanent residence, according to Serbian law, is more than 'long-term residence' (this term used in EU terminology still implies temporary limited stay!) because it establishes closest ties between the alien and Serbia and is granted to persons who are considered to have chosen Serbia as a country of their lasting life interests. Namely, a permanent residence permit is not dependent on specific purposes of residence, and is, therefore, not subject to limitations either with regard to the purpose of residence or length of residence.[189]

§2. Administrative Procedures and Documents

184. According to the General Administrative Procedure Act, the competent authority in administrative matters concerning the personal status issues (which include the issuance of a permanent residence permit) is determined by the applicant's domicile.[190] It follows that if the applicant is domiciled abroad he/she should file the request for permanent residence to the nearest Serbian diplomatic or consular mission. If domiciled in Serbia, permanent residence permit is issued by the relevant Department for Aliens of the Ministry of Interior. Request for approval of permanent residence shall be submitted in person, to the organizational unit of the Ministry of Interior in charge of alien's affairs by place of residence of the foreigner. Request for approval of permanent residence to a minor shall be submitted by one of the parents, adoptive parent or guardian. To obtain a permanent residence permit, an alien always has to file an application; the only permanent residence permit which is issued ex officio is the one issued to children of an alien who has a permanent residence permit.

185. The permanent residence permit is issued in administrative procedure, regulated by the General Administrative Procedure Act. To the procedure of issuing a permanent residence permit, apply the same rules as in the case of a temporary residence permit – with the application, the alien has to enclose all the necessary documents proving that he/she meets the conditions.

186. The required documentation for a permanent residence permit is rather extensive. Whatever the grounds for the request, all applicants must submit a filled-out application form, photocopy of passport, two photographs, birth certificate, wedding certificate (if applicable), proofs of possessing funds for subsistence, proof of secured dwelling, medical certificate not older than six months (issued on the form of the Serbian Medical Society), certificates or other documents on education

188. Article 41 of the Aliens Act.
189. Kogovšek Šalamon, N., *Slovenia – Migration Law, Suppl. 2* 77 (Wolters Kluwer Law & Business September 2011).
190. Article 21 of the General Administrative Procedure Act *(Zakon o opštem upravnom postupku)*, Official Gazette of the Federal Republic of Yugoslavia, Nos 33/1997, 31/2001.

degrees (photocopy of original document with translation in Serbian language by authorized sworn-in court interpreter), as well as proof of payment of requested fees in the total amount of RSD 8,200 (around EUR 70).

187. Specific documents are required depending on the ground of application:

- for the application based on family joining one should submit as well: proof of kinship with the citizen of Serbia or a permanently staying foreign citizen;
- for the application based on marriage one should submit as well: Marriage Certificate (on the form of the competent authority of the Republic of Serbia, not older than six months), Divorce Judgment of previous marriages of both spouses (if applicable), and Birth Certificates of children and proof of citizenship of the spouse (not older than six months);
- for the application on grounds of employment one should submit as well: applicant's Employment Certificate and data regarding salary.

188. The competent administrative body may invite the applicant for a personal interview in order to clarify the facts and circumstances of the applicant. When conducting a procedure and deciding in administrative matters, the authorities should as much as possible facilitate the protection and exercise of rights and legal interests of the parties to the procedure. The competent authority is obliged to adopt a decision not later than ninety days from the submission of an application. If the authority fails to adopt a decision within the specified time period or the request is not answered (administrative silence), the applicant is entitled to file an appeal.[191]

189. An identity card for an alien, who has been granted permanent resident status, shall be issued with a validity period of five years.[192] According to the implementation rules for the Aliens Act, an alien who has been granted the permanent resident status must register his/her domicile and change of address, within eight days from the day of arrival in the domicile or from the day of the change of the address.[193]

§3. Legal Status of Permanent Residents

190. In principle, an alien who has been granted permanent residence has equal treatment with respect to rights and obligations as citizens of Serbia, except with regard to those rights and obligations from which he/she has been exempt, pursuant to the Constitution and law. After obtaining permanent residence an alien shall enjoy the same rights that the nationals are entitled to, except so-called rights reserved exclusively for domestic citizens like, for instance, voting or running for political

191. Article 19 of the Administrative Dispute Act, Official Gazette of the Republic of Serbia, No. 111/2009.
192. Article 66 of the Aliens Act.
193. Rules on More Specific Conditions on Registration of Foreigners' Place of Temporary and Permanent Residence, Change of Address and Termination of Permanent Residence, Official Gazette of the Republic of Serbia, No. 59/2009.

office, holding certain jobs that have a high-level security clearance requirement, possessing travel documents of Serbia, etc.

191. The status of a permanent resident is equivalent to the status of a long-term resident introduced at the EU level. An alien who is granted permanent residence shall be integrated through entitlement to the right to: work and employment, education and vocational training; social assistance, health and social insurance, access labour market and services, freedom of association, relationships and membership in organizations representing the interests of workers or employers. The foreign national is entitled to these rights in accordance with the laws regulating the way in which the above-mentioned rights are exercised. An alien, who is granted permanent residence and is registered with the NES, shall be involved in active employment policy measures. Such an alien shall have the same possibility as a citizen of Serbia who is registered with the NES to be involved in active job seeking (clubs and training centres for active job search), in programmes of additional education and training, and shall be entitled to use subsidies for employment, etc.

192. Rights to social security, under the competence of the Ministry of Labour and Social Policy (pension and disability insurance, social protection and financial support to families and children), shall be provided in accordance with bilateral agreements on social security which provide for coordination of social security.

193. Serbia has concluded social insurance agreements with a number of countries or has overtaken – as one of the SFRY successor states – such agreements of the previous state. Currently applicable social insurance agreements regard the following countries: Austria, Belgium, Bosnia and Herzegovina, Bulgaria, Croatia, Cyprus, Czech Republic, Denmark, Egypt, France, Germany, Hungary, Italy, Libya, Luxembourg, Macedonia, Montenegro, Netherlands, Norway, Panama, Poland, Romania, Slovakia, Slovenia, Sweden Switzerland, and United Kingdom[194]

194. Some of the above-mentioned agreements (mostly those concluded by the former Yugoslavia) are based on the principle of citizenship, i.e., are applied to nationals of contracting states and members of their families, but are also (with some exceptions) applied to refugees and stateless persons as well. Other agreements are based on the principle of insurance and are applied to all persons who are or have been subject to the legislation of the contracting party, as well as to family members of such persons. These agreements cover the basic EU principles and rules, such as: the principle of aggregation of insurance and residence periods necessary for establishing the right to social security benefits, equal treatment of nationals of the contracting states, territorial proportion of contracting states, the principle of preservation of the acquired rights, the principle of payment of pensions within

194. Pension and Disability Insurance Fund of the Republic of Serbia – International Agreements (*Republički fond za penzijski i invalidsko osiguranje – Medjunarodni ugovori*), http://www.pio.rs/lat/medjunarodni-ugovori.html (accessed 14 Sep. 2013).

the territory of another contracting state, the principle of *pro rata temporis* – determining the proportionate benefit, etc. The principle of insurance, rather than citizenship is applied in the system of pension and disability insurance and, to that effect, foreign nationals who are employed or perform activities in Serbia are fully entitled to equal rights and obligations under pension and disability insurance as local nationals. Pensions are paid to beneficiaries pursuant to international agreements or in accordance with the principle of factual or legal reciprocity.

195. Foreign nationals are provided with equal access to the institutions of the Serbian judicial system, without discrimination in relation to citizens of Serbia. As said before, the Constitution of Serbia provides equal protection of all persons in a general way, regardless whether they are foreign or Serbian citizens. All are equal before the Constitution and law and everyone has the right to equal legal protection, without discrimination. All direct or indirect discrimination based on any grounds, particularly on race, sex, national origin, social origin, birth, religion, political or other opinion, property status, culture, language, age, mental or physical disability shall be prohibited. The aliens has the right to use his/her language in the proceedings before the court, other state body or organization performing public powers, when his/her right or duty is decided on. Everyone is guaranteed the right to free assistance of an interpreter if the person does not speak or understand the language officially used in the court. The same is regarding the right to use maternal language in criminal, civil and administrative procedure which stipulates equal protection to all persons, whether they are foreign citizens or citizens of the Republic of Serbia.[195]

196. If an alien is deprived of liberty, according to the Criminal Procedure Code, he/she has, among other, to communicate without impediment with his/her defence attorney, diplomatic or consular representative, or the representative of an international organization and the Ombudsman.

197. The status of a permanent resident offers to the bearer the right to apply for Serbian citizenship, according to conditions on eligibility established by Serbia's Citizenship Act. This Act provides facilitated acquisition of Serbian citizenship, particularly for refugees from the former republics of Yugoslavia and members of the Serbian Diaspora, but stipulates relatively soft requirements to gain citizenship also for other aliens with permanent residence in Serbia. An alien who, in line with the regulations on movement and residence of aliens, was allowed to permanently reside in Serbia can, upon his/her own request, be admitted to citizenship of Serbia if he/she is at least 18 years old and not deprived of the capacity to exercise rights. He/she should be released from the foreign citizenship or submit evidence that he/she will be granted the dismissal if admitted to citizenship of Serbia. However,

---

195. Article 11 of the Criminal Procedure Code (*Zakonik o krivičnom postupku*), Official Gazette of the Republic of Serbia, Nos 46/2006, 72/2011, 101/2011, 121/2012, 32/2013 and 45/2013); Art. 25 of the Civil Procedure Code (*Zakon o građanskom postupku*), Official Gazette of the Republic of Serbia, No. 72/2011; Art. 16 of the General Administrative Procedure Act (*Zakon o opštem upravnom postupku*), Official Journal of the Federal Republic of Yugoslavia, Nos 33/1997 and 31/2001 and Official Gazette of the Republic of Serbia, No. 30/2010.

renouncing or loss of previous citizenship shall not be requested if that is not possible or cannot be reasonably expected. Until submitting the application for citizenship he/she should have at least three years of uninterrupted residence in the territory of Serbia. Additionally an alien should submit a written statement that he/she considers Serbia 'his own state'.[196] According to the Citizenship Act, an alien may be accepted as a Serbian citizen if he/she had been married with a citizen of Serbia for at least three years, and if he/she was allowed permanent settlement in the Republic of Serbia. Conditions under which children of a permanent resident may be admitted to Serbian citizenship are also rather flexible.[197]

§4. Position of Family Members

198. Aliens admitted to Serbia as a lawful permanent resident have the right to reunite with their close family members. According to the Aliens Act, their close family members, i.e., their 'nuclear family' member, may be issued a temporary residence permit for the purpose of family reunification, with a validity of one year; it may be extended and be valid for three years, or until the conditions for obtaining the permanent residence permit are met.[198]

199. The scope of persons who are considered close family members is the same as for those aliens who have a temporary residence permit, which means that close family members include:

– spouses;
– underage children born in or out of wedlock;
– underage adopted children or underage stepchildren.

200. Exceptionally, and mostly for humanitarian reasons, ministers competent for interior affairs and/or social policy may, at their own discretion, regard as a family member also another relative if special circumstances justify family reunification in Serbia.[199] There are no explicit propositions regarding polygamous matrimony spouses, opposite-sex extramarital relationships and same-sex couples registered according to laws of other countries, but the administrative practice applies the interpretation that this scope of persons is not eligible for permanent residence permit on the ground of family reunification.

201. Administrative procedure applied for family members of a permanent resident is identical as in the case of aliens with temporary residence permits who invoke the right to family reunification. They also have to submit documentation with proofs on sufficient means of subsistence of close family members, who intend

196. Article 14 of the Citizenship Act of the Republic of Serbia, Official Gazette of the Republic of Serbia' No. 13/2004.
197. *See more*: Duško Dimitrijević, *Regulisanje državljanstva na prostoru bivše SFR Jugoslavije*, Međunarodni problemi, Vol. LX, No. 2-3, pp. 291–344 (2008).
198. Article 32 of the Aliens Act.
199. *Ibid.*

to reside in the country and include proofs of kinship (Birth Certificate, Marriage Certificate, Certificate of the Embassy, etc. with translation by sworn-in court interpreter).

202. The basic regulations governing the right to social security and family protection in the Republic of Serbia are the Social Protection Act,[200] Financial Support to Families with Children Act[201] and the Family Act.[202] Although the existing Social Protection Act is applied to Serbian nationals, and only exceptionally to aliens, a substantial part of social services falling within measures of social integration (day care for children and the elderly, with a variety of programmes, counselling centres and other services to persons who need additional support for life quality) are under the competence of local self-governments and are provided under same conditions for all citizens who live and work within the territory of a local community, including foreign citizens.

203. The Financial Support to Families with Children Act contributes to the overall measures of social care for children through a special financial support for families with children for improving conditions for satisfying the basic needs of children, but the support and help for aliens is provided only under conditions stipulated in bilateral agreements on social security. Protection of the interests of minor children without adequate parental care, of adults who are unable to represent their interests, as well as protection against family violence, is also ensured for foreign nationals pursuant to the provisions of the Family Act.

204. The right to education is regulated in Article 71 of the Constitution of the Republic of Serbia, Article 6 of the Act on the Foundations of the Education System and by the Higher Education Act. Pursuant to the Constitution, everyone shall have the right to education. Primary education is mandatory and free, whereas secondary education is free. All citizens shall have access to higher education under equal conditions. Foreign nationals and stateless persons have the right to education and upbringing under the same conditions and in the manner prescribed for the citizens of the Republic of Serbia.

205. For the exiled and displaced persons who are not familiar with the language in which the educational programme is carried out, or with certain curricula with relevance to further education, schools organize language training, or preparation for classes and additional classes, according to special instructions. The possibility to organize the native language and culture teaching for children of EU citizens on a reciprocal basis is also provided.

206. Relevant legislation in other areas related in an indirect manner to aliens, in the context of family reunifications, can be found in the Serbian Constitution that

---

200. *Zakon o socijalnoj zaštiti*, Official Gazette of the Republic of Serbia, No. 24/2011.
201. *Zakon o finansijskoj podršci porodici sa decom*, Official Gazette of the Republic of Serbia, Nos 16/2002, 115/2005 and 107/2009.
202. *Porodični zakon*, Official Gazette of the Republic of Serbia, No. 18/2005.

stipulates that children have a right to 'learn about their ancestry', and the right to 'preserve their own identity'.[203] It should also be mentioned that appropriate legislation regulates illicit taking away and retention of the child abroad. In the case of illegally taking away, retention and non-return of a child from abroad, which may be qualified as a violation of the right of custody over the child, i.e., violation of the right to maintaining personal relationships, the provisions of the Convention on the Civil Aspects of International Child Abduction should be applied. Serbia confirmed the European Convention on Recognition and Enforcement of Decisions Concerning Custody of Children and on Restoration of Custody of Children. Serbia has also signed several bilateral agreements on legal assistance between the judicial and other competent authorities (States), in carrying out decisions concerning the care of children, which should contribute to more effective protection of children who were illegally separated from their parents. The Criminal Code also defines the abduction of minors as a criminal offence.[204]

207. Propositions on measures and conditions for family reunification for accepted asylum seekers and person whose right to refuge has been recognized are regulated by the Asylum Act. (*See* Part III, Chapter 3, §5)

203. Article 46 of the Constitution of Serbia, Official Gazette of the Republic of Serbia, No. 98/2006.
204. Article 191 of the Criminal Code of the Republic of Serbia, Official Gazette of the Republic of Serbia, Nos 85/2005, 88/2005, 107/2005.

Part III. Right of Residence for Special Categories of Persons

Chapter 1. Nationals with Preferential Treatment

§1. Returnees under Readmission Agreements

I. Serbia: European Union Readmission Agreement

208. Readmission agreements are agreements between States which undertake to readmit into their territory their own nationals found in an irregular situation in the territory of the other signatory, as well as other third-country nationals and stateless persons who are not their own nationals but who have crossed their territory in transit before being intercepted in the other signatory's territory. These agreements are part of the larger EU return policy. Besides mutual recognition of decisions on the expulsion of third-country nationals, the organization of joint flights, etc. readmission agreements are the main means of executing the common return policy.

209. Serbia signed and ratified such an agreement with the European Union in 2007 and subsequently protocols on the implementation of this Agreement with several EU Member States, as well with a number of non-EU European States. (*See General Introduction, §2, section 44*). Agreement between the Republic of Serbia and the European Community on the Readmission of Persons Residing without Authorization,[205] establishes rapid and effective procedures for the identification and safe and orderly return of persons who do not, or no longer, fulfil the conditions for entry to, presence in, or residence in the territories of Serbia or one of the Member States of the European Union.

210. The readmission obligations set out in the Agreement are drawn up in a reciprocal way, comprising own nationals as well as third-country nationals and stateless persons including, for Serbia, former nationals of the SFRY who have acquired no other nationality.[206] The obligation to readmit own nationals includes also former own nationals who have renounced, or who have been deprived of, their

205. *Sporazum između Republike Srbije i Evropske zajednice o readmisiji lica koja nezakonito borave,* Official Gazette of the Republic of Serbia, International Agreements, No. 103/2007.

206. Articles 2–5 of the Agreement Between the Republic of Serbia and the European Community on the Readmission of Persons Residing Without Authorisation.

nationality without acquiring the nationality of another State. The readmission obligation with regard to own nationals covers also family members (i.e., spouses and minor unmarried children) who hold a nationality other than the person to be readmitted and who do not have an independent right of residence in the requesting state. The obligation to readmit third-country nationals and stateless persons is linked to the following prerequisites: (a) the person concerned holds or at the time of entry held, a valid visa or residence permit issued by the requested state, or (b) the person concerned illegally and directly entered the territory of the requesting state after having stayed on or transited through the territory of the requested state.[207] Exempted from these obligations are persons in airside transit and all persons to whom the requesting state has issued a visa or residence authorization before or after entry to its territory.

211. The former nationals of the SFRY who have acquired no other nationality were treated as a separate category. Their readmission shall be accepted by Serbia provided two conditions are met: their place of birth was in Serbia's territory and their place of permanent residence on the conventional date of the dissolution of the SFRY (i.e., 27 April 1992) was in the territory of that State.[208] The specific conditions for the readmission of this category of persons were applied horizontally in all the readmission agreements with the Western Balkan countries. Both for own nationals, in case of expiry of specified delay, as well as for third-country nationals or stateless persons, in all cases, Serbia has accepted the use of the EU's standard travel document for expulsion purposes.[209]

II. Procedure

212. The Readmission Agreement contains the necessary technical provisions regarding the readmission procedure (the form and content of the readmission application, means of evidence, time limits, transfer modalities and modes of transportation).[210] The procedure is regulated by Articles 6–15 of the Agreement and seven Annexes to the Agreement, which are its integral part and regulate the following issues:

- Annex 1 – Joint list of documents that should be submitted so as to prove the citizenship.
- Annex 2 – Joint list of documents that should be submitted presenting prima facie evidence of citizenship.
- Annex 3 – Joint list of documents presenting proof on the existence of conditions for the readmission of the citizens of third countries or stateless persons.

---

207. Article 3 of the Agreement Between the Republic of Serbia and the European Community on the Readmission of Persons Residing Without Authorisation.
208. *Ibid.*
209. Articles 2(4) and 3(4) of the Agreement Between the Republic of Serbia and the European Community on the Readmission of Persons Residing Without Authorisation.
210. Articles 6–9 of the Agreement Between the Republic of Serbia and the European Community on the Readmission of Persons Residing Without Authorisation.

- Annex 4 – Joint list of documents presenting prima facie evidence on the existence of conditions for the readmission of the citizens of third countries or stateless persons.
- Annex 5 – Joint list of documents presenting evidence or prima facie evidence on existence of conditions for the readmission of the citizens of former SFRY.
- Annex 6 – The Form of the Readmission Application.
- Annex 7 – the Form of Transit Application.

213. Any transfer of an individual to be readmitted must follow an application known as a 'readmission application' submitted by the requesting state to the requested state. Some procedural flexibility is provided by the fact that no readmission will be needed in cases where the person to be readmitted is in possession of a valid national passport and, if he/she is a third-country national, also holds a valid visa or residence authorization of the state which has to readmit him or her.[211]

214. Readmission applications must include the following information and documentation regarding the person concerned: surname, forenames, date and place of birth, last place of residence, documents attesting his/her nationality, photograph, a note as to whether he/she requires help or care, and information on any other protection or security measure which may be necessary for his/her transfer.

215. For the readmission of nationals of the partner country or Member States, readmission agreements list the documents which make it possible to establish:

- proof of nationality without any further investigation being required;
- prima facie evidence of nationality. In such cases, the Member States and the partner country shall consider that nationality has been established unless there is proof to the contrary.

216. For the readmission of third-country nationals, the readmission agreements list the documents which constitute evidence making it possible to establish:

- proof that the readmission conditions have been fulfilled;
- prima facie evidence that the readmission conditions have been fulfilled. In such cases, the Member States and the partner country shall consider that the readmission conditions have been fulfilled unless there is proof to the contrary.

The requesting state must submit readmission applications for third-country nationals one year after becoming aware of the facts at the latest.

217. Replies to applications shall be provided in writing within a set time limit (e.g., twelve days) from the date of receipt of the readmission application. For some readmission agreements this time limit is reduced if the individual is apprehended in the border region of the requesting state. By contrast, it may also be extended by

211. Article 6(2) of the Agreement Between the Republic of Serbia and the European Community on the Readmission of Persons Residing Without Authorisation.

a maximum of six days in certain circumstances. If there is no reply within the extended time limit, the transfer shall be deemed to have been approved. If the application is rejected, the readmission shall not take place. Rejection decisions must be justified by the requested State. If the application is accepted, the readmission shall take place. In principle, transfers are organized within the three months following acceptance. This deadline may be extended.

218. Before repatriating a person, the authorities of the partner country and the Member State concerned shall agree matters in advance in writing, particularly as regards the date of the transfer, the entry point and any escorts which may be required. Repatriation may take place by air or over land. Air transport may take place on scheduled or charter flights. In readmission operations, all transport costs as far as the border of the state of final destination shall be covered by the requesting state. Joint committees are set up to monitor implementation of each agreement.

III. Humanitarian Aspect

219. The whole readmission process has been followed by massive rejecting of asylum applications and forced or voluntary return to the country of origin. There are no official data of the Serbian state institutions (Ministries, competent services) on the number and structure of returnees. According to unverified assessments, in the period 2008–2011 around 17,000 persons had been forcibly returned to Serbia (without Kosovo). The total number of people from Serbia (including Kosovo) with no legal residence title abroad is estimated at up to 100,000 persons, 53,000 in Germany alone, of which 38,000 are assumed to belong to the Roma, Ashkali and Egyptian communities.[212] Having in mind that asylum seekers from Serbia are the majority of asylum seekers in certain countries of the EU and that their number has been gradually decreasing, it can be supposed that after the enforcement of the Readmission Agreement, the greatest number of illegal migrants will be returned.

220. Process of returning people on the ground of the Readmission Agreement raises some human rights concerns, the most important ones being respect for the right to asylum and the principle of *non-refoulement*.[213] The right to asylum may be infringed if a Member State returns a protection seeker to a safe third country with which the protection seeker has a connection, without investigating his or her asylum application, based on the assumption that the protection seeker would have obtained protection there. It is not unthinkable that the safe third country does not investigate the asylum application either. Readmission agreements do not provide any protection in this regard. It should be considered to be inserted in any future agreement that a readmission application must explicitly mention the special status

212. The Strategy of Returnees' Reintegration Based on the Readmission Agreement, Official Journal of the Republic of Serbia, Nos 55/2005, 71/2005-correction, 101/2007 and 65/2008.
213. Kim Gillade, *Readmission Agreements Concluded by the EU*, p. 92, Masterproef van de opleiding 'Master in de rechten', Universiteit Gent (2011), http://lib.ugent.be/fulltxt/RUG01/001/787/173/RUG01-001787173_2012_0001_AC.pdf (accessed 19 Oct. 2013).

of the returnee, foremost whether he/she is an asylum seeker, but also if the returnee belongs to another vulnerable category, such as an unaccompanied minor.[214]

221. While the legal basis of readmission is mostly defined, its implementation raises a number of social and humanitarian issues. Namely, the greatest number of returnees is facing serious existential troubles upon their return. A great number of returnees do not have any personal documents necessary for the regulation of their status in Serbia. Therefore, they have problems in terms of regulating the place of residence, due to the lack of a permanent address and living in improvised settlements. Researches show that the housing problems and unemployment are the biggest problems of returnees under readmission agreements. Joint for all returnees is that they now live in worse conditions than they had in Western Europe. Continuation of education is a problem characteristic of their children. A certain number of them do not speak Serbian well, or they do not know Serbian at all, so that they need extra courses, in order to understand the lectures in school. For successful reintegration and social inclusion of returnees, it is necessary to solve the problem of their access to health and social services. Giving humanitarian aid to returnees presents an integral part of measures with a view to solving their urgent problems.

222. After the Readmission Agreement with the European Union came into in force, the Government of Serbia has revised and amended its Strategy for Returnees' Reintegration Based on the Readmission Agreement in order to speed up the process of social and economic reintegration of returnees. According to this document, expected results of its implementation should be:

- Viable integration of returnees with full respect of social and cultural aspects of integration, creating the conditions for admission and taking care of returnees.
- Active inclusion of local self-government and developing the network of support services according to the needs of returnees in the area of social protection.
- Prevention of new poverty.
- Prevention of secondary migrations, migration control.
- Prevention of human trafficking.
- Inclusion of competent returnees in the labour market in order to decrease the unemployment rate.
- Development of rural and depopulated areas.
- Building trust and interethnic tolerance.

223. The Council for Reintegration of returnees based upon the Readmission Agreement, as a government body, has been formed. Implementation and coordination tasks were assigned to the Commissariat for Refugees and Migrations and the Ministry of Labour and Social Policy. They use important financial support from EU IPA funds, as well from UNHCR and a number of EU Member States. Visible outcomes of this strategy are still in a very early stage.

214. *Ibid.* at 93.

224. After visa liberalization with the EU, an increasing number of Serbian citizens requested asylum in EU countries; they were returned to Serbia on the ground of the Readmission Agreement. This increasing number of unfounded asylum seekers caused reaction in EU which indicated the possibility of endangering the Serbian free-visa regime with the Schengen states. In order to discourage its citizens to abuse the institution of asylum, the Serbian government formed the 'Committee for the preservation of a visa-free regime with the EU' at the beginning of 2011. The task of this inter-ministerial committee was to monitor the implementation of the free-visa regime. The competent authorities in Serbia have increased the campaign to inform citizens about the rights that flow from the visa liberalization, but above all of its limitations, and on non-existence of grounds for seeking asylum in the EU. On the other hand, it was suggested to the EU Member States to reduce or eliminate cash benefits to asylum seekers that motivate the poor citizens of Serbia to seek unfounded asylum. Other measures included the introduction of stricter controls at border crossings when leaving the country, relating to the possession of funds, accommodation and return tickets. These measures, however, have been controversial from the point of view of human rights, and as such have been criticized by some NGOs.

§2. Internally Displaced Persons

I. Definition and Legal Status

225. 'Internally displaced persons' (IDPs) are defined in the UN *Guiding Principles on Internal Displacement* as:

> persons or groups of persons who have been forced or obliged to flee or to leave their homes or places of habitual residence, in particular as a result of or in order to avoid the effects of armed conflict, situations of generalized violence, violations of human rights or natural or human-made disasters, and who have not crossed an internationally recognized State border.[215]

The involuntary nature of their departure and the fact that they remain within the borders of their own country are the two main elements determining them as an internally displaced person.

215. The Guiding Principles on Internal Displacement is a document prepared by experts that were presented by the Representative of the UN Secretary-General on internally displaced persons to the UN Commission on Human Rights at its 55th session in 1998 (E/CN.4/1998/53/Add.2) as an addendum to his annual report (E/CN.4/1998/53). Since then, the Heads of State and Governments assembled at the World Summit in New York in September 2005 have recognized the Guiding Principles as 'an important international framework for the protection of internally displaced persons.' (General Assembly. Resolution. 60/L.1, 132, U.N. Doc. A/60/L.1) The Guiding Principles on Internal Displacement as such is not a binding instrument that could be ratified by States. However, it reflects and is consistent with international human rights law and international humanitarian law. To the extent that States have ratified the human rights and humanitarian instruments upon which the Guiding Principles are based, they are bound by the corresponding principles. States also can opt, as some have done, to make them binding by incorporating them into their domestic law.

226. While no international convention on the rights of IDPs exists, they enjoy the same human rights as all other people within their own country of citizenship or residence. These rights may be articulated in the domestic constitution and legislation as well as international human rights instruments and customary law. The *Guiding Principles on Internal Displacement* restate in explicit terms the rights of IDPs that are implicit in the more general guarantees of existing international human rights and humanitarian law relevant to the IDPs. The Principles identify rights and guarantees relevant to the protection of persons from forced displacement and to their protection and assistance during displacement as well as during return or resettlement and reintegration.

II. IDPs in Serbia

227. As of December 2012, there were an estimated 225,000 IDPs from Kosovo within Serbia, including an estimated 15,000 displaced Roma who have never been registered as displaced.[216] These numbers are the consequence of events in 1999, when over 245,000 members of local minority communities fled from or within Kosovo in fear of reprisals from the majority Albanian population after NATO air strikes had forced the withdrawal of Serbian troops. UN Security Council Resolution 1244 established the United Nations Interim Administration Mission in Kosovo (UNMIK), but deferred judgment on the issue of the final status of the Serbian province. UNMIK's mandate was to provide a transitional administration pending a final settlement, support the development of provisional democratic self-government institutions (known as Provisional Institutions of Self-Government or PISG) and create an environment in which refugees and IDPs could return home. From Serbia's perspective, Kosovo's current status remains ambiguous despite the increasing number of states that have recognized it. The border between Kosovo and Serbia is therefore not considered an internationally recognized state border by Serbia. As a result, persons who fled Kosovo to Serbia continue to be considered IDPs.

228. Around 20% of IDPs are minorities, approximately half of them Roma. This does not include unregistered Roma IDPs whose numbers are estimated by some to be as high as 15,000. The Serbian Government, as well as the international community, has pledged to facilitate the Roma social inclusion. In April 2009, a Roma National Strategy (RNS) was adopted as Serbia chaired a meeting of the Decade for Roma Inclusion, a commitment by European governments to improve the socio-economic status and social inclusion of Roma people. It includes recommendations on Roma IDPs, forced returnees and personal documentation, but lacks a clear time frame and benchmarks.

229. Various analysis of the status of IDPs indicate that their major problems concern housing, access to information and employment, due to a long period of inactivity and lack of required qualifications and contacts, as well as a lack of basic

216. The Internal Displacement Monitoring Centre (IDMC), Country Summaries, Serbia, 12 Mar. 2013, http://www.internal-displacement.org/countries/serbia (accessed 25 Sep. 2013).

documents which enable exercise of other rights. The number of persons who have returned to Kosovo is very small, as well as the number of displaced persons who have found some other long-term solution. The main reasons for such a low rate of IDPs return lay in the lack of security in Kosovo, restricted freedom of movement, limited access to public services and schools for children, lack of economic perspective for returnees and difficulties they face in restitution of their own property.

230. Property issues are among the key obstacles to return. IDPs face significant obstacles to restitution of land and property in Kosovo, both residential and agricultural. There has been widespread illegal occupation and expropriation of houses and land of IDPs, mainly Kosovo Serbs. The restitution process for those seeking to return has been slow. The Kosovo Property Agency (KPA) took over from the Housing and Property Directorate (HPD) in 2006 as the main body mandated to address property claims dating back to the 1999 conflict and before. It works with enforcement agencies to enforce claims and to evict secondary occupants when necessary. To date it has processed over 34,000 claims from over 42,000 received; more than 85% of these relate to agricultural or business properties. Local courts are also processing some property claims.[217]

231. The Serbian government has in recent years focused attention on identifying the needs of IDPs in displacement, closing collective centres and providing alternative housing through the extension of programmes initially designed for the integration of refugees from Croatia and Bosnia. In the last four years progressive steps to address the situation of those displaced have been put in place.

232. The Serbian Commissariat for Migration and Refugees and the Office for Kosovo and Metohija are the two Serbian government institutions responsible for IDPs from Kosovo. In 2012, the Ministry of Kosovo and Metohija was restructured as the Office of Kosovo and Metohija, mandated to address questions of IDPs and returnees in northern Kosovo and other Serbian enclaves where Serbian institutions operate in parallel with Kosovo institutions. The Serbian Commissariat for Migration and Refugees focuses on the problems of IDPs in displacement in Serbia and has also been restructured to meet requirements for Serbian accession to the European Union.

233. A new Migration Management Strategy was adopted in July 2009, covering economic and conflict induced migration in light of Serbian accession obligations. In May 2011, an Action Plan was elaborated in which the Serbian Commissariat for Migration and Refugee's role in addressing IDP issues was highlighted.

---

217. The Internal Displacement Monitoring Centre (IDMC), Norwegian Refugee Council (NRC), Serbia: Integration stalled, 12 Mar. 2013, http://www.internal-displacement.org/ 8025708F004BE3B1/ %28httpInfoFiles%29/650F7E7EF84456A1C1257B2C004B2267/$file/ serbia-overview- mar2013 .pdf. (accessed 11 Aug. 2013).

234. In 2011, Serbia revised its National Strategy, placing greater emphasis on mechanisms to improve living conditions of those displaced. Yet despite considerable progress there continues to be a discrepancy between the situation of many IDPs and their host communities. Though the Serbian government policy has been principally to promote return, it has undertaken and enacted various strategies to address the situation of IDPs in protracted displacement. The National Strategy for Resolving the Problems of Refugees and IDPs of 2002, while placing emphasis on return, highlighted the need for voluntary choice of durable solutions. Local integration programming has been essentially oriented towards refugees rather than IDPs. It has, nonetheless, addressed situations of displacement as have various other policies including the Poverty Reduction Strategy (2003), the National Strategy for Sustainable Development (2008) and the Migration Management Strategy (2009).[218] These have progressively addressed the situation of employment, access to health services, education, social welfare and services as well as improving access to documentation.

235. These initiatives, however, have had modest impact. While they have not discouraged integration per se, efforts have often been belated and hesitant, emphasizing the need – as state policy describes it – to improve living conditions, and avoiding any reference to integration whether temporary or permanent. This terminology has often obscured important distinctions, for example between the urgent need for permanent local integration of particularly vulnerable IDPs – those who are unlikely to return under any circumstances – and interim measures to increase the self-reliance and sustainable return prospects of other IDPs should the circumstances later permit.[219]

§3. Serbian Diaspora

236. Serbian immigration law provides a number of benefits for the members of the Serbian Diaspora in relation to the conditions for right to residence and admission to the citizenship. According to the Aliens Act, having 'ancestral links to the territory of the Republic of Serbia' is the ground for permanent residence permit.[220] That means that a Diaspora member will be granted a permanent residence permit without meeting other usual conditions required for permanent residence (previous residence on the ground of temporary residence, or marriage with Serbian citizen) if he/she proves his/her Serbian roots (for instance, birth place of his/her ancestors in direct line).

237. Also, the 2004 Citizenship Act of the Republic of Serbia[221] facilitates the procedure for admission to Serbian citizenship members of the Serbian Diaspora and their descendants. According to Article 18 of this Act an immigrant and his/her

218. *Ibid.*
219. *Ibid.*
220. Article 37 of the Aliens Act.
221. *Zakon o državljanstvu Republike Srbije*, Official Gazette of the Republic of Serbia No. 135/2004.

descendant can be admitted to citizenship of the Republic of Serbia if they are 18, if they are not deprived of legal capacity and if they submit a written statement that they consider Serbia their own state. A spouse of the person who acquired citizenship of the Republic of Serbia on the ground of this proposition can be admitted to Serbian citizenship if upon submission of a written statement that he/she considers Serbia his/her own state. The member of Serbian Diaspora is defined in the Citizenship Act as 'an expatriate' i.e., 'person who emigrated from the Republic of Serbia with an intention to reside permanently abroad'.[222]

238. According to the 2009 Diaspora and Serbs of the Region Act (*Zakon o dijaspori i Srbima u regionu*)[223] the term 'Serbian diaspora' refers to two categories of people: (a) Serbian citizens and their descendants living abroad and (b) 'Serbs in the region', i.e., members of the people with Serbian roots and their descendants who live in the 'region', i.e., in the neighbouring countries (Slovenia, Croatia, Bosnia and Herzegovina, Montenegro, Macedonia, Romania, Albania and Hungary). In some of these countries, this latter group is recognized the minority status. The particular right provided by the above-mentioned Act to Serbian Diaspora and 'Serbs of the Region' is the right to compensation for learning the Serbian language and the Cyrillic alphabet.[224]

239. The Strategy of Preserving and Strengthening Relations between the Motherland and Diaspora and between the Motherland and Serbs of the Region (*Strategija očuvanja i jačanja odnosa matične države i dijaspore i matične države i Srba u regionu*)[225] is a programmatic document adopted in 2011 by the Serbian parliament, which contains a series of declarations of intentions of the Government aimed to strengthen ties between Serbia and its diaspora. Among the objectives of this strategy are various measures to encourage investment of the Serbian diaspora, to preserve cultural, religious and linguistic heritage and identity, returning and reducing the emigration of highly skilled people from Serbia (*brain drain*), etc., but these intentions for the time being are not translated into an *ius positum*.

---

222. Article 18 of the Citizenship Act of the Republic of Serbia.
223. Diaspora and Serbs of the Region Act, Official Gazette of the Republic of Serbia No. 88/2009.
224. Article 37 of the Diaspora and Serbs of the Region Act.
225. Strategy of Preserving and Strengthening Relations between the Motherland and Diaspora and between the Motherland and Serbs of the Region, Official Gazette of the Republic of Serbia Nos 4/2011, 14/2011.

Chapter 2. Students and Researchers

240. A residence regime for foreign students and researchers is common, and is covered by the same basic and implementing legal acts. The right of an alien to reside in Serbia for the purpose of studies and/or scientific research is provided for in Article 31 of the Aliens Act, which enables issuing a temporary residence permit for this purpose. The Act lists purposes sufficient for application for temporary residence: enrolling to a school, university or advanced education course, scientific research, practical training, participation in the programmes of international exchange of pupils or students, and/or other scientific/education activities. Also, an alien is obliged to present proofs of fulfilment of the basic conditions requested for temporary residence, i.e., that he/she possesses sufficient financial means to sustain him/her; that he/she has health insurance and that his/her reasons for temporary residence are justified and in compliance with the declared purpose of temporary residence. The fulfilment of specific requests for granting temporary residence to foreign students and researchers is stipulated in a regulation issued by the minister competent for education and the minister competent for science.[226]

241. According to a relevant implementing act,[227] foreign students and researchers should accompany their request for temporary residence visa by appropriate proofs depending upon the grounds on which the residence permit is requested. The following proofs are requested:

- For enrolling to a *school, university or advanced education course*: certificate (acknowledgment) of university/school that such foreign student was accepted.
- For *specialization*: a certificate (acknowledgment) of the appropriate authority or institution organizing specialized studies.
- For *scientific research*: the certificate (acknowledgment of the institution where an alien has performed scientific research.
- For *practical training*: certificate (acknowledgment) of the institution/company which carries out the practical training, and document of registration of that institution/company.
- For *participation in international exchange programmes for students*: Certificate (acknowledgment) of organization dealing with international exchange of students.
- For *participation in other scientific and educational activities*: Certificate (acknowledgment) of scientific and educational institutions in which the activity is carried out.

226. Article 31 of the Aliens Act.
227. Rules on Fulfillment of the Conditions for Granting Temporary Residence of Aliens for the Purpose of Enrolling to School, University or Advanced Education Course, Scientific Research, Practical Training, Participation in the Programmes of International Exchange of Pupils or Students, and/or other Scientific/Education Activities (*Pravilnik o ispunjenosti uslova za odobravanje privremenog boravka stranca radi školovanja, studiranja ili specijalizacije, naučno-istraživačkog rada, praktične obuke, učestvovanja u programima međunarodne razmene učenika ili studenata, odnosno drugim naučno-obrazovnim aktivnostima*), Official Gazette of the Republic of Serbia No. 59/2009.

242. According to general rules on temporary residence (*see* Part II, Chapter 3, §1) the permit for this type of residence in Serbia is approved for a period of up to one year and may be extended for the same period. However, for students and researchers it may be extended for the term of maximum two years after the expiry of the period prescribed for attending a school, university, advanced education or practical training course.[228]

243. In practice, before a residence permit may be granted on the basis of studies/research, Serbian education and research institutions could have their own requirements in order to accept a foreign student/researcher. Thus, it is often required that the applicant in fact is accepted as a student to a Serbian university only after passing various entrance exams, interviews or likewise, which the applicant should pass before filing any application for a residence permit. These additional requests for students and research residence may complicate the applicants' situation because they should, prior to applying for temporary residence, meet requests from educational or research institutions and for that reason are often forced to first come to Serbia on the basis of short stay visa.

244. According to the rules of Serbian universities on admission of foreign students, applicants who apply for higher degrees of studies, have to submit a recognized (validated) diploma of his/her previous school enrolment, pay university/school fees, unless an international agreement or a bilateral agreement between the universities determined otherwise, and provide an evidence of competence in the Serbian language in accordance to the Universities' statutes. Serbia is the signatory of the CoE Convention on the Recognition of Qualifications concerning Higher Education in the European Region.[229] Recognition procedure is carried out in accordance with the Higher Education Act, if an international agreement does not provide otherwise, and it is often time consuming.

245. Although basic Serbian legal instruments declare that foreign nationals (and stateless persons) shall have the right to education under the same conditions and in the manner prescribed for the citizens of Serbia,[230] in practice there are discriminatory practices that should be corrected in the forthcoming harmonization of Serbian law with *acquis communautaire*. The Universities' tuition fee for aliens is higher than the fees paid by Serbian nationals and so are the alien's taxes for diploma recognition.

246. Applications for temporary residence permits for studies or research should be submitted to a Serbian diplomatic or consular mission if an alien residing out of

---

228. Article 31 of the Aliens Act.
229. Convention on the Recognition of Qualifications concerning Higher Education in the European Region, CETS No. 165, Council of Europe, http://conventions.coe.int/Treaty/ Commun/ChercheSig.asp?NT=165&CM=8&DF=10/17/2007&CL=ENG (accessed 12 Sep. 2013).
230. Article 71 of the Constitution of the Republic of Serbia, Official Gazette of the Republic of Serbia, No. 98/2006; Art. 6 of the Foundations of the Education System Act, Official Gazette of Republic of Serbia, No. 72/2009; Art. 8 of the Higher Education Act, Official Gazette of Republic of Serbia, Nos 76/2005, 100/2007, 97/2008, 44/2010.

Serbia, or to the Police office nearest to his/her Serbian registered address if he/she is already resident of Serbia on other grounds (short stay). Decisions on the applications for residence permits based on studies and/or research are made by the Ministry of Interior Aliens Department.

247. The parts of the EU Directives on students (2004/114/EC)[231] and researchers (2005/71/EC)[232] relating to the approval of temporary residence, refusal of entry, and disapproval of application for temporary residence to students and researchers are incorporated in the provisions of the Aliens Act. However, in Serbian legislation no provisions are in place for regulating the temporary residence of highly skilled persons. Their status is regulated by application of provisions of the Aliens Act governing the requirements for approval of temporary residence in the Republic of Serbia. With regard to the application of the Directive on students (2004/114/EC), since there are no specific provisions that relate to the employment of students, students have the right to get involved in economic activity, namely to establish employment or self-employment, in accordance with local regulations governing the residence, employment and work of aliens. The NES issues work permits to the students who establish employment in the territory of the Republic of Serbia, provided their residence has been regulated, in accordance with the Aliens Act.

---

231. Council Directive 2004/114/EC of 13 Dec. 2004 on the Conditions of admission of third-country nationals for the purposes of studies, pupil exchange, unremunerated training or voluntary service, Official Journal of the European Union L 153M.

232. Council Directive 2005/71/EC of 12 Oct. 2005 on a specific procedure for admitting third-country nationals for the purposes of scientific research, Official Journal of the European Union L 289/15, 3 Nov. 2005.

Chapter 3. Labour and Economic Migration

§1. Labour Employment

248. General rule is that an alien can establish an employment provided that he/she has obtained temporary or permanent residence and an appropriate work permit, in accordance with the Aliens Employment Act. Under the conditions of this Act an alien may be employed albeit without authorization for temporary or permanent residence if he/she has a residence registration in accordance with the Aliens Act and the appropriate application for work registered with the NES. *(See Part VII., Chapters 1 and 2).*

§2. Seasonal and Temporary Workers

249. As described before, in order to have the right to engage in any type of work available for aliens' in Serbia, at least a temporary residence permit is required. Permits for movement and stopping in the zone of a border crossing – which are issued to the border area population – as well as permits given to those engaged in cross-border services, in legal terms are not residence permits under the Aliens Act.

250. The Aliens Act regulates carrying out of temporary and occasional jobs that last less than ninety days, but to perform this type of work a temporary residence permit is also required. These provisions apply mostly to foreign workers engaged for seasonal agriculture works (planting, harvest). Applications for such residence permit should be submitted to the Police office nearest to the applicant's registered address. An employment or service contract with a person that owns rural property should be enclosed, together whit proofs that such property is the only source of income for its owner. If the alien is engaged by a legal person, the ruling on the legal person's registration and agreement for agricultural works should be enclosed with the certificate that agriculture is the basic activity of that legal person.[233] In practice, this legal request is rarely respected and seasonal or temporary workers work in Serbia mostly on the short stay residence basis which is strictly unlawful, or on the basis of permanent residence that they obtained earlier on different grounds.

251. Employment of foreign citizens in Serbia is regulated by the Conditions for Foreign Citizens Employment Act. Foreign citizens may be employed if they have temporary or permanent residency in Serbia and if they obtain approvals for establishing a 'labour relationship' (employment). This approval, which is commonly called 'work permit', is issued by the competent employment service. The

233. E-Government Portal of the Republic of Serbia, http://www.euprava.gov.rs/en/ individuals/ temporary_stay_terms (accessed 3 Sep. 2013).

application for issuance of a work permit for a foreign citizen with granted temporary residence is submitted by the employer, while foreign citizens with permanent residence should submit applications by themselves.[234]

252. Bearing in mind that the Conditions for Employment of Foreign Citizens Act was adopted in 1978, a new wording of the Aliens Employment Act has been drafted and is currently pending adoption by the Serbian Parliament. Under Article 4 of the said Draft Law, an alien employed in Serbia has the same rights and obligations in terms of work, employment and self-employment that citizens of Serbia have in accordance with the law. According to the Draft Law, nationals of Member States of the European Economic Area (EEA) and Swiss Confederation will have free access to the labour market as well as members of their families who are not nationals of these states but have permission for temporary or permanent residence because of their family members in those states. The Draft Law stipulates a new model of granting a work permit for aliens. (*See* Part VII, Chapter 2, §3) According to the mentioned Draft Law, a work permit for 'special cases of employment' shall be issued for the following:

- performing seasonal jobs in the field of agriculture, forestry, civil engineering and other activities characterized by temporary significant increase in the workload;
- vocational training, specialization, obtaining qualifications or training;
- expatriate workers;
- movements within the company registered abroad;
- independent professionals;
- pupils and students under 26 years of age; and
- daily migrant workers.[235]

253. For more detailed information about the conditions to acquire residence permits for the purpose of work and employment *see* above Part II, Chapters 1, 2, 3, and below Part VII, Chapter 2, §2, §3 and §5.

§3. Independent Economic Activities

254. Conditions for independent economic activities and self-employment of aliens in Serbia are regulated mostly within the same sources of law as employment of aliens in general. General regime of residence permits applicable for employment of aliens is applicable also for self-employed aliens. (*See* Part VIII, Chapters 1 and 2).

---

234. *Zakon o uslovima za zasnivanje radnog odnosa sa stranim državljanima*, Official Journal of the SFR of Yugoslavia, Nos 11/1978 and 64/1989, Official Gazette of the Federal Republic of Yugoslavia, Nos 42/1992, 24/1994 and 28/1996 and Official Gazette of the Republic of Serbia, No. 101/ 2005.

235. Article 16 of the Aliens Employment Act, *See* Ivana Krstić, *Protecting the Rights of Migrants in the Republic of Serbia* 51 (International Organization for Migration – Mission to Serbia, Belgrade 2012).

§4. Investment Activities

255. There are no specific provisions regarding residence permits regime for foreign nationals, as well as stateless persons who are entrepreneurs, founders or company members, although they do not get work permits in the NES, but they get the so-called business license in the Ministry of Interior of the Republic of Serbia. (*See* Part VII, Chapter 1, §1 and Part VIII, Chapters 1 and 2).

Chapter 4. Humanitarian Status

§1. Humanitarian or Compassionate Grounds

256. Humanitarian and/or compassionate grounds exist when unusual, undeserved or disproportionate hardship would be caused to a person seeking consideration. As an exception of general rules for granting residence permits, there are number of situations when a residence seeker can obtain a residence status on humanitarian or compassionate grounds. These exceptions are:

- Short stay visa can be issued at the Border Crossing Point without meeting all requests, if 'serious humanitarian reasons' and urgency of the trip exist if an 'emergency medical assistance or intervention is needed, if humanitarian aid is transported over the territory of Serbia and if immediate presence of an alien in Serbia for personal, professional or other reasons is needed'. (*See* Part I, Chapter 2, §3).
- For the same reasons transit visa for a single transit can be issued; (*see* Part I, Chapter 2, §3).
- It is possible to extend a visa expiration date in exceptional cases, namely if required by humanitarian, professional or personal reasons. (*See* Part I, Chapter 2, §3).
- According to the Aliens Act, the application for obtaining the permission for temporary residence for the purpose of reunification the family should be submitted only by an alien who is a 'nuclear family' member of a citizen of Serbia, or a 'nuclear family' member of an alien who has been given the permit for permanent residence or temporary residence. Exceptionally, other relatives may also be considered as members of the nuclear family, provided that there are especially important personal or humanitarian reasons for family reunification in Serbia. (*See* Part I, Chapter 3, §1).
- Exceptionally, and mostly for humanitarian reasons, ministers competent for interior affairs and/or social policy may, at their own discretion, regard as a family member also another relative if special circumstances justify family reunification in Serbia.[236] (*See* Part 2, Chapter 4, §4).
- Permanent residence may be granted to the foreigners who have been granted a temporary resident status, if so required by humanitarian reasons or if this is in the interest of the Republic of Serbia.[237] (*See* Part II, Chapter 4, §1).
- In the process of cancellation of residence permit, the competent authority prescribes a deadline of maximum thirty days within which an alien shall be obliged to leave the country, but, as an exception, the time limit within which the foreigner is obliged to leave Serbia may be extended, for humanitarian reasons, for up to six months. (*See* Part II, Chapter 4, §1)

236. *Ibid.*
237. Article 37 of the Aliens Act.

§2. NON-ACCOMPANIED OR SEPARATED MINORS

257. As said above, the Asylum Act defines a non-accompanied minor as an alien under 18 years of age who was unaccompanied by parents or guardians on his/her arrival in the Republic of Serbia, or who became unaccompanied by parents or guardians, i.e., separated after arriving in Serbia.

258. According to UNHCR, since 2008 to June 2012, 1147 minor asylum applicants were registered in Serbia, of which 783 were non-accompanied or separated.[238] Like most other asylum-seekers, they often leave Serbia before a first-instance decision is reached. Based on the overall migration trends and increase in asylum-seekers in the region, it is possible that a number of non-accompanied or separated minors remain undetected and without institutional support while transiting through Serbia. Until today, no unaccompanied or separated minor was given the status for any asylum-seekers.

259. The Asylum Act establishes the principle of providing care for asylum-seekers with special needs, including children. According to independent sources from Serbia, in most cases, when identified, non-accompanied and separated minors with special needs are accorded this special care.[239]

260. UNHCR reports that there are problems with the process of identification of non-accompanied minors. The police typically identify and make initial contacts with non-accompanied children without the support of qualified civilian staff such as social workers or child welfare personnel. In addition, interpreters are rarely available at this point of initial contact. An additional serious concern is that there are no formal age assessment procedures. Very often it is only during the first interview with a free legal adviser and thanks to the presence of interpreters that the applicant has the opportunity to assert that he/she is a minor.[240]

261. Non-accompanied minor asylum-seekers identified during their first contact with the police are referred to a local Social Care Centre where a temporary guardian is appointed. Accompanied by the temporary guardian, minors are then transferred to the Centre for Accommodation of Underage Aliens Non-accompanied by Parents or Custodians,[241] one of the units within the Institute for Education of Children and Adolescents in the city of Belgrade or, alternatively, to its branch office in the city of Nis; together, they have an accommodation capacity of twenty-two children. These institutions are able to accommodate only male children between seven and eighteen years of age. Separate ad hoc arrangements are made for non-accompanied female children, as necessary. In practice, however,

238. UNHCR, Serbia as a Country of Asylum, Observations on the Situation of Asylum-Seekers and Beneficiaries of International Protection in Serbia, s. 48 (August 2012).

239. Group 484, *Underage asylum-seekers in Serbia: At the Verge of Dignity* 7 (2011).

240. UNHCR, Serbia as a Country of Asylum, *ibid.* at s. 50.

241. The Centre is a separate unit, founded according to the Decision on the Social Protection Institution Network of the Government of the Republic of Serbia, Official Gazette of the Republic of Serbia, No. 51/2008.

despite these provisions, once a temporary guardian from the social welfare centre is appointed, both non-accompanied and separated children are transferred to the Asylum centres.

262. Non-accompanied asylum-seeking minors often arrive in asylum centres in poor physical condition, most commonly with skin diseases. The Government provides resources for the treatment of all uninsured patients, including asylum-seekers although during the initial reception phase, only basic medical examinations are performed. Immediately after the initial reception phase, non-accompanied and separated children are informed about their rights and obligations during their stay in the institution. In the case that they express an intention to seek asylum, which most of them do immediately after admission to a reception facility, they are provided with an interpreter and given the possibility to consult with representatives of a NGO providing free legal assistance within the shortest possible time. The expenses of interpretation are covered by UNHCR.[242]

263. There is no separate asylum procedure for a non-accompanied or separated child, asylum-seeker. After expressing the intention to apply for asylum, the non-accompanied and separated minor asylum seekers are taken to the police, specifically to the Department for Aliens in Belgrade, where the employees of the Asylum Office implement all steps set out in the first-instance asylum procedure. First the applicants are registered (the child is photographed and fingerprinted in the presence of the responsible adult); next they are issued identity cards, so that they can apply for asylum. After this, they can be interviewed. The law requires that the legal representatives, UNHCR, and the interpreter are present during the interview of non-accompanied and separated children.

264. The Asylum Act regulates that a guardian for an unaccompanied minor, or a person without legal capacity who does not have a legal representative, should be appointed by the guardianship authority before the submission of an asylum application. This guardian should be present in the course of an interview with mentioned minors[243] and this rule is applied in practice.

§3. Victims of Human Trafficking

265. Under Serbian immigration law, victims of human trafficking have, under precisely defined conditions, a particular status in regard to the right of residence in the country. The Aliens Act regulates that the permission for temporary residence may be granted to an alien who is a victim of human trafficking if it is in the interest of a court proceeding regarding the criminal act of human trafficking.[244] In such a case, temporary residence will be granted even though an alien does not meet basic requirements for entry and temporary residence permit in Serbia, i.e., does not

242. UNHCR, Serbia as a Country of Asylum, *ibid.* at s. 48.
243. Article 16 of the Asylum Act.
244. Article 28 of the Aliens Act.

possess a valid travel document and/or visa (if required), sufficient financial means to sustain him/her and, logically, requirements relating to 'justified purpose of residence'. Alien with the status of a victim of human trafficking will be granted temporary residence even in the case that he/she does not meet requirements from Article 11 of the Aliens Act, (*see* Part I, Chapter 3, §1) i.e., if he/she is in transit, but does not meet the requirements to enter the third country, if the protective measure of removal or the security measure of deportation against him/her is in effect, or if his/her permission to stay was cancelled. Such protection to the victim of human trafficking will be denied in just two cases: if so required by reasons related to protection of the public order or the safety of the Republic of Serbia and its citizens, and if there is reasonable doubt that an alien could take advantage of the stay for purposes other than those declared.[245]

266. An alien who is a victim of human trafficking will be granted special treatment regarding the residence in Serbia only in the case that he/she is a victim of activity defined as 'trafficking in persons' pursuant to the Protocol to Prevent, Suppress and Punish Trafficking in Persons, Especially Women and Children,[246] supplementing the United Nations Convention against Transnational Organized Crime (so called Trafficking Protocol), which Serbia ratified in 2001.[247] According to this Protocol, as human trafficking is considered:

> recruitment, transportation, transfer, harbouring or receipt of persons, by means of the threat or use of force or other forms of coercion, of abduction, of fraud or deception, of the abuse of power or of a position of vulnerability, or of the giving or receiving of payments or benefits to achieve the consent of a person having control over another person, for the purpose of exploitation.
>
> Exploitation includes, at a minimum, the exploitation of the prostitution of others or other forms of sexual exploitation, forced labour or services, slavery or practices similar to slavery, servitude or the removal of organs.[248]

Human trafficking exists even in spite of possible consent of a victim of trafficking, i.e., this consent is irrelevant where any of the above-mentioned means have been used.[249]

245. *Ibid.*
246. Protocol to Prevent, Suppress and Punish Trafficking in Persons, especially Women and Children, General Assembly resolution 55/25 of 15 Nov. 2000, http://www.unodc.org/documents/treaties/UNTOC/Publications/TOC%20Convention/TOCebook-e.pdf (accessed on 11 Oct. 2013).
247. Official Gazette of the Federal Republic of Yugoslavia – International Treaties No. 6/2001.
248. Article 3 of the Protocol to Prevent, Suppress and Punish Trafficking in Persons, especially Women and Children.
249. The Criminal Code of the Republic of Serbia in the Art. 388, para. 1, contains the legal definition of trafficking in human beings which fully draws upon the definition provided by the 2000 Protocol to Prevent, Suppress and Punish Trafficking in Human Beings, especially Women and Children (Art. 3 of the Protocol).

267. Ministry of Interior's *Instruction on the conditions for granting temporary residence to foreign nationals – victims of human trafficking*[250] regulates the conditions and procedure on treatment of aliens who are victims of human trafficking and on these grounds were granted humanitarian protection. According to this Instruction, a temporary residence permit may be granted for a period of three months, six months or one year depending on the case. When applied for the first time, temporary residence is usually granted for a period of three months in order to provide for the protection and recovery assistance of the victims and their return to their country of origin or previous residence (period of recovery and reflection). A victim of human trafficking may be granted temporary residence for a period of six months, if he/she cooperates with authorities in the investigation of criminal offences and perpetrators. Temporary residence for a period of one year is granted to a victim of human trafficking if he/she actively participate in the proceedings as a witness or is injured, or when so required for reasons of personal safety.[251] In the cases where a victim of human trafficking at the time of the request does not have a passport, a temporary residence permit will be granted on the basis of special decision of the competent office of the Ministry of Interior.

268. The Serbian *Criminal Procedure Code*[252] includes a number of provisions important for the prevention of human trafficking and protection of victims when they appear as witnesses in criminal investigation. When there are circumstances demonstrating that a witness or a close person's public testimony may substantially endanger his/her life and limb, health, freedom or property (particularly in cases dealing with organized crime, corruption and other serious criminal acts), the court may issue a decision to award special protection measures by granting the witness the status of a protected witness.[253] The special protection measures imply a special proceeding for questioning the witness, which imply relevant conditions and applying methods which will ensure the confidentiality of the witness's identity as well as the security measures for safeguarding the witness's physical integrity in the course of the proceedings.[254]

269. The *Health Care Act of the Republic of Serbia* includes provisions that ensure protection and assistance to aliens, victims of human trafficking. In Article 241 of this Act, there is a provision that medical institutions shall be refunded for their medical services from the budget of Serbia, according to the pricelist established by the organization in charge of the compulsory health insurance for the medical services provided to different categories of aliens (such as those who have been granted asylum in Serbia) in case they have no financial support, or in case

---

250. *Uputstvo o proceduri odobrenja privremenog boravka stranim državljanima žrtvama trgovine ljudima*, Ministry of Interior of the Republic of Serbia, UP, No. 03/1 br. 26-1658/04, 20 Sep. 2004.
251. *Ibid.*
252. *Zakonik o krivičnom postupku*, Official Gazette of the Republic of Serbia, Nos 72/2011, 101/2011, 121/2012, 32/2013 and 45/2013.
253. Article 162 of the Criminal Procedure Code.
254. For further details *see* M. Kostić & A. Mihajlović, *Counteracting and Preventing Human Trafficking in the Republic of Serbia*, 10 Facta Universitatis, Series: L. & Pol. 101–110 (2012).

they have been victims of human trafficking.[255] Some additional protection is also provided in the Administrative Taxes Act which prescribes that an alien who is a human trafficking victim is exempted from paying the administrative tax for being issued a travel document.[256]

270. The victim of human trafficking who was granted a temporary stay is provided with appropriate accommodation, food and living conditions if he/she does not have enough financial means to sustain himself/herself during the temporary stay. The victims are accommodated in confidential shelters for victims of human trafficking (the shelters can be under the jurisdiction of government services, as well as under the jurisdiction of non-governmental organizations), or at some other secret location if the (foreign national) victim of human trafficking does not wish to be held in the shelter during the whole stay in the Republic of Serbia. Apart from these official shelters, there are also private homes offered by NGOs for the purpose of emergency assistance to victims of human trafficking. This type of facilities is already in use in Belgrade, Novi Sad and Niš.

271. For victims of human trafficking, of special importance during their stay in Serbia in terms of support is the state sponsored Legal Aid Office for the Coordination of Protection of Victims of Human Trafficking as part of the Institute for Education of Children and Adolescents in Belgrade. The Office's assignment is to offer legal, medical and psychosocial services which are essential in the process of assisting human trafficking victims. Duties of this Office are defined by the Rules on Tasks and Assignments of the Institution for Education of Children and Adolescents in Belgrade:

– Identification of a victim after the police reports the case.
– Conversation with the victim and getting him/her acquainted with the aid programme and is/her rights.
– Reaching a decision with the victim on what should the next steps on protection be.
– Organization of transportation to shelters or to the town where the victim lives.
– Cooperation with the competent centre for social work.
– Cooperation with the police and establishing an estimate of the victim's safety and information on whether criminal charges will be pressed against the perpetrator.
– Cooperation with the judicial bodies from which it receives information during the proceedings and organizing the victim's transport to the court.
– Providing legal aid to the victim, also in the form of legal representation during the proceedings.
– Issuing a document which states that a person is a victim of human trafficking so that the person could exercise his/her right to health care services in primary care facilities, or with a recommendation of a doctor in other health care providers.

255. *Zakon o zdravstvenoj zaštiti Republike Srbije*, Official Gazette of the Republic of Serbia, Nos 99/2010 and 57/2011.
256. *Zakon o administrativnim taksama*, Official Gazette of the Republic Serbia, No. 70/2011.

- Cooperation with embassies in the case when an alien does not have personal documents.
- Cooperation with international and NGOs through which it provides the necessary help to victims.
- Making a plan for individual reintegration of every victim in line with his/her needs and in accordance with available resources and programmes.
- Establishing communication between a victim and his/her family.
- Gathering documentation needed in order to apply for a temporary residence permit for aliens, travel document and/or visa.
- Escorting the victim to the airport or to the border when needed, and waiting for and collecting the victim at the airport or the border.[257]

272. For the status of victims of human trafficking, the Strategy for Combating Human Trafficking in the Republic of Serbia, which was adopted in 2006, is highly relevant.[258] It consists of series of measures and activities which should be undertaken with the aim of making a timely and comprehensive response to the problem of human trafficking in the Republic of Serbia, with special emphasis on protection of victims' human rights. The Strategy helped establish the national mechanism for coordination of activities and creation of a policy for the fight against human trafficking. Institutional framework that has been established for the coordination of activities and policy-making in this field consists of two levels: (a) the central-strategic, which includes the Council on Combating Human Trafficking, the Coordinator for Combating Human Trafficking and the Republic Team for Countering Human Trafficking; and (b) the operational one that includes the judicial bodies, the police and the Agency for the Coordination of the Protection of Human Trafficking Victims.

§4. OTHERS

273. Humanitarian motives play a certain role in regulations of residence of returnees under Readmission Agreements and IDPs. However, being nationals, to these groups Aliens Act provisions regarding residence regime are not applicable. (*See* Part III, Chapter 1, §1, III for Returnees and Part III, Chapter I, §2 for IDPs)

---

257. Ivana Krstić, *Protecting the Rights of Migrants in the Republic of Serbia* 82–83 (International Organization for Migration – Mission to Serbia, Belgrade 2012).
258. *Strategija za suzbijanje trgovine ljudima u Republici Srbiji*, Official Gazette of the Republic of Serbia, No. 111/2006.

Chapter 5. Asylum

§1. General Framework

274. The Republic of Serbia is a state party to the UN Convention on the Status of Refugees of 1951 and an Additional Protocol on the Status of Refugees of 1967, and is thus bound to respect and implement provisions of these agreements. Serbia is also bound by the Stabilization and Association Agreement with the European Communities (SAA) and their Member States. In SAA Serbia is committed to harmonize her legislation in the relevant sectors to that of the Community, and to effectively implement it. The Serbian government has set the establishment of the asylum system as one of the important tasks in all the key documents within European integration. Although Serbia is still not formally bound by the standards established by the EU directives and regulations regarding asylum, the Asylum Act was being developed in compliance with the EU standards. However, Serbia is still not part of the Dublin II Regulation.

275. The Asylum Act was adopted as part of legislation that was to be enacted to fulfil the 'Schengen Criteria', in November 2007. As said before, the Act was harmonized with EU Council Directive 2003/09/EC on minimum requirements for admission of asylum seekers, with EU Council Directive 2004/83/EC on minimum requirements and status of third-country citizens or stateless persons for acquisition of refugee status, and with EU Council Directive 2001/55/EC on minimum requirements for provision of temporary assistance in cases of mass inflows of displaced persons. The Act came into force on 1 April 2008. Before this date, the UNHCR carried out full responsibility for refugee status determination procedure (RSDP) and for asylum applicants within the territory of Serbia, pursuant to the SaM 2005 Asylum Act[259] and, partly, the 1980 Movement and Stay of Aliens Act[260] which before the adoption of the Asylum Act in Serbia in 2007 were applied in asylum matter. After entering into force of the Asylum Act of 2007, they ceased to have effect.

276. Apart from the right to asylum, which comprises the right to refuge and the right to subsidiary (humanitarian) protection, the Act also provides for temporary protection, which is extended in case of a large-scale influx of people, when it is impossible to review individual asylum applications. Besides, it is important to stress that this Act is not applicable to refugees who were granted that status under the 1992 Refugees Act which deals with refugees from ex-Yugoslav republics.[261]

277. From that moment the Asylum Act has been applied; there was a steady increase in the number of registered asylum seekers in Serbia. Beyond the legacies of regional displacement, Serbia at present is primarily a country of transit for

259. *Zakon o azilu*, Official Gazette of Serbia and Montenegro, No. 12/2005.
260. Official Journal of the Socialist Federal Republic of Yugoslavia, Nos 56/1980, 53/1985, 30/1989, 26/1990, 53/1991 and Official Gazette of the Federal Republic of Yugoslavia, No. 68/2002.
261. Official Gazette of the Republic of Serbia, Nos 18/1992 and 45/2002.

mixed migratory flows from Asia and the Middle East towards EU Member States. Government sources have conveyed their view to UNHCR that approximately one-third of irregular migrants arriving in Serbia apply for asylum in order to avoid detention that would otherwise apply to them as irregular migrants. The number of undocumented migrants who find themselves unable to leave Serbia has been increasing, due to reinforced Schengen border controls with Hungary. The behavioural pattern of the majority of these individuals provides the basis for the claim that in most cases, according to asylum applications (expressed intent), they were the so-called irregular migrants without real intention to seek asylum in the Republic of Serbia. (This does not lead to the conclusion that among them there is not and will not be persons who have proper grounds for seeking asylum). Asylum seekers reach the competent authorities of Serbia mostly through the territory of Macedonia or Kosovo, transferred from the territory of Greece (to Greece they usually come from Turkey). In addition to nationals of Afghanistan, who are the most numerous, the nationals of Palestine, Somalia and Pakistan use a similar 'route'.

278. Since 2008 until June 2013, 6,506 individuals expressed the intention to seek asylum in Serbia. During the same period, three persons were granted asylum. So far, five people have been granted the status of subsidiary protection, for one year, with the possibility of extension.[262]

279. The asylum system is a complex problem in Serbia because of the situation in Macedonia and Greece. Macedonia is neither willing to provide asylum to migrants, nor is it attractive to them in any way. On the other hand, Greece is not able to provide shelters and adequate services to further flows of asylum seekers. Apart from the issue of asylum seekers coming from third countries, Serbia has to solve the problem of IDPs and returnees coming back to the country on the basis of re-admission agreements with neighbouring countries and EU Member Countries.[263]

§2. Conditions

I. Refugee Status

280. The Asylum Act prescribes the principles, conditions and procedure for the granting and cessation of asylum, as well as the status, rights and obligations of asylum seekers and persons granted the right to asylum in Serbia. The Act offers an interpretation of the meaning of the main notions regarding asylum, that are relevant for assessing conditions for a refugee status.

262. Danilo Rakić (ed.), *Challenges of Forced Migration in: Serbia: Position of Refugees, Internally Displaced Persons, Returnees and Asylum Seekers* 4 (Group 484 2011).
263. Ewelina Tylec, *Serbian Asylum System in the Wake of EU Accession – Challenges and Opportunities* 51 (Belgrade Centre for Human Rights 2013).

281. Asylum is defined as the right to residence and protection accorded to an alien (and stateless person) to whom, on the basis of a decision of the competent authority deciding on his/her application for asylum in Serbia, refuge or another form of protection provided for by the Asylum Act was granted.[264] According to the Act, *an asylum seeker* is an alien who has filed an application for asylum on the territory of Serbia, on whose application a final decision has not been taken. *A refugee* is defined as a person who, on account of well-founded fear of persecution for reasons of race, sex, language, religion, nationality, membership of a particular social group or political opinions, is not in the country of his/her origin, and is unable or unwilling, owing to such fear, to avail him/herself of the protection of that country (as well as a stateless person who is outside the country of his/her previous habitual residence). Consequently, *refuge* is designated as the right to residence and protection granted to a refugee who is on the territory of Serbia, with respect to whom the competent authority has determined that his/her fear of persecution is well founded.[265]

282. Besides, the Asylum Act includes an *asylum seeker family member* and an *unaccompanied minor* in the scope of, by this Act, protected persons. As family members are recognized: minor child, adopted child or stepchild, who is not married; a spouse, provided that the marriage was contracted before the arrival in Serbia, and a parent or an adoptive parent that the asylum seeker is legally obliged to support. The status of a family member may also be granted to other persons in exceptional circumstances, particularly taking into account the fact that they were supported by the person who has been granted refuge or subsidiary protection.[266]

283. An *unaccompanied minor* is an alien under 18 years of age who was unaccompanied by parents or guardians on his/her arrival in Serbia, or who became unaccompanied by parents or guardians after arriving in Serbia.[267]

284. According to the Asylum Act, conditions for acquiring the refugee status, the reasons for its cessation, as well as the fundamental rights and obligations of asylum seekers should be based on the following basic principles:

- *The principle of non-refoulement* which means that no person shall be expelled or returned against his/her will to a territory where his/her life or freedom would be threatened on account of his/her race, sex, language, religion, nationality, membership of a particular social group or political opinions. However, this principle is not applicable to a person with respect to whom there are reasonable grounds to believe that he/she constitutes a threat to national security, or who has been convicted of a serious crime by a final court judgment, for which reason he/she constitutes a danger to the public order. Notwithstanding this provision, no person may be expelled or returned against his/her will to a territory where

264. Article 2 of the Asylum Act.
265. *Ibid.*
266. *Ibid.*
267. *Ibid.*

there is a risk of his/her being subjected to torture, inhumane or degrading treatment or punishment.[268]

– *The principle of non-discrimination* means that in the asylum procedure in Serbia, any discrimination on any grounds is prohibited, and in particular on the grounds of race, colour, sex, nationality, social origin or a similar status, birth, religion, political or other beliefs, financial standing, culture, language, age, mental, sensory or physical disability.[269]
– *The principle of non-punishment for unlawful entry or stay* prohibits the punishment of an asylum seeker for unlawful entry or stay in Serbia, provided that he/she submits an application for asylum without delay and offers a reasonable explanation for his/her unlawful entry or stay.[270]
– *The principle of family unity* obliges competent authorities to take all the available measures for the purpose of maintaining family unity during the asylum procedure and after granting the right to asylum. Persons granted asylum are entitled to family reunification, in accordance with the provisions of this Act.[271]

A. Asylum Application

285. The general rule is that an alien who is in the territory of the Republic of Serbia has the right to file an application for being granted asylum in the Republic of Serbia. Under the Asylum Act, asylum is understood as the right to residence and protection accorded to an alien to whom, on the basis of a decision of the competent authority deciding on his/her application for asylum in Serbia, refuge or another form of protection provided for by this Act was granted. The Asylum Office shall issue a decision by virtue of which the right to refuge is granted to an alien (or stateless person) once it has been established that the person who has filed an asylum application meets the requirements for being granted the right to refuge, if no reasons to deny the right to refuge exist.[272]

286. Pending the adoption of the final decision on asylum applications, asylum seekers are provided with accommodation and basic living conditions at the Asylum Centre, which is managed by the Commissariat for Refugees and Migrations as a special organization, organized in accordance with the 2012 Migration Management Act.[273]

287. Asylum application may be considered unfounded, denied or refused by the reasons that are listed in the Asylum Act.

---

268. Article 6 of the Asylum Act.
269. Article 7 of the Asylum Act.
270. Article 8 of the Asylum Act.
271. Article 9 of the Asylum Act.
272. Article 28 of the Asylum Act.
273. 2012 Migration Management Act (*Zakon o upravljanju migracijama*), Official Gazette of the Republic of Serbia, No. 107/2012.

B. Unfounded Asylum Applications

288. An asylum application shall be considered unfounded if it has been established that a person who filed the application does not meet the requirements prescribed for granting the right to refuge, and in particular:

- if the asylum application is based on untruthful reasons, fraudulent data, forged identification papers or documents, unless the applicant can provide valid reasons for that;
- if the statements given in the asylum application regarding facts of relevance to the decision on asylum contradict the statements made in an interview with the asylum seeker in question or other evidence gathered in the course of the procedure (if, contrary to the statements given in the application, it has been established in the course of the procedure that the asylum application was submitted for the purpose of postponing deportation, that the asylum seeker has come for purely economic reasons and the like);
- if the asylum seeker refuses to make a statement regarding the reasons for seeking asylum or if his/her statement is unclear or does not contain information indicating persecution.[274]

C. Denying the Right to Asylum

289. The right to asylum may be denied, i.e., not recognized, to an asylum seeker with respect to whom there are serious reasons to believe that:

- he/she has committed a crime against peace, a war crime, or a crime against humanity, according to the provisions of international conventions adopted with a view to preventing such crimes;
- he/she has committed a serious non-political crime outside the Republic of Serbia prior to entering her territory;
- he/she is responsible for acts contrary to the purposes and principles of the United Nations.

290. Also, the right to asylum shall not be recognized to a person who enjoys protection or assistance from some of the institutions or agencies of the United Nations, other than UNHCR, as well as to a person to whom the competent authorities of Serbia already recognize the same rights and obligations as to the citizens of the Republic of Serbia, on the other grounds.[275]

---

274. Article 30 of the Asylum Act.
275. Article 31 of the Asylum Act.

D. Rejection of Asylum Applications

291. The Asylum Office shall reject an asylum application without examining the eligibility of an asylum seeker for the recognition of asylum if it has established:

- that the asylum seeker could have received effective protection in another part of the country of origin, unless he/she cannot be reasonably expected to do so in view of all the circumstances;
- that the asylum seeker enjoys the protection of, or receives assistance from, an agency or a body of the UN, other than UNHCR, or has been granted asylum in some other country;
- that the asylum seeker has the citizenship of a third country;
- that the asylum seeker can receive protection from a safe country of origin, unless he/she can prove that it is not safe for him/her;
- that an asylum application, which the asylum seeker has submitted in another country that complies with the Geneva Convention was refused, and the circumstances upon which the application was based have not changed in the meantime, or if he/she has already filed an asylum application in another country observing the Geneva Convention;
- that the asylum seeker has come from a safe third country, unless he/she can prove that it is not safe for him/her;
- that the asylum seeker has deliberately destroyed a travel document, an identification paper or some other written official communication, which could have been of relevance to the decision on asylum, unless he/she can quote valid reasons for that.

292. Before issuing a decision on rejecting an asylum application, the Asylum Office should duly question the asylum seeker with respect to all the circumstances which exclude the reasons for rejecting an asylum application.[276]

E. Implementation of Concepts of 'Safe Third-Country' and 'Safe Country of Origin'

293. The Asylum Act accepts the concepts of 'Safe Third-Country' and 'Safe Country of Origin'. A 'safe country of origin' is defined as:

> country from a list established by the Government whose national an asylum seeker is, and if the person concerned is stateless, a country where that person had previous habitual residence, which has ratified and applies international treaties on human rights and fundamental freedoms, where there is no danger of persecution for any reason which constitutes grounds for the recognition of the right to refuge or for granting subsidiary protection, whose citizens do not

276. Article 29 of the Asylum Act.

leave their country for those reasons, and which allows international bodies to monitor the observance of human rights.

A 'safe third country', according to the Act, shall mean a 'country from a list established by the Government, which observes international principles pertaining to the protection of refugees contained in the 1951 Convention on the Status of Refugees and the 1967 Protocol on the Status of Refugees, where an asylum seeker had resided, or through which he/she had passed, immediately before he/she arrived in the territory of Serbia and where he/she had an opportunity to submit an asylum application, where he/she would not be subjected to persecution, torture, inhumane or degrading treatment, or sent back to a country where his/her life, safety or freedom would be threatened'.[277]

294. As said before, the Asylum Act regulates that competent authorities are entitled to reject an asylum application without examining the eligibility of an asylum seeker for the recognition of asylum if it has established that the asylum seeker could have received effective protection in another part of the country of origin (unless he/she cannot be reasonably expected to do so in view of all the circumstances), that can receive protection from a safe country of origin (unless he/she can prove that it is not safe for him/her) or that the asylum seeker has come from a safe third country, (unless he/she can prove that it is not safe for him/her).[278]

295. According to the Serbian Government Decree on Establishing a List of Safe Countries of Origin and Safe Third Countries, safe countries of origin for asylum seekers are all countries-members of the European Union, Bosnia and Herzegovina, Macedonia, Montenegro, Norway, Iceland, Liechtenstein, Switzerland, Monaco, Russia, Belarus, Australia, New Zealand, Japan, Canada, USA, Argentina, Paraguay, Uruguay, Chile, Costa Rica, Mexico, Seychelles, Mauritius, Kenya, Tunisia and Turkey. Safe third country are all the above listed countries except Russia, Belarus, Argentina, Paraguay, Uruguay, Chile, Costa Rica, Mexico, Seychelles, Mauritius, Kenya, Tunisia and Turkey.[279]

296. The Government's list of 'safe countries of origin' deserves sharp criticism. It is known that in Macedonia asylum seeker requests were treated inefficiently and without fair process; Tunisia and Belarus are countries which were accused of grave violations of human rights; in Greece, systematic violations of human rights during the procedure for asylum was confirmed by the European Court of Human Rights, and Turkey has made a reservation to the Protocol to the Convention on refugees 1967, which limits the application of the Convention only to persons who have become refugees because of events that occurred on European soil.

277. Article 2 of the Asylum Act.
278. Article 33 of the Asylum Act.
279. Decree on Establishing a List of Safe Countries of Origin and Safe Third Countries (*Odluka o utvrđivanju liste sigurnih zemalja porekla i sigurnih trećih država*), Official Gazette of the Republic of Serbia, No. 67/2009.

297. The Belgrade Centre for Human Rights, a prestigious Serbian NGO dealing with asylum seekers' rights, submitted to the Constitutional Court an initiative for the assessment of constitutionality of the Decree on Establishing a List of Safe Countries of Origin and Safe Third Countries. In the initiative it was stated that the disputed Decree (declared by the Government in 2009 and not updated since then) was developed based on ambiguous criteria and that it affects the essence of the right to asylum by denying it in practice. In addition, the choice of certain countries as safe countries of origin and safe third countries is criticized in the initiative, and examples from the international court's practice and suggestions of criteria based on which safe countries should be chosen are listed. In April 2013, the Constitutional Court rejected the initiative on ground of its incompetence, based on the provision that the disputed Decree, in form and content, is not a general legal act, whose compliance with the Constitution and the Law is to be determined by the Constitutional Court. Namely, based on the assumption that the disputed Decree determines only the list of safe countries of origin and safe third countries, the Constitutional Court has judged that this act is not in character a general legal act, as it does not contain general norms which can regulate an issue in a general and abstract manner.[280] According to the opinion of a number of legal experts, this Constitutional Courts' Decision remains controversial.

298. The Hungarian Helsinki Committee (HHC) examined whether it is justified to apply to Serbia the concept of the safe third country, fuelled by a significant increase in the number of asylum seekers returned by the Hungarian authorities to Serbia in 2011. Hungary modified its Asylum Act in December 2010 and introduced the concept of a safe third country among the criteria examined in the admissibility procedure. The result of this research demonstrated that asylum seekers arriving in Hungary through Serbia may be returned to Serbia without an in-merit examination of their claim. HHC concluded that the current Serbian asylum system is not sufficiently functional and is neither able to ensure the proper determination of international protection needs for an increasing number of asylum seekers, nor does it provide an effective protection for those qualifying for refugee status. The above being a precondition for considering a country as a safe third country, HHC assessed that Serbia cannot be regarded as such, stressing that 'Hungarian asylum authorities wrongly consider Serbia as a safe third country in their daily practice and wrongly exclude asylum seekers arriving in Hungary through Serbia from an in-merit determination of their protection needs'. According to HHC, Hungary's practice of applying the safe third country concept to Serbia is in breach of the European Convention on Human Rights, namely of Article 3, by exposing asylum seekers to the risk of torture, inhuman or degrading treatment or punishment (through *refoulement*), and of Article 13, by failing to provide an effective remedy.[281]

---

280. Constitutional Court of the Republic of Serbia, Decision No. I.Uo-812/2012 of 24 Apr. 2013, in Belgrade Centre for Human Rights (Beogradski centar za ljudska prava), *Asylum in the Republic of Serbia: Report for the Period January – June 2013* 14 (Belgrade June 2013).

281. Anikó Bakonyi, Júlia Iván, Gruša Matevžic & Tudor Rosu, *Serbia as a Safe Third Country: A Wrong Presumption* (Report based on the Hungarian Helsinki Committee's field mission to Serbia, 8–10 Jun. 2011, Budapest, September 2011).

II. Subsidiary Protection Status

299. The Asylum Act recognizes the notion of subsidiary protection. It is defined as a form of protection which the Republic of Serbia grants to an alien (or stateless person) who, if returned to the country of origin, would be subjected to torture, inhumane or degrading treatment, or where his/her life, safety or freedom would be threatened by generalized violence caused by external aggression or internal armed conflicts, or massive violation of human rights. The Asylum Act stipulates that in the case that an alien is not eligible for being granted the right to refuge (asylum), the competent authorities should consider ex officio whether there exist conditions for granting subsidiary protection.[282]

300. It should be noted that the Act has overtaken standards for eligibility of aliens or stateless persons as beneficiaries of subsidiary protection from the European Union Directive 2011/95/EU.[283] A difference that can be found in the Asylum Act is the deletion of 'danger of sentencing to or enforcement of capital punishment' as a ground for such protection. However, one of the possible reasons for denying the right to subsidiary protection are 'serious reasons to believe' that the protection seeker has committed a crime against peace, a war crime, or a crime against humanity, according to the provisions of international conventions adopted with a view to preventing such crimes, or has committed a serious non-political crime outside the Republic of Serbia prior to entering its territory, or if he/she is 'responsible for acts contrary to the purposes and principles of the United Nations'.[284]

301. In principle, beneficiaries of subsidiary protection enjoy conditions and rights which are equal or similar to those which are granted to persons who are recognized as refuges. The only exception is the situation in which families are reunited. Namely, family reunification in the case of persons granted asylum is governed by the Asylum Act, whilst people granted subsidiary protection may exercise the right to family reunification 'pursuant to regulations on the movement and residence of aliens', i.e., pursuant to the Aliens Act.[285]

III. Temporary Protection Status

302. Temporary protection as a pragmatic and flexible protection framework to protect persons that are forced to flee in mass influx situations is provided under the

282. Article 27 of the Asylum Act.
283. Article 15 of Directive 2011/95/EU of the European Parliament and of the Council on Standards for the qualification of third-country nationals or stateless persons as beneficiaries of international protection, for a uniform status for refugees or for persons eligible for subsidiary protection, and for the content of the protection granted on 13 Dec. 2011, Official Journal of the European Union L 337/9 20 Dec. 2011.
284. Article 31 of the Asylum Act.
285. Article 49 of the Asylum Act.

Asylum Act. It was adopted following the transposition of the EU Temporary Protection Directive 2001/55/EC.[286] Temporary protection is granted in the case of a massive influx of persons from a country where their life, safety or freedom are threatened by generalized violence, external aggression, internal armed conflicts, massive violation of human rights or other circumstances that have seriously affected public order.[287]

303. Temporary protection is given on a prima facie basis, without the individual procedure for determining the status. Namely, it is provided that temporary protection shall be accorded when it is not possible to carry out an individual procedure for granting the right to asylum due to the above-mentioned situation. According to the Asylum Act, it will be granted 'in line with the social, economic and other capacities of the Republic of Serbia'. A decision on the provision of temporary protection is taken by the Government of Serbia.[288]

304. Temporary protection is an extraordinary measure and may last for up to one year, and if the reasons for providing temporary protection continue to apply, it may be extended. Aliens to whom temporary protection has been granted have the right to submit an asylum application. Possible negative decision on that request shall not affect the rights conferred on the basis of temporary protection.

305. Temporary protection may also be accorded to those persons who lawfully resided in Serbia at the time when such circumstances occurred, but their residence right expired before the reasons for the provision of temporary protection ceased to apply, if other statutory requirements have been met.

306. Temporary protection shall cease upon the expiry of the period for which it was granted, or when the reasons for which it was granted have ceased to exist, which shall be decided by the Government. Temporary protection may cease to apply to an alien, at any moment, on the basis of a decision taken by the Asylum Office, if it has been established that in such alien's case reasons exist for which the right to refuge may be denied.

307. The Aliens Act regulates that an alien who has been granted temporary protection shall be equal in terms of obligations with persons whose right to refuge has been recognized. The Act lists these rights:

- residence during the period of the validity of temporary protection;
- a personal document confirming his/her status and residence right;
- health care, in accordance with the regulations governing health care for aliens;

286. Council Directive 2001/55/EC of 20 Jul. 2001 On minimum standards for giving temporary protection in the event of a mass influx of displaced persons and on measures promoting a balance of efforts between Member States in receiving such persons and bearing the consequences thereof, Official Journal of the European Communities L 212/12, 7 Aug. 2001.
287. Article 36 of the Asylum Act.
288. *Ibid.*

- free primary and secondary education in public schools, in accordance with a special regulation;
- legal aid, under the conditions prescribed for asylum seekers;
- freedom of religion, under the same conditions that apply to the citizens of the Republic of Serbia;
- accommodation, in accordance with a special regulation;
- affordable accommodation, in the case of handicapped persons.[289]

308. Regarding the family reunification of a person granted temporary protection, the Asylum Act stipulates that the competent authorities may, in justifiable cases, allow family reunification and also grant temporary protection to family members of a person enjoying temporary protection in Serbia.[290]

§3. PROCEDURES

I. Asylum Procedure

A. *Competent Authorities*

309. The Asylum Office, a competent organizational unit of the Ministry of the Interior, conducts the asylum procedure with respect to asylum applications and the cessation of the right to asylum and takes all decisions in the first instance.[291]

310. The Asylum Commission decides in the second instance on complaints lodged against the decisions taken by the Asylum Office. It comprises the Chairman and eight members appointed by the Government for a four-year term. A person may be appointed the Chairman or a member of the Asylum Commission if he/she is a citizen of Serbia, has a university degree in law and a minimum of five years of work experience as a practicing lawyer, and is familiar with regulations in the field of human rights. The Asylum Commission is an independent body and decides by a majority vote of the overall number of its members.[292]

B. *Asylum Centres*

311. Pending the adoption of the final decision on asylum applications, asylum seekers are provided with accommodation and basic living conditions at the asylum centres which are a part of the governmental body, the Commissariat for Refugees and Migrations. (*See* General Introduction, §2.). The Government of Serbia has so

289. Article 38 of the Asylum Act.
290. Article 50 of the Asylum Act.
291. Article 19 of the Asylum Act.
292. Article 20 of the Asylum Act.

far established two asylum centres: the Asylum centre in Banja Koviljača (established 15 December 2008) and the Asylum centre in Bogovadja (established 23 May 2011) both situated around 100 km from Belgrade.

312. Pending adoption of the final decision on asylum applications, asylum seekers are provided with accommodation and basic living conditions at the Asylum Centre. Code of conduct of asylum seekers is defined in the House Rules of the Asylum Centre. All other issues significant for the functioning of centres are regulated by the Rules on the Conditions for Accommodation and Provision of Basic Living Conditions in the Asylum Centre.[293] According to the Rules, an asylum seeker may be accommodated in the asylum centre if he/she was previously recorded or registered and referred to the Asylum Centre by the Ministry of Interior, if the medical examination has been performed in accordance with the regulation passed by the Minister of Health, and if the accommodation capacity of the Centre so allows. If there is no available accommodation, the Centre is not obligated to accept and accommodate asylum seekers. Also, asylum centres are not able to accept asylum seekers in need of another person's assistance and care, mentally ill individuals and individuals in need of health care of an appropriate specialized medical institution.[294]

C. Procedural Principles

313. The Asylum Act lists the principles that should govern the asylum procedure. These principles are recommended in the UNHCR Handbook and Guidelines on Procedures and Criteria for Determining Refugee Status. These principles are:

- *The principle of providing information and legal aid*: It implies that an alien who has expressed his/her intention to seek asylum in Serbia should be entitled to being informed about his/her rights and obligations in the course of the entire asylum procedure. An asylum seeker has the right to free legal aid and representation by UNHCR and NGOs whose objectives and activities are aimed at providing legal aid to refugees.[295]
- *The principle of providing free translation services* is provided for an asylum seeker who does not understand the official language of the procedure. He/she should be provided with free services for the purpose of translation into the language of the country of origin or a language he/she can communicate in. An asylum seeker may also engage an interpreter of his/her own choice and at his/her expense, if he/she thinks this is a better solution. The obligation of providing free

293. *Pravilnik o uslovima smeštaja i obezbeđivanju osnovnih životnih uslova u Centru za azil*, Official Gazette of the Republic of Serbia, No. 31/2008.
294. Article 6 of the Regulation on the Conditions for Accommodation and Provision of Basic Living Conditions in the Asylum Centre.
295. Article 10 of the Asylum Act.

translation services shall apply also to the use of gestural language and the availability of materials in the Braille alphabet and other accessible formats.[296]

- *The principle of free access to UNHCR* means that an asylum seeker has the right to contact the authorized UNHCR staff at any stage of the asylum procedure.[297]
- *The principle of personal delivery* means that any written official communication in the procedure should be delivered to an asylum seeker or his/her legal representative in person. A written official communication should be considered delivered when either of the above-mentioned persons had received it.[298]
- *The principle of gender equality* means, in terms of the Asylum Act, that it should be ensured that an asylum seeker is interviewed by a person of the same sex or provided with a translator or an interpreter of the same sex, unless this is not possible or is associated with disproportionate difficulties for the body conducting the asylum procedure. This principle should always be applied in the cases of conducting a search, body checks and other actions in the procedure presupposing physical contact with an asylum seeker.[299]
- *The principle of providing care for persons with special needs* is foreseen by Article 15 of the Asylum Act and implies that care should be taken in the asylum procedure of the specific situation of persons with special needs who seek asylum. The scope of such persons encompasses: minors, or persons completely or partially deprived of legal capacity, children separated from parents or guardians, handicapped persons, elderly people, pregnant women, single parents with minor children and persons who were subjected to torture, rape or other serious forms of psychological, physical or sexual violence.[300]
- *The principle of representation of unaccompanied minors and persons without legal capacity* implies that before the submission of an asylum application for an unaccompanied minor or a person without legal capacity who does not have a legal representative, a guardian should be appointed by the guardianship authority. It is mandatory that the guardian be present in the course of an interview with such persons.[301]
- *The principle of directness* means that any alien who has filed an asylum application has the right to a verbal and direct interview, carried out by an authorized officer of the organizational unit of the Ministry of the Interior in charge, regarding all the facts relevant to the recognition of the right to refuge or to the granting of subsidiary protection.[302]
- *The principle of confidentiality* obliges competent authorities to provide that the data on an asylum seeker obtained in the course of the asylum procedure are confidential (classified) information and access to it may be allowed only to persons authorized by law. These data must not be disclosed to the country of origin of an asylum seeker, unless he/she has to be forcibly returned to the country of origin

296. Article 11 of the Asylum Act.
297. Article 12 of the Asylum Act.
298. Article 13 of the Asylum Act.
299. Article 14 of the Asylum Act.
300. Article 15 of the Asylum Act.
301. Article 16 of the Asylum Act.
302. Article 17 of the Asylum Act.

upon the completion of the procedure, his/her asylum application having been rejected.[303]

D. Phases in Asylum Procedure

314. According to the Asylum Act, the procedure for granting asylum is implemented in several phases:

315. In the first one, an asylum seeker should, verbally or in writing, express his/her intention to seek asylum to an authorized officer of the Ministry of Interior. He/she can do that during a border check in the course of entering Serbia, or later, inside its territory.

316. In the second phase, after an asylum seeker has expressed intention, an authorized officer of the Ministry of Interior, to whom this intention was expressed, should make a record of it and direct the asylum seeker to the Asylum Office, i.e., into the Asylum Centre. The entry into records includes the issuance of a prescribed certificate containing the personal data that the alien has provided about himself or that can be established on the basis of the identification papers and documents available on his/her person. The certificate serves as proof that the asylum seeker has expressed an intention to seek asylum and that he/she has the right to reside in Serbia for seventy-two hours. The asylum seeker is obliged to contact, within seventy-two hours, an authorized officer of the Asylum Office, i.e., the Asylum Centre. If the authorized officer of the Ministry of Interior suspects that one of the reasons for the restriction of movement applies to this asylum seeker, such officer may escort an alien to the Asylum Office or the Asylum Centre. The authorized police officer is entitled to perform personal search of the asylum seeker and his/her personal belongings for the purpose of finding identification papers and documents required for the issuance of the certificate. All identification papers and documents which have been found are recorded in the certificate.

317. The next step begins when the authorized officer of the Asylum Office registers an alien and his/her family members. The registration includes establishing identity, taking a photograph and fingerprints, and the temporary seizure of all identification papers and documents which can be of relevance in the asylum procedure, of which a certificate is issued to an asylum seeker.

318. The form of the asylum application is printed in Serbian Cyrillic script and in English. The content of the form of the asylum application is translated orally into the language the asylum seeker understands. The form of the asylum application should (preferably) be completed in the language in which it is printed. If the asylum seeker does not understand the language(s), he/she may complete it in the language he/she understands.

303. Article 18 of the Asylum Act.

319. The procedure for granting asylum continues by submitting an asylum application to an authorized officer of the Asylum Office on a prescribed form, within fifteen days of the day of registration. In justified cases, the Office may extend this time limit at the request of an asylum seeker. However, an alien may lose the right to reside in Serbia if he/she unjustifiably fails to abide by the defined time limit. Before the submission of the asylum application, the asylum seeker should be informed of his/her rights and obligations.

320. The authorized officer of the Asylum Office should interview an asylum seeker in person as soon as possible. An asylum seeker may be interviewed more than once. It is allowed to organize an audio recording of an interview, provided that the asylum seeker in question has been informed of this. A legal representative of an asylum seeker and a UNHCR representative may be present at an interview, provided that the asylum seeker does not object to that. An authorized officer of the Asylum Office endeavours during the interview to establish all the facts of relevance to making a decision on an asylum application, and in particular on the identity of the asylum seeker and the grounds on which his/her asylum application is based.

E. Suspension of the Procedure and Restitutio in Integrum

321. In legally defined cases, the Asylum Office may decide to suspend the asylum procedure. The procedure for granting asylum shall be suspended ex officio if an asylum seeker:

- withdraws his/her asylum application;
- despite having received a duly served summons, fails to appear for an interview or declines to make a statement, without providing a valid reason for doing so;
- without a valid reason, fails to notify the Asylum Office of a change of address at which he/she resides within three days of the said change, or if he/she prevents the service of a summons or another written official communication in some other way;
- leaves Serbia without the approval of the Asylum Office.[304]

In its decision to suspend the procedure, the Asylum Office should set a time limit within which an alien who has no other grounds for residing must leave Serbia. If he/she fails to do so, he/she shall be forcibly expelled, in accordance with the law governing the stay of aliens.

322. An asylum seeker may, within three days of the date when the reasons for his/her failure to respond to the summons for an interview or to report a change of address in a timely manner ceased to apply, submit a proposal for restoration to the original condition (*restitutio in integrum*). A decision on the proposal for restoration to the original condition shall be taken by the Asylum Office.

---

304. Article 34 of the Asylum Act.

II. Review of the Decision Rejecting the Application for Asylum

323. After conducting the procedure, the Asylum Office should pass a *first instance* decision. The Office may decide that an asylum seeker fulfils legal conditions and then adopt the application recognizing to the asylum seeker the right of refuge or extending to him/her a subsidiary protection. The Asylum Office may also conclude that the application was unjustified and take decision on refusing an asylum application and ordering an alien to leave Serbia within the set time limit, unless he/she has some other grounds for residence. The reasons for denying the status should also be justified. (For the reasons for refusal and rejection of asylum application see above).

324. First-instance decisions on asylum applications may be appealed within fifteen days from the day they are served.[305]

325. The Asylum Commission that reviews in *second-instance* the appeals of the Asylum Office should decide within two months from the date the appeal was filed. The decision of the Asylum Commission can be positive, when the appeal was adopted and asylum or subsidiary protection granted, or negative, i.e., confirming the first instance decision of Asylum Office.

326. An Asylum Commission decision may be challenged in an administrative dispute before the Administrative Court, (*see more*: Part VI, Chapter 1).

327. An alien whose asylum application was previously refused in the Republic of Serbia may file a new application if he/she provides evidence that the circumstances relevant for the recognition of the right to refuge, or for granting subsidiary protection, have substantially changed in the meantime. If he/she fails to do so, the application shall be rejected.[306]

328. According to the EU Commission 2013 Serbia Progress Report which assesses Serbia's achievements in the process of accession to EU, a number of weak points of Serbian asylum system need to be overcome and adapted to *acquis communautaire*. Among other things, asylum claims are still temporarily processed by the Border Police Asylum Unit, and the Asylum Office intended to operate as the first instance body has yet to be definitively established in line with the Asylum Act. A unified national database for checking the personal data and fingerprints of aliens, including asylum seekers, is being developed but remains to be put in operation. From over 2,723 applications in 2012 (3,134 in 2011), only three of those that were maintained were granted positive protection decisions (none in 2011). The criteria of safe countries of origin and the list of safe non-EU countries have yet to be fully aligned with the *acquis*. The lack of adequate asylum processing, where applicants are neither referred to nor registered in the asylum procedure as the Asylum Act requires, tends to encourage asylum applicants to see Serbia as a transit country for

305. Article 35 of the Asylum Act.
306. Article 32 of the Asylum Act.

illegally entering the EU. Additional reception facilities with adequate conditions for asylum seekers are also needed, especially since access to the asylum procedure is dependent on accommodation at an asylum centre. 'Overall, Serbia continues to be in the early stages of aligning with EU asylum policy'.[307]

329. According to the most recent UNHCR Report, with the existing legislative framework and national reception system Serbia's national asylum system, in particular the Asylum Office as currently set up, cannot process the significant increase of asylum-seekers. This can be attributed to several factors, particularly to an over-reliance on the 'safe third country concept'. The primary obstacle to ensuring the quality of the asylum procedure is the fact that the Asylum Office is currently still operating on an ad hoc basis under the Border Police Directorate of the Interior Ministry. Besides, the Asylum Office lacks a sufficient number of qualified personnel to adjudicate asylum claims in an efficient yet thorough manner. Another concern is that the Asylum Office, based within the Border Police Directorate, is not independent from the police structure. Asylum procedures are conducted by police officers who are often inadequately trained in the principles and application of international refugee protection. While Article 19 of the Asylum Act stipulates that authorized officers conducting the asylum procedure in the Asylum Office should be specially trained for performance of these tasks, their primary expertise, as professional police officers, is in criminal law enforcement and border control; they lack sufficient training on issues related to the asylum procedure and refugee protection. Placing police in the role of the interviewer during the asylum procedure may additionally undermine the perception of confidentiality and impartiality, which is crucial in creating conducive conditions for applicants during the personal interview. UNHCR recommends that a civilian authority be assigned this role, along with responsibility for taking decisions, under future development of the asylum system.[308]

III. Unaccompanied Minor Asylum Claimants

329.1. *See* Part III, Chapter IV, §2.

IV. Safe Country of Origin and Safe Third Country

329.2. *See* Part III, Chapter V, §2, E.

---

307. *Serbia 2013 Progress Report*, p. 50, Commission Staff Working Document SWD (2013) 412 final in: *Enlargement Strategy and Main Challenges 2013-2014*, Communication from the Commission to the European Parliament and the Council COM (2013) 700 final (Brussels, 16 Oct. 2013).
308. UNHCR, Serbia as a Country of Asylum, Observations on the Situation of Asylum-Seekers and Beneficiaries of International Protection in Serbia, p. 6 (August 2012).

§4. LEGAL POSITION

330. One should distinguish the legal position of the recognized refugee, i.e., an alien who is granted asylum by the Asylum Office and the legal position of the asylum seeker during the asylum application procedure.

I. A Person with Recognized Refugee Status

331. As regards the legal position of a recognized refugee, the Asylum Act mostly takes over solutions of the 1951 Convention Relating to the Status of Refugees and 1967 Protocol.

332. The Asylum Act regulates that persons whose right to refuge in Serbia has been recognized shall have rights equal to those of the citizens of Serbia with respect to intellectual property protection rights, free access to courts of law, legal aid, exemption from the payment of court fees and other fees payable to state organs, and the right to freedom of religion.[309]

333. All other rights of refugees are equal to those of permanently residing aliens. According to the Asylum Act, persons whose right to refuge in Serbia has been recognized shall have rights equal to those of permanently residing aliens with respect to the right to work and rights arising from employment, entrepreneurship, the right to permanent residence and freedom of movement, the right to movable and immovable property, and the right of association.[310] Besides, a person who has been granted asylum shall have equal rights to health care, right to free primary and secondary education and the right to welfare benefits in accordance with the regulations governing health care, i.e., education for aliens.

334. To persons whose right to refuge or subsidiary protection has been recognized, accommodation should be provided commensurately with the capacities of the Republic of Serbia, but not for longer than one year from the final decision on status recognition. Accommodation implies the provision of a certain habitable space for use, or of financial assistance necessary for housing.[311]

335. A recognized refugee has also the right to an identity card in Serbia, valid for up to five years (and up to one year for a person granted subsidiary protection) and the right to a travel document for a person over 18 years of age (available to persons with subsidiary protection in exceptional cases), as well the right to family reunification.

336. The Asylum Act also foresees an exemption of refugee from possible reciprocity measures. This exemption applies when a refugee had resided in Serbia at

309. Article 42 of the Asylum Act.
310. Article 43 of the Asylum Act.
311. Article 44 of the Asylum Act.

least for three years from the date of recognition of his/her refugee status, in respect of rights due to him/her according to the law.[312] This regulation is harmonized with the 1951 Convention Relating to the Status of Refugees that stipulates that 'after a period of three years residence, all refugees shall enjoy exemption from legislative reciprocity in the territory of the Contracting States'.[313]

337. The Asylum Act regulates that the Republic of Serbia should create, commensurate with its capacities, conditions for the inclusion of refugees in its social, cultural and economic life, and enable the naturalization of refugees. (For the conditions of naturalization *see* General Introduction, section 2, II).

338. The general obligation of every recognized refugee is to respect duties toward the Republic of Serbia, which require in particular that he/she conform to Serbia's laws and regulations, as well as to measures taken for the maintenance of public order.

339. It should be again pointed out that the Serbian 1992 Refugees Act does not apply to aliens who were granted asylum according to the Asylum Act because the 1992 Refugees Act regulates the status, position and rights specifically for refugees coming from the territory of one of the republics of the former SFR of Yugoslavia and does not apply to other aliens. (*See* Part III, Chapter 6).

II. Asylum Seeker Status

340. Legal status and rights of asylum seekers are regulated by the Asylum Act and other relevant laws. Asylum seekers rights during asylum procedure should be in accordance with the principles listed in the Asylum Act (*see* Part III, Chapter 3, §3).

341. As said above, an asylum seeker cannot be punished for unlawful entry or stay in Serbia, provided that he/she submits an application for asylum without delay and offers a reasonable explanation for his/her unlawful entry or stay.[314] Further, the competent authorities are obliged to take all the available measures for the purpose of maintaining family unity during the asylum procedure (as well as after granting the right of asylum). If the asylum seeker so requests, the right to refuge will be granted to his/her family members who are outside of Serbia.

342. An asylum seeker shall have the right to reside in Serbia for the duration of the procedure and, if necessary, he/she shall be entitled to accommodation at the Asylum Centre during that period. Upon admission to the Asylum Centre, all asylum seekers should undergo a medical examination in accordance with a regulation passed by the Minister in charge of public health. At the Asylum Centre, in addition

312. Article 45 of the Asylum Act.
313. Article 7 of the 1951 Convention Relating to the Status of Refugees.
314. Article 8 of the Asylum Act.

to accommodation, the basic living conditions are provided to asylum seekers: clothes, food, financial assistance and other conditions, in conformity with special regulations and the principles of the asylum procedure. If an asylum seeker possesses his/her own financial assets or if they have been provided to him/her in some other manner, he/she shall be obliged to co-finance the costs of accommodation at the Asylum Centre, and at his/her request, if there are no reasons for restriction of movement as defined in Article 52 of the Asylum Act (*see below*), the Asylum Office shall allow him/her to reside outside the Asylum Centre.[315]

343. In accordance with the above-mentioned principles, an alien who has expressed his/her intention to seek asylum in Serbia is entitled to be informed about his/her rights and obligations in the course of the entire asylum procedure. He/she is also entitled to free legal aid and to contact authorized UNHCR staff or NGOs whose objectives and activities are aimed at providing legal aid to refugees at any stage of the asylum procedure. An asylum seeker who does not understand the official language of the procedure should have an interpreter, or, as has already been said, may engage an interpreter of his/her own choice and at his/her expense. Any written official communication in the procedure should be delivered to an asylum seeker or his/her legal representative in person. It is ensured that an asylum seeker is interviewed by a person of the same sex or provided with a translator or interpreter of the same sex, unless this is not possible or is associated with disproportionate difficulties.

344. Any alien who has filed an asylum application is entitled to a verbal and direct interview, carried out by an authorized officer of the competent organizational unit of the Ministry of Interior, regarding all the facts relevant to the recognition of the right to refuge or to the granting of subsidiary protection. The data on the asylum seeker obtained in the course of the asylum procedure should be treated as confidential.

345. An asylum seeker has rights to health care, in accordance with the regulations governing health care for aliens. In accordance with the Health Care Act the expenses of health care services provided to aliens having been granted an asylum in Serbia will be covered by the budget of the Republic of Serbia if they are financially insecure.[316] An asylum seeker has the right to free primary and secondary education and the right to welfare benefits, in accordance with a special regulation. Detailed conditions under which the right to welfare benefits is realized are defined by the Rules on Social Assistance for Asylum Seekers or Persons who Have Been Granted Asylum.[317] According to the Regulation, monthly financial benefits may be received by an asylum seeker or his/her family members, provided that they are not accommodated in the Asylum Centre and that this person and his/her family members have no income or that this income is below the limit set by this Regulation.

315. Article 39 of the Asylum Act.
316. Article 241 of the Health Care Act.
317. *Pravilnik o socijalnoj pomoći tražiocima azila i osobama kojima je odobren azil*, Official Gazette of the Republic of Serbia, No. 44/2008.

A request for exercising the right to monthly financial benefit is decided by Social Care Centers in the municipality of residence of the asylum seeker (or person granted asylum).

346. Also, the asylum procedure should take care of the specific situation of persons with special needs who seek asylum, such as minors, or persons completely or partially deprived of legal capacity, children separated from parents or guardians, persons with disabilities, elderly people, pregnant women, single parents with minor children and persons who were subjected to torture, rape or other serious forms of psychological, physical or sexual violence.

347. An asylum seeker has to fulfil a number of obligations in order to enjoy the above-mentioned rights. According to the Asylum Act an asylum seeker is obliged:

- to adhere to the measures for restriction of movement referred to in Article 52 of this Act, if they have been imposed;
- to inform the Asylum Office in writing of any change of address within three days of such a change of address;
- to abide by the House Rules, if he/she is accommodated at the Asylum Centre;
- to respond to the summons and cooperate with the Asylum Office and other competent authorities at all stages of the asylum procedure;
- to hand over to an authorized officer his/her identification papers, travel document and other documents, which can be of relevance for his/her identification;
- to cooperate with authorized staff during his/her registration and medical examination;
- to stay in the territory of the Republic of Serbia pending the completion of the procedure for granting asylum;
- to leave the Asylum Centre after the final decision on asylum application has been taken.[318]

348. According to the Asylum Act, restriction of movement of an alien, asylum seeker, can be implemented by ordering accommodation at the Reception Centre for Aliens under intensified police surveillance or by imposing a ban on leaving the Asylum Centre, a particular address and/or a designated area. These restrictions can last for as long as the reasons for them exist, but not for longer than three months.[319]

§5. Position of Family Members

349. The Asylum Act regulates in Chapter VII issues regarding family reunification and legal status of asylum seekers and their family members. By these provisions the right to family reunification of a person whose right to refuge has been recognized. At the explicit request of the recognized refugee, the Asylum Office

318. Article 47 of the Asylum Act.
319. Article 52 of the Asylum Act.

should also grant the right to refuge to his/her family members who are outside the territory of the Republic of Serbia, unless there are statutory reasons to deny them that status.[320]

350. The same right is recognized also to persons who were granted subsidiary protection. Although the Aliens Act does not apply in principle to aliens who applied for or were granted asylum in Serbia, the provisions of this Act apply to family reunifications of people granted subsidiary protection.[321]

351. Given that temporary protection is considered as an exceptional measure, a person granted temporary protection may enjoy the right to family reunification only 'in justifiable cases'. This should decide the competent authorities implementing asylum procedures.[322]

352. As previously stated, welfare benefits for refugee family members are regulated by the Rules on Social Assistance for Asylum Seekers or Persons who Have Been Granted Asylum.[323] According to these Rules, monthly financial benefits may be received by an asylum seeker's family members, provided that they are not accommodated in the Asylum Centre and that this person and his/her family members have no income or that this income is below the limit set by these Rules.

---

320. Article 48 of the Asylum Act.
321. Article 49 of the Aliens Act.
322. Article 50 of the Aliens Act.
323. *Pravilnik o socijalnoj pomoći tražiocima azila i osobama kojima je odobren azil*, Official Gazette of the Republic of Serbia, No. 44/2008.

Chapter 6. Others

§1. Refugees from the Republics of SFR Yugoslavia (Refugees under the 1992 Refuge Act)

353. A special category of persons enjoying a (specific) refugee status in Serbia are the persons coming to Serbia from the republics of former SFR Yugoslavia due to armed conflicts during the 1990s. According to combined data of the Serbian Commissariat for Refugees and Migrations and UNHCR, in the period 1991–1996 a total of 537,937 persons entered Serbia, fleeing from war. From Croatia came 290,667, from Bosnia and Herzegovina 232,974 and from other former Yugoslav Republics 14,296 persons.[324] The number of these refugees decreased by more than 80% in the period between 1996 and 2010. While 232,974 persons were listed in the census of refugees and war-affected persons in 1996, 346,000 persons in the census of 2001, and 104,246 persons in the registration of refugees in 2004/2005 – in 2010 Serbia had 82,600 registered refugees, of which 61,200 from Croatia and 21,400 from Bosnia and Herzegovina. The reduction of the number of refugees was the result of their integration into Serbia (around 300,000 refugees have acquired Serbian citizenship), their return to Croatia and Bosnia and Herzegovina (around 150,000) or getting refugee status in third countries (around 50,000).[325] To refugees from former Yugoslav republics, generally ethnic Serbs, refugee status was recognized prima facie under the 1992 Refugees Act.[326]

354. The Serbian Parliament passed in 1992 the Refugees Act, which includes a narrow definition of the term refugee: limiting it only to persons originally coming from territories of the former republics of the SFRY. According to this Act, the refugee status was recognized to:

> Serbs and citizens of other nationalities, who were forced, on account of the pressure from the Croatian authorities, or the authorities of other Republics, a threat of genocide, as well as persecution and discrimination on the grounds of their religion and nationality or political opinion, to leave their places of residence in those republics and take refuge in the territory of the Republic of Serbia for the purpose of meeting their basic subsistence needs and providing them social security.[327]

324. UNHCR and the Commissariat for Refugees, *Refugees in Serbia according to the Previous Place of Residence and Time of Arrival*, 1996, Census Data on Refugees and War-affected Persons, http://www.kirs.gov.rs/articles/navigate.php?type1=19&lang=ENG&date=0 (accessed 23 Jul. 2013).
325. Network Migration in Europe, *Forced Migration In Serbia*, http://migrationeducation. de/26.0.html (accessed 12 Oct. 2013).
326. For definition of prima facie refugee status determination *see* Matthew Albert, *Prima Facie Determination of Refugee Status – An Overview and Its Legal Foundation*, 18, Working Paper Series No. 55 (Refugee Studies Centre, Oxford Department of International Development, University of Oxford January 2010).
327. Article 1 of the 1992 Refugees Act.

It was regulated that the Republic of Serbia shall provide care to refugees pending the creation of conditions for their return to the places of origin, i.e., pending the creation of conditions for their durable social security. Under Article 2 it was said precisely that persons with refugee status determined in keeping with the provision of this Act shall include organized reception, temporary accommodation, aid in food, appropriate health care and material and other assistance. At the time when the Refugees Act was adopted, the aim was primarily to provide the legal framework for humanitarian protection of persons (mostly with Serbian ethnic roots) who found refuge in the territory of Serbia due to the war in Croatia and Bosnia and Herzegovina. As the time was passing by, it became clear that refugee crisis turns into a long-term problem because a large number of refugees decided to stay in Serbia. Therefore, the Refugees Act was amended only in May 2010 with the objective to create improved legal framework for the integration of persons who acquired Serbian citizenship. The most important provision of the amended Act regard the definition of refugee, i.e., the scope of persons to whom the Act should be applied. According to the amended Act, as refugees were understood:

> persons who due to the events taking place in the period 1991–1998 and their consequences were persecuted from former Yugoslav republics, or took refuge in the territory of the Republic of Serbia, and are unable to return to the country of their former habitual residence owing to the fear from persecution or discrimination, including persons who opted for integration.[328]

The person who opted for integration implies the person who submitted the application for the citizenship of the Republic of Serbia. The new definition of the term ‘refugee’ has thus included the persons who are determined to integrate. In accordance with this, refugees are being assisted in the process of integration as well as in housing, in order to satisfy their basic life needs.[329]

355. Under the 1992 Refugees Act, the Commissariat for Refugees and Migrations was established as a specialized body for carrying out professional and other tasks associated with the provision of care, return and integration of refugees. The Commissariat for Refugees and Migrations decided in the first instance on the recognition and cessation of the refugee status. An appeal may be lodged against the decision of the Commissariat within fifteen days from the day of the receipt of the decision and the Ministry of Interior decides on such appeal. On the basis of the decision on the recognition of the refugee status, the Ministry of Interior issues a refugee identity card, presenting a public document proving the identity of its holder, on the basis of which a refugee exercises the rights pertaining to him under the law.[330]

---

328. Article 1 of the Law on Amendments to the Refugees Act, Official Gazette of the Republic of Serbia, No. 30/2010.
329. Ivana Krstić, *Protecting the Rights of Migrants in the Republic of Serbia* 66 (International Organization for Migration – Mission to Serbia 2012).
330. Article 5 of the 1992 Refugees Act.

356. In accordance with the Act, refugees have the rights to employment and education, in keeping with the law, and they shall have the duty to do military service, i.e., fulfil the labour obligation, on the same terms as citizens of the Republic of Serbia.[331]

357. Several by-laws have been adopted in addition to the 1992 Refugees Act:

- Regulation on the Provision of Care to Refugees.[332]
- Regulation on the Manner of Provision of Care to the Persecuted People.[333]
- Rules on Keeping Records of Refugees.[334]
- Rules on Refugee Identity Card.[335]
- Rules on the Form of Refugee Identity Card.[336]
- Regulation on Detailed Conditions and Defining Priorities related to the Resolving of the Housing Needs of Refugees.[337]

358. In accordance with regulations, temporary accommodation and aid in food to refugees may be provided by organizing collective accommodation (collective centres). If an individual cannot adapt to collective accommodation owing to his/her psycho-physical condition (elderly persons and persons with disabilities, children, etc.), the Commissariat for Refugees and Migrations provides to this person accommodation in social welfare institutions. In accordance with regulations, refugees are occasionally provided in-kind assistance in the form of food and clothing and, in exceptional circumstances, in the form of money and monetary coupons.[338]

359. Until 2010 amendments, the 1992 Refugees Act contained a number of provisions that were in conflict with the 1951 Convention Relating to the Status of Refugees and, especially, with the 1967 Protocol Relating to the Status of Refugees binding Serbia as one of the successor states of SFRY. The 1951 Convention pertains to the very definition of refugee. Contrary to the 1951 Convention and 1967 Protocol the Article 1 of the 1992 Refugees Act maintained the incomplete definition of the term 'refugee', with additional deficient alterations. The target group was defined in a slightly discriminatory manner (Serbs and citizens of other ethnicities) as a certain category within the entire refugee population (referring to the internationally recognized meaning of that term), the category that emerged from the precisely defined time and geographical area (period 1991–1998; former Yugoslav republics). Temporal and geographical limitations in determining the refugee status

---

331. Article 2 of the 1992 Refugee Act.
332. Official Gazette of the Republic of Serbia, Nos 20/1992, 70/1993, 105/1993, 8/1994, 22/1994, 34/95 and 36/2004.
333. Official Gazette of the Republic of Serbia, No. 47/1995.
334. Official Gazette of the Republic of Serbia, No. 23/1992.
335. Official Gazette of the Republic of Serbia, Nos 23/1992 and 139/2004.
336. Official Gazette of the Republic of Serbia, Nos 23/1992, 22/94 and 61/1994.
337. Official Gazette of the Republic of Serbia, No. 58/2011.
338. Ivana Krstić, *ibid.* at 66.

and defining a refugee are clearly contrary to the 1967 Protocol which corrected criteria for defining a refugee stipulated by the 1951 Convention.[339]

360. Contrary to the spirit and letter of the 1951 Convention Relating to the Status of Refugees has been also the provisions of Article 2 and Article 18 of the 1992 Refugees Act. As already stated, Article 2 stipulated the duty of refugees to do military service in Serbia and by Article 18 it was regulated that the refugee may lose the rights stipulated in this Act if he/she has refused to return to the place of his/her permanent residence once objective conditions to do so have been created. By the Decision of the Federal Constitutional Court of the FRY of 25 July 2002 it was established that both provisions were not in accordance with the FRY Constitution and with the 1951 Convention Relating to the Status of Refugees.[340]

361. After adoption of the Asylum Act in 2007, the 1992 Refugees Act has been gradually omitted in practice, becoming a 'dead letter' that has outlived its relevance. However, it is formally still a part of Serbian applicable immigration law. In the future process of harmonization of Serbian law with *acquis communautaire* this Act will be, very likely, abolished or substantially changed. Once again, it should be pointed out that the Asylum Act stipulates that its provisions should be implemented with regard to the refugees who were granted their status by the 1992 Refugees Act only when this Act cannot be applied. (*See* Part III, Chapter 3, §1).

362. In addition to regulations, the National Strategy for Resolving the Problems of Refugees and IDPs for the period 2011–2014 was adopted by Serbia's Government in March 2011.[341] The Strategy relates to two target groups: refugees whose status is defined in accordance with the 1992 Refugees Act, and IDPs from the territory of Kosovo, which reside in Serbia outside Kosovo (*see* Part III, Chapter 5, §2). In relation to refugees, this Strategy established two main, parallel courses of action, which allow refugees to choose the most favourable long-term solution – return or integration. Regarding the refugees, the Strategy is based on two strategic goals:

- 'To promote the conditions necessary for the safe and dignified return of refugees to the Republic of Croatia and the Republic of Bosnia and Herzegovina, as well as institutional mechanisms for full and timely implementation of acquired rights in countries of origin'; and
- 'Creating necessary conditions for the refugees, particularly the most vulnerable categories of refugees – individuals and families who have chosen to live in the Republic of Serbia, in order to provide equal opportunities for

339. Praxis, *Brief Comment on Draft Law on Amendments to Refugees Law*, 10 Aug. 2006, http://www.praxis.org.rs/index.php/en/praxis-in-action/migration/item/290-praxis_brief-comment-on-draft-law-on-amendments-to-refugee-law (accessed 12 Dec. 2012).

340. Federal Constitutional Court of the Federal Republic of Yugoslavia, Decision No. I.U.253/2002 of 29 Jun. 2002, Official Gazette of the Republic of Serbia, No. 45/2002 and Official Gazette of the Federal Republic of Yugoslavia, No. 42/2002.

341. *Nacionalna strategija rešavanja problema izbeglica i interno raseljenih lica za period 2011–2014*, Official Gazette of the Republic of Serbia, No. 17/2011.

them and all other citizens, to solve their basic problems and integrate into the local community'.[342]

363. The Sarajevo Declaration process, initiated in 2005, is an international programme aimed to find long-lasting solutions for refugees and displaced persons following the 1991–1995 conflicts in the territory of the former Yugoslavia. The process involves four countries: Bosnia and Herzegovina, Croatia, Montenegro and Serbia. International organizations with UNHCR in the lead, the EU, the Organisation of Security and Cooperation in Europe (OSCE) as well as the United States have been closely involved in supporting the countries in addressing the issues. After a period of stalemate, the Sarajevo Process was reactivated in March 2010, when a ministerial meeting was held in Belgrade which brought together the four participating countries, the UNHCR, the EU and the OSCE. At this meeting, the countries committed themselves to work towards solutions of a number of outstanding issues, including data exchange and statistics, pensions and con-validation rights, housing and property issues. In November 2011, the four Ministers of Foreign Affairs of the participating countries signed a Joint Declaration together with a Framework Programme in which it was agreed that a Regional Housing Programme (RHP) should be established. The objective of the RHP is to make a substantial contribution to the satisfactory resolution of the protracted problem of the remaining refugees and displaced persons in the participating countries by providing long-lasting, sustainable housing solutions.

342. *Ibid.*

Part IV. Loss of Right of Residence

Chapter 1. Conditions under Which the Right of Residence Might Be Lost

§1. General Framework

364. Loss of aliens' right of residence may occur in two basic situations: first, when the alien resides legally and with required residence permits in the country but the grounds of his/her right have been disrupted; and second, when the alien continues his/her stay after the residence permit or other legal grounds for residing in Serbia have elapsed. Conditions under which the right of residence may be lost differ with regard to the type of alien's legal status and with regard to the ground for which the residence permit has been granted.

365. Loss of residence can be the consequence of the facts like the expiration of validity or death of the bearer, but also of the action of the competent authority as its reaction to changes in the residence grounds. From the procedural point of view there are basically two forms of competent authority action which leads to the alien's loss of right to residence: annulations and cancelation of permit of residence. The difference between these two forms lies in the reasons for which the residence is abridged as well in the range of the discretionary power of the competent authority. The cancellation can be effective on the ground of the discretionary power of competent authority, but the annulation may be imposed only *ex lege*, on the ground of the reasons explicitly established by law. In the continuation, the specific conditions for losing the right of residence on the basis of a visa, temporary residence permit, permanent residence permit, refugee status, subsidiary protection and temporary protection will be addressed.

366. According to the 2009 Aliens Act reasons for loss of the aliens' right to all types of residence in Serbia (short stay until ninety days, temporary residence and permanent residence) are as follows:

- if the term of validity of visa has expired;
- if the visa was cancelled; and

– if the protective measure of removal, or the security measure of deportation, was imposed against an alien.[343]

§2. Loss of Right to Short Stay

367. Alien's short stay in Serbia is allowed on the ground of the obtained Serbian visa (if it is necessary regarding the aliens citizenship). Although a visa is not a residence permit *in stricto sensu* but only the permit of entry, visa cancellation de facto means that the alien lost the of right to short stay.

368. The short stay may be contested to aliens who have entered the country both with or without a visa if it is afterwards established that some of the obstacles for lawful entry in Serbia exist. These obstacles are listed in Article 11 of the Aliens Act (*see* Part II, Chapter 1, §1). For instance, a visa can be revoked if the competent authority (border police officer) assesses that an alien cannot prove the purpose of his/her stay in Serbia. If the alien is refused entry into Serbia on any ground despite the existence of the visa, the visa is revoked as a result of such refusal of entry. If the alien on the grounds of the particular ground for stay in Serbia is required to present evidence of a valid health insurance or sufficient means for stay, the visa can be revoked if such evidence cannot be presented.[344] However, it is not provided by law that the validity of visa can be shortened, or the amount of days of stay under the visa permit reduced.

§3. Loss of Right to Temporary Residence

369. According to the Aliens Act, general reasons for cancellation of an alien's temporary residence permit are:

- Term of validity of residence permit has expired.
- Against an alien was imposed the protective measure of removal or the security measure of deportation.
- An alien was granted permit of residence on the basis of a false personal document or this document in the meantime ceased to be valid.
- An alien no longer has the means of subsistence and his/her subsistence in Serbia has not been provided for in another way.
- An alien no longer has health insurance.
- An alien no longer has a place of residence.
- The competent authority has found that cancellation of an alien's residence is required by reasons related to the protection of the public order or the safety of Serbia and its citizens.
- An alien is registered as an international felon in the relevant records.[345]

343. Article 36 of the Aliens Act.
344. Article 21 of the Aliens Act.
345. Article 11 of the Aliens Act.

370. The basic ground for temporary residence in Serbia is a justified purpose of residence. Consequently, temporary residence to an alien will be cancelled if – after the permit has already been issued – it is subsequently found that there had been reasons for refusal of temporary residence permit, or an alien intentionally provided false data on his/her identity or other false information, or has intentionally concealed the circumstances relevant for the issue of a temporary residence permit. An alien may lose his/her temporary residence also if there are proofs that he/she has taken advantage of the stay for purposes other than those declared, or if he/she has altered the previously declared purpose of stay in Serbia. (*See* Part II, Chapter 2)

371. Like the short stay permit, temporary residence permit also may be cancelled if it is in a later stage detected that some of the obstacles listed in the Article 11 of the Aliens Act exist. (*See* Part II, Chapter 1, §1). As an exception to this rule, temporary residence in Serbia will be not contested to an alien who is the victim of human trafficking although if he/she does not have a valid travel document, unless the competent authority assesses that the alien's stay is undesirable by reasons related to the protection of the public order, or establishes that he/she intends to stay for the purposes other than those declared.[346]

372. Specific reasons for loss of temporary residence depend on the different purposes of residence. For instance, for the foreign citizen who has been granted the right to work, or his/her permission for temporary residence is a precondition for exercising such right, in accordance with the regulations governing the work of aliens in Serbia temporary residence may be cancelled if the term of approved labour contract in Serbia has expired. Also, the loss of residence is possible if an alien and his/her employer do not reach an employment or service contract.[347]

§4. Loss of Right to Permanent Residence

373. According to the Aliens Act, two ways lead to an alien's loss of permanent residence. The first one is elaborated in Article 40 'Cancellation of permanent residence', and the second one in Article 41 'Termination of the right to permanent of the Aliens Act'.

374. Cancellation of permanent residence in Serbia is applied against an alien who has been granted permanent residence in Serbia in the following cases:

- If an alien, upon release from prison, has received the final unconditional sentence of imprisonment for more than six months for a criminal offence for which perpetrators are prosecuted ex officio.
- If the protective measure of removal or security measure of deportation has been imposed on an alien.

346. Article 28, of the Aliens Act.
347. Article 8 of the Conditions for Foreign Citizens Employment Act.

- If this is required for reasons of safeguarding public order or security of the Republic of Serbia and its citizens.
- If an alien no longer has the means of subsistence and his/her subsistence in Serbia has not been provided for in another way.
- If an alien no longer has health insurance.
- If an alien no longer has a place of residence.
- If an alien has provided false data regarding his/her identity or has concealed circumstances relevant to issuing the permit.[348]

375. Termination of the alien's right to permanent residence is effective if:

- It has been ascertained that an alien has moved out of the Republic of Serbia or that he/she has stayed abroad in continuity for longer than one year and has failed to notify this fact to the competent authority.
- The alien's stay has been cancelled.
- An alien has renounced the right to permanent residence.[349]

§5. The Cessation of the Refugee Status

376. General and specific conditions for the cessation of an alien's refugee status are prescribed by the Asylum Act. For refugees from the former Yugoslav republics for whom the refugee status was recognized by the 1992 Refugees Act, cessation of right to residence in Serbia and loss of refugee status is regulated by this Act. As already said above, the Asylum Act does apply to refugees who have been granted that status under the 1992 Refugees Act except in situations when this Act cannot be applied.

377. According to the 2007 Asylum Act, an alien's right to refuge shall cease for the following reasons:

- If a person has voluntarily re-availed him/herself of the protection of his/her country of origin.
- If, having lost his/her citizenship, a person has voluntarily re-acquired it.
- If a person has acquired a new citizenship, and thus enjoys the protection of the country of his/her new citizenship.
- If a person has voluntarily returned to the country he/she had left or outside which he/she has remained owing to fear of persecution or ill-treatment.
- If a person can no longer, because the circumstances that led to granting protection to him/her have ceased to exist, continues to refuse to avail himself/herself of the protection of his/her country of origin.[350]

---

348. Article 40 of the Aliens Act.
349. Article 40 of the Aliens Act.
350. Article 54 of the Asylum Act.

378. The Aliens Act specifies that the above listed conditions for the cessation of refugee status shall not apply to a person who is able to give compelling reasons, arising out of past persecution or ill-treatment, for refusing to avail himself/herself of the protection of his/her country of origin.

379. The Asylum Act also provides conditions for revoking a decision on granting asylum. According to Article 55, the Asylum Office shall ex officio revoke a decision on granting asylum if it is established that the above listed reasons for cessation already exist, as well as in other cases defined by law.[351]

380. The cessation of asylum is also possible by cancelling a decision on granting asylum. According to Article 56 of the 2007 Asylum Act, the Asylum Office shall ex officio cancel a decision on granting asylum if it is subsequently established:

- that a decision on granting asylum was taken on the basis of falsely presented facts or of concealment of facts by an asylum seeker and that, due to the above reason, at the time of the submission of the asylum application he/she was not eligible for being granted asylum; and
- that there exist reasons for which, on the basis of the law, he/she would have been denied the right to refuge, had these reasons been known at the time of the submission of the asylum application.[352]

381. As said above, in legally defined cases the Asylum Office may decide to suspend ex officio the asylum procedure. For the reasons for such suspension of the asylum procedure *see* Part III, Chapter 3, §3.

382. The 1992 Refugees Act regulates the conditions for cessation of the refugee status and cessation and/or reduction of refugee's right to welfare and other assistance. According to the Act, a refugee may lose the rights stipulated in this Act if he/she:

- has supplied incorrect information when applying for refugee status recognition or when exercising particular refugee rights;
- has failed to report changes in his/her refugee status, which are of relevance to the exercise of refugee rights, or failed to report a change in his/her habitual residence;
- has declined offered accommodation, i.e., replacement, or has declined accommodation permanently.[353]

As already said, by the Decision of the Federal Constitutional Court of the FRY, the provision of the 1992 Refugees Act related to the reasons for the cessation of refugee status because of refusing to do Serbian military service and refusing to

351. Article 55 of the Asylum Act.
352. Article 56 of the Asylum Act.
353. Article 18 of the 1992 Refugees Act.

return to the place of the refugee's permanent residence once objective conditions to do so have been created have been suspended as unconstitutional and contrary to the UN Convention Relating to the Status of Refugees. (*See* Part III, Chapter 6, §1).

383. The refugee shall be denied the right to provision of care if he/she:

- has returned to the place of origin or if the permanent accommodation has been secured to him/her in another specified place;
- has found a full-time job;
- has been provided for through acquisition of ownership of real estate, which can secure durable accommodation to him/her;
- has been provided for in that he/she, or his/her 'nuclear family' member, has established a business, thus ensuring durable social security.[354]

384. Welfare assistance as part of care for refugees, provided by the Office of the Commissioner to a refugee, may be reduced or terminated when:

- temporary employment has been secured to a refugee – until the expiry of the period of his/her employment, i.e., until the expiry of the period during which employment was secured to him/her;
- assistance as part of the provision of care through a humanitarian or another organization has been afforded to a refugee;
- conditions have been created for him/her to generate income from movable or immovable properties or other sources.[355]

§6. The Cessation of Subsidiary Protection

385. An alien who has been granted subsidiary protection is, in principle, equal in terms of obligations to persons whose right to refuge has been recognized. Grounds for cessation or lose of this status are, consequently, *mutatis mutandis* applicable to aliens with subsidiary protection status.[356]

§7. The Cessation of Temporary Protection

386. Given that the temporary protection is an extraordinary measure which may last for up to one year, it ceases upon the expiry of the period for which it was granted. However, it may be extended. Also, temporary protection may cease when the reasons for which it was granted have ceased to exist. The Government of Serbia decides whether or not such reasons exist. Besides, temporary protection may

354. Article 17 of the 1992 Refugees Act.
355. Article 16 of the 1992 Refugees Act.
356. Article 27 of the Asylum Act.

cease to apply to an alien, at any moment, on the basis of a decision taken by the Asylum Office, if it has been established that in a given case there are reasons for which the alien may be denied the right to refuge. Otherwise, an alien who has been granted temporary protection is equal in terms of obligations to persons whose right to refuge has been recognized.

Chapter 2. Legal and Administrative Procedures

387. It is very important to strictly respect the basic principles regulating administrative procedure when it comes to cancellation of residence. Namely, the right to residence is in itself a very sensitive issue, having in mind that loss of residence necessarily has serious and negative consequences for the individual. Competent authorities (police) should respect the principles of procedure regulated by the General Administrative Procedure Act,[357] providing that when acting in these matters they must take decisions pursuant to the law and – if legally empowered to make discretionary decisions – should remain within the scope and the purpose for which the powers have been given. Also, when conducting a procedure and deciding in the matters of residence cancellation, the authorities must as much as possible facilitate the protection and exercise of the rights and legal interests of the parties to the procedure, ensuring that the exercise of their rights is not detrimental to the rights and legal interests of other persons or in contravention of the legally established public interests, etc. Parties should always be informed about the method of conducting the proceedings and about the consequences, they have for them. Every civil servant should act in the interest of a migrant, resolving a case as quickly as possible with due consideration of the migrant's rights and consequences of non-exercising those rights.

388. On the other hand, state authorities, legal and natural persons are obliged to notify immediately the competent authority about an alien residing unlawfully or for whom there are conditions for rescinding of residence in the Republic of Serbia. The authority that instituted misdemeanour or criminal proceedings against an alien is obliged to notify immediately the competent authorities on the fact of unlawful stay of an alien.[358]

389. Competence for deciding on residence permit cancellation belongs to the Ministry of Interior unit responsible for aliens' affairs.[359]

390. If the competent authority decides to cancel the residence permit it should, in the process of cancellation, prescribe a deadline of maximum thirty days within which an alien shall be obliged to leave Serbia and the period during which the alien shall be prohibited to re-enter.[360]

391. The competent authority has a discretionary power when deciding on alien's short stay and visa issuance. Therefore, there is no right of appeal against the decision to refuse one's application for visa or the decision to cancel a visa. Also, such decision shall not require a statement of grounds.

---

357. Articles 5–9 of the General Administrative Procedure Act.
358. Article 45 of the Aliens Act.
359. Article 38 of the Aliens Act.
360. Article 35 of the Aliens Act.

392. In the same way will be decided also in the procedure of cancellation of the temporary residence and permanent residence, but in these cases an alien has a right on appeal. (*see more* in the Part VI, Chapter 1 on legal remedies). Under the procedure of cancellation of a permanent residence it is possible, as an exception, and out of humanitarian reasons, to extend the deadline within which an alien must leave Serbia for up to six months.[361]

393. The cancellation of stay and the prohibition of entry shall be entered in the aliens travel document if he/she possesses one; otherwise, it shall be entered into the alien identification card in the way stipulated by the Minister competent for interior affairs.

394. In its decision to suspend ex officio the procedure of granting asylum (see Part III, Chapter 3, §2) in legally defined cases, the Asylum Office can decide to suspend the asylum procedure. The Asylum Office should set a time limit within which an alien who has no other grounds for residing must leave Serbia. If he/she fails to do so, he/she shall be forcibly expelled, in accordance with the law governing the stay of aliens. However, an asylum seeker may, within three days of the date when the reasons for his/her failure to respond to the summons for an interview or to report a change of address in a timely manner ceased to apply, submit a proposal for restoration to the original condition (*restitutio in integrum*). A decision on the proposal for restoration to the original condition shall be taken by the Asylum Office.[362]

395. The statement on renunciation of the right to permanent residence as one of the reasons for the cessation of this type of residence is strictly formal. It should be written in the special form prescribed by the Minister competent for interior affairs.

361. Article 43, para. 3 of the Aliens Act.
362. Article 34 of the Asylum Act.

Part V. Sanctions

§1. General Remarks

396. Up to the adoption of the 2005 Misdemeanour Act,[363] in Serbia sanctions imposed for misdemeanours or small offences were considered as administrative sanctions because they were ruled in an administrative rather than criminal procedure. After 2005, misdemeanours offences are processed under judicial competences, in the framework of the newly established network of Misdemeanour courts. Ever since sanctions imposed by these courts are considered as a kind of 'soft' penal sanctions because are regulated under the penal/criminal law system. A prison sentence, fine, community service as well as a number of so-called precautionary measures may be prescribed as sanctions for a misdemeanour. For one misdemeanour, both a prison sentence and a fine may be prescribed and both may be imposed together. A prison sentence may be imposed only as the main penalty. If a fine and a prison sentence are prescribed alternatively, a prison sentence shall be imposed only for the misdemeanour, which has caused grave consequences or for the misdemeanours that point to a higher degree of guilt of the offender. A prison sentence may not be prescribed for any duration shorter than one or longer than sixty days. A prison sentence may not be imposed on a pregnant woman, after she reaches three months of pregnancy, or on a mother until her child reaches 1 year of age.[364] If a convicted individual, within a certain time period, fails to timely pay a fine in full or in part, the fine or the unpaid portion of the fine shall be substituted by community service or by a prison sentence.[365] Misdemeanour sanctions may be imposed against individuals (natural persons) and against legal persons. Misdemeanour offences are not codified. Such offences related to migration issues are listed in specialized laws like the Aliens Act, Asylum Act, State Border Protection Act, etc.

397. Precautionary (protective) measures may be imposed for misdemeanour offences, among them, also a measure of removal of aliens from the territory of Serbia. According to the 2005 Misdemeanour Act, removal of aliens from the territory of Serbia may be imposed on a person who has committed a misdemeanour due to which his/her further stay in the country is undesirable. This precautionary measure may be imposed for any duration from six months to three years. Duration of the

363. Misdemeanour Act (*Zakon o prekršajima*), Official Gazette of the Republic of Serbia, No. 101/2005.
364. Article 32 of the Misdemeanour Act.
365. Articles 28–31 of the 2005 Misdemeanour Act.

imposed measure shall run from the date of the legally binding judgment, whereby the time spent serving a prison sentence shall not be counted in the duration of the measure.[366]

398. Penal sanctions include criminal sanctions against persons violating provisions on entry and the cross-border regime and rules of residence, as well as against persons dealing in human smuggling and human trafficking. These penal sanctions are stipulated by the Criminal Code of the Republic of Serbia (2005).[367] According to this Code, penal sanctions may be: punishment (imprisonment), caution, security measures and rehabilitation measures. One of the security measures provided by this Code is the expulsion of an alien from the country that may be applied if an offender has already been pronounced penalty or suspended sentence.[368] The court may order expulsion from Serbia of an alien who committed a criminal offence for a period of one to ten years. In deliberating to order this measure, the court should take into consideration the time and gravity of a committed offence, motives for the which the offence was committed, manner of commission and other circumstances relevant for declaring an alien a *persona non grata* in Serbia.

399. It is also important to note that the criminal legislation of Serbia is applicable to an alien who commits a criminal offence against Serbia or its citizen outside the territory of Serbia, if they are found in Serbian territory or if extradited to Serbia.[369] Criminal legislation of Serbia shall also apply to an alien who commits a criminal offence abroad against a foreign state or foreign citizen, when such offence is punishable by five years' imprisonment or a heavier penalty, pursuant to laws of the country of commission, if such person is found in the territory of Serbia and is not extradited to the foreign state. In such cases the court, in principle, shall not impose a penalty heavier than set out by the law of the country where the criminal offence was committed.[370]

366. Article 57 of the 2005 Misdemeanour Act.
367. *Krivični Zakonik Republike Srbije*, Official Gazette of the Republic of Serbia, Nos 85/2005, 88/2005 and 107/2005.
368. Article 88 of the Criminal Code.
369. Article 9 of the Criminal Code.
370. *Ibid.*

Chapter 1. Sanctions Related to the Violation of Entry and/or Cross-Border Regime

§1. Administrative Sanctions

400. There is no administrative sanctions for the violation of entry and/or cross-border regime which are imposed by administrative courts in the administrative procedure. For such violations only penal (misdemeanours) sanctions imposed following criminal (misdemeanours) procedure are in place. (*See above:* Part V, §1.)

§2. Penal Sanctions

401. Sanctions for the violation of entry and cross-border regime are provided by the Aliens Act and State border Protection Act.

I. Sanctions against Natural Persons

402. According to the Aliens Act an alien shall be fined RSD 10,000–50,000 (around EUR 90–450) if he/she enters Serbia unlawfully.[371] Entry into Serbia is considered illegal if it is performed beyond the place or time prescribed for crossing the state border and thus avoiding the border control. Using another person's invalid, and/or forged travel or other document, and providing incorrect information to the border police, are also considered as offence.[372] However, according to the Asylum Act an asylum seeker shall not be punished for unlawful entry or stay in the Republic of Serbia, provided that he/she has submitted an application for asylum without delay and offered a reasonable explanation for his/her unlawful entry or stay.[373]

403. State Border Protection Act prescribes a fine of RSD 5,000–50,000 (EUR 45–450) or up to thirty days imprisonment that shall be imposed on a natural person committing an offence by:

- crossing or trying to cross the state border outside a certain border crossing point, outside working hours at the border crossing point or contrary to the purpose of the border crossing point; or, crossing or trying to cross the state border at a border crossing point without valid travel or other document prescribed for crossing of the state border;
- not possessing a document prescribed for crossing the state border or refusing to present it to the police officer, i.e., refusing to submit to the border control, or leaving the zone of the border crossing point before the border control is completed, or trying to evade border control in some other way;

371. Article 84 of the Aliens Act.
372. Article 10 of the Aliens Act.
373. Article 8 of the Asylum Act.

- failing to declare weapons for hunting purposes, i.e., weapons for shooting sports purposes, and ammunition which are brought into the Republic of Serbia;
- debarking or embarking a vessel, upon its arrival from abroad or upon departure from the Republic of Serbia outside a border crossing point.[374]

404. According to the Aliens Act, an alien may be fined also RSD 6,000–30,000 (EUR 50–250) for the misdemeanour if he/she:

- refuses to present an identification document to a police officer;
- gives his/her ID to another person to use, or uses an invalid ID, or uses someone else's ID as his/her own;
- travels or stays in a particular area in contravention of the restriction or prohibition of movement under Article 5 of the Aliens Act that regulates that movement and stay in a specific territory in the Republic of Serbia may be limited or prohibited to an alien if this is necessary due to reasons related to protection of public order and/or safety of the Republic of Serbia and her citizens, or pursuant to an international treaty.[375]

405. A fine of RSD 3,000–30,000 (EUR 25–250) or up to fifteen days imprisonment may be imposed on an individual committing an offence by:

- crossing the state border outside a border crossing point due to force majeure, and failing to immediately inform the border police;
- moving and stopping in the zone of a border crossing point without necessary permit or failing to act at the border crossing point and its zone according to orders and instructions given by police officers;
- failing to carry identification card in plain sight while moving and stopping in the zone of the border crossing point;
- failing to explain to the police officer conducting the border control any circumstances relevant to crossing of the state border, and failing to act according to the instructions and orders given by the police officer;
- as shipmaster in international traffic, failing to inform immediately the frontier police directorate, i.e., police station of the place of docking of the vessel, which docks due to force majeure outside an international border crossing point;
- as shipmaster in international traffic, failing to inform immediately the nearest authority of the embarking and debarking of persons outside a border crossing point for rescue purposes;
- as shipmaster, allowing at the port, without approval of the border police, the debarking from the vessel of person/persons not possessing documents prescribed for crossing of the state border, or embarking of such persons on the vessel without the shipmaster's approval;

374. Article 66 of the State Border Protection Act.
375. Article 85 of the Aliens Act.

- hunting or fishing in a certain zone along the borderline, but fails to submit to the border police a written announcement of this activity forty-eight hours before the hunting starts, i.e., twenty-four hours before the fishing starts at the latest.[376]

406. The Aliens Act lists a number of sanctions for misdemeanour offences committed against rules of lawful residence and administrative obligations of aliens related to these rules.

407. An alien may be fined RSD 10,000–50,000 (EUR 90–450) for misdemeanour offences if he/she:

- fails to leave the Republic of Serbia within the set time limit after the cancellation of his/her permit to stay and after the measure of prohibition of entry into Serbia was issued;
- leaves the detention centre without permission or fails to observe the house rules and rules of stay in the detention centre;
- leaves the place of stay ordered by the competent authority, or fails to report regularly to the competent authority on the ground of the decision on imposing a travel restriction order requiring the stay in a particular place on an alien who has residence and means of subsistence and who cannot be forcibly removed immediately.[377]

408. An alien may be fined RSD 6,000–30,000 for an infraction if he/she:

- Stays on the territory of Serbia unlawfully, i.e., without a visa, permission for temporary residence or other legal grounds, according to provisions of the Aliens Act.
- Stays in Serbia for purposes other than those for which he/she has been issued a visa or granted a temporary or permanent residence.
- Travels or stays in a particular area in contravention of the restriction or prohibition of movement and stay in a specific territory in Serbia limited or prohibited to an alien due to reasons related to protection of public order or safety of the state, or pursuant to an international treaty.
- Refuses to present an identification document to a police officer.

Gives his/her ID to another person to use, or uses an invalid ID, or uses another's ID as his/her own.[378]

409. An alien shall be fined RSD 3,000–15,000 for an infraction if he/she:

- fails to file an application for the extension of temporary residence within the prescribed time limit;

376. Article 66 of the State Border Protection Act.
377. Article 84 of the Aliens Act.
378. Article 85 of the Aliens Act.

- fails to file an application with the competent authority for issuing an alien identity card within the prescribed time limit;
- fails to file an application with the competent authority for replacement of the alien identity card within the prescribed time limit;
- fails to return the alien identity card to the competent authority in case he/she has acquired citizenship of Serbia, or is relocating out of Serbia or his/her temporary or permanent residence permit has been revoked;
- fails to report the loss or disappearance of documents issued by the competent authority of Serbia;
- fails to register his/her stay or change of address with the competent authority within twenty-four hours upon arrival in the place of temporary residence or upon a change of address in the place of temporary residence, as appropriate, in contravention of the Aliens Act provisions related to registration of temporary and permanent residence, change of address and termination of permanent residence;[379]
- wears a foreign military, police or the customs service uniform during his/her stay in the Republic of Serbia in contravention of the Aliens Act special provisions on the movement of aliens in uniforms and requirements related to wearing foreign military, police or customs service uniforms.[380]

410. In addition to the fine for all above listed offences, an alien may also receive the protective measure of removal from the territory of Serbia.

II. Sanctions against Legal Entities

411. The Aliens Act and the State Border Protection Act provide a number of sanctions for misdemeanour offences of legal entities related to various violations of the entry and border crossing regime.

412. A legal entity or sole trader shall be fined RSD 100,000–500,000 (EUR 900–4,500) for infraction if they transport an alien into the territory of Serbia or refuse to transport him/her therefrom in contravention of the Aliens Act provisions on obligations of carriers regarding the transport of foreign nationals to border crossing points. They may be also fined if due to their fault in the organization of a tourist or business trip, an alien stays unlawfully in the territory of Serbia.[381] According to Article 22 of the Aliens Act, a carrier may transport an alien to a border crossing only if none of the reasons for denial of entry of such alien to Serbia exist. In case that such reasons exist and entry was denied, a carrier is obliged to provide transportation free of charge without delay or, if immediate transportation

379. A natural person, Serbian citizen, who fails to register an alien's stay with the competent authority within twenty-four hours of the moment of alien's arrival for a visit is fined RSD 5,000 to 25,000 (EUR 45–230).
380. Article 86 of the Aliens Act.
381. Article 81 of the Aliens Act.

is not possible, to bear the costs of the stay and removal of such alien. This provision also applies to the carrier who brought an alien into the international transit area of an airport if another carrier has refused to transport him/her into the destination country, or if entry into the destination country is denied to the foreign national. An agency organizing a tourism or business related travel is obliged to reimburse the incurred costs if these cannot be charged to the alien and if his/her illegal stay resulted from a fault on part of the agency that organized the trip.[382]

413. According to the 2008 State Border Protection Act, a fine of RSD 100,000–1,000,000 (EUR 900–9,000) may be imposed on a legal entity found responsible for one of the following misdemeanour offences:

- constructing and installing, without consent of the Ministry, facilities, installations, equipment and devices in the zone of a border crossing point;
- failing to submit to the border police a written application for issuing a permit for movement and stopping at the border crossing point for its employee, before the employee begins to work in the zone of a border crossing point;
- failing to provide an identification card for the employee who has a permit for movement and stopping in the zone of a border crossing point;
- if its vehicle leaves the zone of the border crossing point before executed border control prescribed by State Border Protection Act;
- failing to provide during border control at the border crossing point, i.e., in the means of transport, conditions necessary for the work of the border police;
- failing to provide conditions or enable unhindered border control in accordance with provisions of the State Border Protection Act (Article 36), regulating obligations of the operator, owner and user of the means of transport;
- failing to ensure that the passengers do not leave the zone of the border crossing point before completion of border control, i.e., that upon performed border control other persons do not get on board or get off;
- failing to provide at the airport open to international traffic appropriate facilities that enable differentiation between international-flight passengers and other passengers, as well as facilities for foreign nationals who do not fulfil entry requirements in compliance with special law;
- if its train, which enters i.e., exits from the territory of Serbia, (except in the event of force majeure or if it is necessary for regulating railroad traffic), stops in the section between the border line and the zone of the border crossing point;
- if its railroad staff fails to immediately inform the border police that the train in international traffic, which is entering, i.e., exiting the territory of Serbia, stopped due to force majeure or emergency reasons; and if its railroad staff fails to ensure that passengers do not leave the train, i.e., that other persons do not get on board the train;
- if its vessel in international traffic crosses the state border outside the border crossing point open to international river traffic;

382. Article 22 of the Aliens Act.

- if its vessel in international traffic, (except in case of force majeure), docks outside the determined river or lake border crossing point without the necessary approval;
- if its shipmaster allows and embarks persons without valid document prescribed for crossing of the state border, or embarks or debarks persons outside the border crossing point except for rescue purposes;
- if its shipmaster upon arrival from abroad or before departure fails to give to the border police a copy of the list of crew members and the list of passengers on the vessel, i.e., does not provide inspection of their documents prescribed for crossing of the state border;
- if its shipmaster upon arrival into the port fails to fulfil the prescribed obligation under Article 42 of the State Border Protection Act regulating obligations of a shipmaster in international traffic. (Article 42 of the State Border Protection Act prescribes that upon arrival from abroad or before departure a shipmaster in international traffic must give to the border police a copy of the list of crew members and the list of passengers on the vessel, unless otherwise provided by international agreement, and provide the inspection of their documents prescribed for crossing of the border. Upon arrival into the port a shipmaster must report to the border police all persons found on the vessel without documents prescribed for crossing of the state border, as well as persons who embarked on the vessel without the shipmaster's approval.);
- if the aircraft captain in international traffic, who due to force majeure or emergency reasons, lands the aircraft outside the zone determined for international air traffic, fails to immediately inform the nearest police directorate, i.e., police station on such aircraft landing;
- if a crew member of its vessel, train or aircraft, who does not have the necessary visa, is moving during stopping of the vessel, train or aircraft in the zone of a border crossing point;
- navigating, hunting, fishing, flying by aircraft or other flying devices, moving or stopping along the border line, when this is prohibited or limited by the act of Government;
- hunting or fishing in a certain zone along the border line, but fails to submit to the border police a written announcement of this activity forty-eight hours before the hunting starts, i.e., at the latest twenty-four hours before the fishing with the use of a vessel starts.[383]

414. A fine of RSD 5,000 (EUR 45) shall be imposed on a natural person on the spot for driving a vehicle when crossing the state border if he/she does not observe all signs and instructions and orders of the police officer, or if he/she does not agree, i.e., does not pull over the vehicle in a certain area of the border crossing point or if he/she leaves the area before border control is performed, i.e., if he/she upon border control does not leave the zone of the border crossing point.[384]

383. Article 64 of the 2008 State Border Protection Act.
384. Article 67 of the 2008 State Border Protection Act.

415. The Criminal Code does not recognize criminal offences that explicitly address acts of violation of the rules of aliens' residence and movement in Serbia. Violations of provisions regulating aliens' rights on entry, movement and residence are mostly regulated by misdemeanour legislation. However, in case of offences indirectly related to this matter considered may be the application of sanctions provided for other criminal offences which are most often in relation to the aliens like, for instance: '*Violation of Freedom of Movement and Residence*' (Article 133 of the Criminal Code) '*Violation of the Right to Employment and during Unemployment*' (Article 164), '*Abuse of the Right to Social Security Benefits*' (Article 168), '*Failure to Act Pursuant to Health Regulations During Epidemic*', (Article 248), '*Transmitting Contagious Disease*', (Article 249), '*Forging a Document*' (Article 355), etc.

§3. Detention

I. Reasons and Time Limits

416. Detention measures may be imposed on aliens violating provisions of the immigration law. Pursuant to the Misdemeanour Act, the police may order twenty-four-hour custody of an offender caught in the commission of a misdemeanour who cannot be immediately taken before a judge and there are reasons to believe that he/she will abscond or continue with the commission of the misdemeanour.[385]

417. Unlawful entry and stay in Serbia and other acts of illegal immigration are the most often reasons for enforcement of detention measures against aliens. According to the report of the Belgrade Centre for Human Rights, a total of 2,522 people served sentences in Serbian penitentiaries in the first five months of 2012 for violating Article 10(2), Article 65(1), Article 41(1) or Article 65(4) of the State Border Protection Act or Article 85(1(3)) of the Aliens Act.[386]

418. Detaining an alien is stipulated by the Aliens Act as an exception, if that is necessary for reasons of a secure forced removal of the alien. An alien may be detained on the premises of the competent authority, for the period not exceeding twenty-four hours.[387] Detention of an alien is subject to provisions of the Police Act.[388]

II. Accommodation in the Immigration Detention Centre

419. The Aliens Act stipulates that an alien, who cannot be forcibly removed immediately, or an alien whose identity has not been ascertained or who does not

385. Article 167 of the Misdemeanour Act.
386. Belgrade Centre for Human Rights, *BCHR Report: Status of Asylum Seekers in Serbia* (2012).
387. Article 48 of the Aliens Act.
388. *Zakon o policiji*, Official Gazette of the Republic of Serbia, No. 101/2005.

possess a travel document, shall be ordered to stay in the temporary holding facility, immigration detention centre of the Interior Ministry, under close police surveillance, pursuant to a decision to be issued by the competent authority. An alien with health-related or other special needs shall be assigned other appropriate accommodation.

420. Accommodation at the immigration detention centre shall last until the forced removal of the foreign national, for a period not exceeding ninety days. The foreign national may have his/her stay at the detention centre extended if his/her identity has not yet been established, if he/she intentionally obstructs forced removal procedure, or if, during the forced removal procedure, he/she has submitted an asylum application, for the purpose of avoiding forced removal, whereupon the total period of detention may not exceed 180 days.[389]

421. During the stay in the detention centre, the procedure for precise identification of alien's data and identity is conducted, and his/her travel documents or funds required for his/her expulsion are obtained through the diplomatic or consular mission of the country whose citizenship that person holds.

422. The Aliens Act also defines the methods of termination of stay at the temporary holding facility. Stay in the detention centre shall be terminated:

- upon the alien's departure from Serbia;
- upon expiry of the set time limit for such stay;
- upon revocation of the decision on ordering or extending the stay in the detention centre;
- upon the alien's acquisition of the right to asylum;
- by release from the detention centre in the case that an alien's identity has been ascertained and he/she discharged from the detention centre if it is expected, on reasonable grounds, that forced removal of the alien will not be possible.[390]

An alien is obliged to observe the house rules and rules of stay in the detention centre, which he/she may not leave without official's permission.

III. Travel Restriction Order

423. The competent authority may issue a decision on imposing a travel restriction order requiring the stay in a particular place of an alien whose identity is known, who has residence and means of subsistence and who cannot be forcibly removed immediately. An alien subject to a travel restriction order is obliged to remain at a particular address and to regularly report to the nearest police station. When there are justified reasons, the alien may temporarily leave the place specified by the travel restriction order, only on condition that he/she is allowed to do so

389. Article 50 of the Aliens Act.
390. Article 53 of the Aliens Act.

by decision of the competent authority. The duration of travel restriction order may not exceed 180 days. The travel restriction order shall be entered into the alien's travel document. An alien who does not possess a travel document shall be issued with a temporary identification card.[391]

424. The travel restriction order shall be terminated:

- upon the alien's departure from the Republic of Serbia;
- upon expiry of the time period for which the travel restriction order was imposed;
- by declaring the decision void in the appeal procedure;
- when the competent authority declares the decision void in case that grounds for imposing the travel restriction order have ceased;
- upon expiry of 180 days.[392]

IV. Detention of Minors

425. The Aliens Act specifies that a minor foreign national shall be accommodated at a detention centre with his/her parent(s), or other legal representative, unless the competent custodial authority evaluates that another accommodation might be more suitable for him/her. The minor foreign national may not return to his/her country of origin or a third country willing to admit him/her, until an adequate admission is provided.[393]

§4. Expulsion and Removal

426. The Serbian law recognizes the measure of expulsion or removal of an alien. The Misdemeanour Act regulates that the purpose of applying a 'precautionary measure' of removal of aliens from the territory of Serbia shall be to eliminate conditions that enable or encourage an offender to commit a new misdemeanour.[394] The Criminal Code lists aliens' expulsion among measures whose function is to eliminate circumstances or conditions that may have influence on an offender to commit criminal offences in the future.[395] (*see more* in the Part V, Chapters 1 and 2). The main Serbian immigration acts, the 2009 Aliens Act and Asylum Act, also stipulate expulsion in situations in instances established by law.

391. Article 54 of the Aliens Act.
392. Article 55 of the Aliens Act.
393. Article 52 of the Aliens Act.
394. Article 45 of the Misdemeanour Act.
395. Articles 7 and 8 of the Criminal Code.

I. Reasons and Time Limits

427. Expulsion is a protective measure against the alien whose stay in Serbia is or became unlawful. It is applied when the alien continues to stay in Serbia after the residence permit, the registered right to stay or other legal grounds for residing in Serbia have elapsed. In some cases it can be also applied as a type of sanction for criminal and/or misdemeanour acts against an alien whose right of residence is valid. Expulsion is as distinct from the refusal of entry: while expulsion is aimed to correct an unlawful situation, i.e., an alien's unlawful stay in the country, the refusal of entry constitutes a preventive measure against creation of an unlawful situation.

428. As said above, stay in the territory of Serbia without a visa, permit for temporary residence or other legal grounds shall be regarded as unlawful residence. An alien who unlawfully stays in the Republic of Serbia is obliged to leave het territory immediately or within a set time limit

429. The time limit within which an alien who is unlawfully staying in Serbia is obliged to leave her territory shall be set by the decision issued by the competent authority. When setting the time limit referred, the competent authority shall take into account the time necessary for the alien to leave the territory of the Republic of Serbia; such time limit may not be longer than thirty days from the day of issuing the decision. The responsible authority may set a new time limit to an alien who has not left the Republic of Serbia within the set time limit for justifiable reasons. An alien on whom a protective measure of removal or a security measure has been imposed, as well as an alien who should be repatriated pursuant to an international agreement, shall be granted extension of time limit for leaving the state only if there are justifiable reasons for doing so.[396]

430. If considered necessary, an exact border crossing point may be determined for the expulsion of the alien, and his/her obligation to report to a police officer at the border crossing.

II. Forced Removal

431. The Aliens Act regulates that the responsible authority shall forcibly remove an alien if the alien unlawfully resides in Serbia or in case the alien has failed to leave the country within the set time limit. Also, an alien on whom a protective measure of removal or a security measure of deportation has been imposed, as well as an alien who is to be repatriated pursuant to an international agreement, may be forcibly removed immediately.[397]

432. The Aliens Act also stipulates the prohibition of forced removal of an alien to a territory where he/she would be under threat of persecution on the grounds of

396. Article 43 of the Aliens Act.
397. Article 46 of the Aliens Act.

his/her race, sex, religion, nationality, citizenship, membership of a particular social group or his/her political views. This rule will not be applied to an alien who is, on reasonable grounds, regarded as a threat to the security of Serbia or to an alien who was finally convicted of a grave criminal offence, wherefore he/she represents a threat to public order. However, even such a person may not be forcibly removed to a territory in which he/she would be under threat of torture, inhuman or degrading treatment or punishment.[398]

433. Throughout the removal procedure, the competent authority should take into consideration the specific situation of aliens with special needs, such as: minors, persons fully or partially deprived of their legal capacity, children separated from their parents or legal guardians, persons with disabilities, elderly persons, pregnant women, single parents with underage children and persons who have been subjected to torture, rape or other grave forms of psychological, physical or sexual violence. In the course of execution of official actions in respect of such aliens, the competent authority is obliged to act in conformity with regulations governing the status of persons with special needs and with international treaties.[399]

434. In order to ensure the enforcement of the protective measure of removal, alien's travel or other documents and travel tickets may be temporarily confiscated. A certificate of confiscation of these documents should be issued.[400]

III. Expulsion of Asylum Seekers

435. The Asylum Act provides that an alien whose asylum application has been refused or rejected, or whose asylum procedure has been suspended, and who does not reside in the country on some other grounds, shall be obliged to leave the Republic of Serbia within the time limit specified in the official decision regulating his/her status. The time limit within which an asylum seeker shall be obliged to leave the Republic of Serbia shall not be longer than fifteen days upon the receipt of this decision. If an alien fails to voluntarily leave Serbia within the specified time limit, he/she shall be forcibly expelled in accordance with the provisions of the law governing the movement and stay of aliens (Aliens Act). The measure of expulsion will be also applied in the case that an alien, during the asylum granting procedure, unjustifiably fails to abide by the time limit of fifteen days within which an asylum seeker after registration must submit an asylum application to an authorized officer of the Asylum Office. Pending his/her expulsion from Serbia this asylum seeker may be placed at the Reception Centre for Aliens.[401]

398. Article 47 of the Aliens Act.
399. Article 58 of the Aliens Act.
400. Article 57 of the Aliens Act.
401. Article 57 of the Asylum Act.

IV. International Legislation

436. Serbian immigration laws regarding the issue of aliens' expulsion are mostly harmonized with relevant international and European legislation in this matter. Principle of '*non-refoulement*' of the 1951 UN Convention relating to the Status of Refugees, as said in the previous chapters, is fully respected, as well as Article 3 of the UN Convention against Torture and Other Cruel, Inhuman or Degrading Treatment or Punishment which prohibits to State parties to 'expel or extradite a person to a State where there are substantial grounds for believing that he/she would be in danger of being subjected to torture'.[402] This obligation also results from the jurisprudence of the European Court of Human Rights.

437. Serbia has ratified Protocol No. 4 to the Convention for the Protection of Human Rights and Fundamental Freedoms which prohibits collective expulsion of aliens.[403] European Court of Human Rights has defined 'collective expulsion' as any measure compelling aliens, as a group, to leave a country, except where such a measure is taken on the basis of a reasonable and objective examination of the particular case of each individual alien of the group.[404]

402. Article 3 of the UN Convention against Torture and Other Cruel, Inhuman or Degrading Treatment or Punishment.

403. Article 4 of the Protocol No. 4 to the Convention for the Protection of Human Rights and Fundamental Freedoms.

404. European Court of Human Rights, *Collective Expulsions*, August 2013, http://www.echr.coe.int/Documents/FS_Collective_expulsions_ENG.pdf (accessed 12 Oct. 2013).

Chapter 2. Sanctions against Persons Helping Illegal Immigrants or Residents

§1. HUMAN SMUGGLING

438. The Criminal Code recognizes the criminal offence of '*Illegal crossing the state border and people smuggling*', as belonging to the group of offences against the public order and peace.[405] This criminal offence is related to human smuggling of aliens unlawfully crossing state borders.

439. The sanction for this criminal offence is designed against any person who without a required permit crosses or attempts to cross the border of Serbia, under arms or by use of force, and is punished by imprisonment up to one year. The perpetrator who enables illegal crossing of Serbia's border or illegal stay or transit through Serbia to a person who is not a Serbian citizen and has the intention to acquire a benefit for himself/herself or another person, shall be punished by imprisonment of three months to six years. If this offence is committed by an organized group, by abuse of authority or in a manner endangering the lives and health of persons whose illicit crossing of the border, stay or transit is being facilitated or if a larger number of persons is being smuggled, the perpetrator shall be punished by imprisonment from one to ten years.[406]

§2. HUMAN TRAFFICKING

440. The Serbian Criminal Code, apart from the offence of '*Illegal crossing the state border and people smuggling*', incriminates also a number of activities aimed at human trafficking, belonging to the offences against humanity and other rights guaranteed by International Law.

441. According to the provisions of Article 338 of the Criminal Code, a criminal offence of '*Human trafficking*' provides that whoever by force or threat, deception or maintaining deception, abuse of authority, trust, dependency relationship, difficult circumstances of another, retaining identity papers or by giving or accepting money or other benefit, recruits, transports, transfers, sells, buys, acts as intermediary in sale, hides or holds another person with intent to exploit such person's labour, forced labour, commission of offences, prostitution, mendacity, pornography, removal of organs or body parts or service in armed conflicts, shall be punished by imprisonment of two to twelve years. When this offence is committed against a minor, the offender shall be punished by the penalty prescribed for that offence even if there was no use of force, threat or any of the other mentioned methods of perpetration. If the offence is committed against a minor, the offender shall be punished by imprisonment of minimum three years. If this has resulted in grave

405. Article 350 of the Criminal Code.
406. *Ibid.*

bodily injury of a person, the offender shall be punished by imprisonment of three to fifteen years and if it resulted in death of one or more persons, the offender shall be punished by imprisonment of a minimum of ten years. Whoever habitually engages in offences of human trafficking or if the offence is committed by an organized group, shall be punished by imprisonment of minimum five years.[407]

442. Criminal offence '*Trafficking in Children for Adoption*' provided by Article 389 of the Criminal Code stipulates that whoever abducts a child under 14 years of age for the purpose of adoption contrary to laws in force or whoever adopts such a child or mediates in such adoption or whoever for that purpose buys, sells or hands over another person under 14 years of age or transports such a person, provides accommodation or conceals such a person, shall be punished by imprisonment of one to five years. Whoever habitually engages in such activities or if the offence is committed by an organized group, shall be punished by imprisonment of minimum three years.

443. Criminal acts of human trafficking and smuggling most often include a violent deprivation of a victim's free movement and are accompanied by various forms of abuse and violence. Article 390 of the Criminal Code includes the offence '*Holding in Slavery and Transportation of Enslaved Persons*' and prescribes that whoever in violation of international law enslaves another person or places a person in similar position, or holds a person in slavery or similar position, or buys, sells, hands over to another person or mediates in buying, selling and handing over of such person or induces another person to sell his/her freedom or freedom of persons under his/her support or care, shall be punished by imprisonment of one to ten years. If the perpetrator transports persons in slavery or other similar position from one country to another, shall be punished by imprisonment of six months to five years. In the case that such offences are committed against minors, such offender shall be punished by imprisonment of five to fifteen years.[408]

444. In addition to the substantive criminal legislation, the legislation on misdemeanours also contains some provisions pertaining to trafficking in human beings. The most frequent misdemeanours which most often are direct results of human trafficking are prostitution and (illegal) residence of foreign nationals in Serbia. Therefore, it sometimes happens that women who have become victims of human trafficking for prostitution purposes are not recognized as the victims of human trafficking. Instead, they are prosecuted for engaging in prostitution and regarded as perpetrators of criminal or misdemeanour offences against public peace and order.[409]

---

407. Article 388 of the Criminal Code.
408. Article 389 of the Criminal Code.
409. M. Kostić & A. Mihajlović, *Counteracting and Preventing Human Trafficking in the Republic of Serbia*, 10 Facta Universitatis, Series: L. & Pol. 104 (2012).

Part VI. Legal Remedies and Procedural Safeguards

Chapter 1. Legal Remedies in Case of Refusal of Right to Enter, Stay or Reside

§1. Administrative Legal Framework

445. Decisions of competent authorities regarding the rights of aliens in the field of immigration are, by its legal nature, 'administrative acts'. Therefore it is important to present the baseline of Serbian administrative law that apply in immigration procedures.

446. According to the Serbian legal theory, as an 'administrative act' is considered an individual, concrete legal act of an authority of a government agency, which unilaterally determines in an authoritative manner questions of rights, obligations or legal interests of a particular individual or legal person.[410]

447. The right of everyone to lodge legal remedies and have a process safeguard against administrative acts is guaranteed by Serbian Constitution. Article 22 of the Constitution regulates that every individual is guaranteed the right to appeal or to apply other legal remedy against a decision concerning his/her right or interest founded on law.[411]

448. In other words, that means that aliens, as every individual, have a right of judicial control of administrative actions and acts. That control is conducted according to principles and conditions regulated in two basic laws: Administrative Disputes Act[412] and General Administrative Procedure Act,[413] both adopted in the former Yugoslavia and later amended within Serbian legislation.

449. Principle of two-tier proceeding (principle of deciding in two instances) is, among others, one of the basic principles governing administrative procedure including matters of legal remedies and process safeguard relevant also for aliens

410. Vuk Cucić, *Administrative Appeal in Serbian Law*, 32 E Transylvanian Rev. Admin. Sci. 52 (2011).
411. Article 22 of the Constitution of the Republic of Serbia.
412. *Zakon o upravnim sporovima*, Official Gazette of the Federal Republic of Yugoslavia, No. 46/1996.
413. *Zakon o opštem upravnom postupku*, Official Gazette of the Republic of Serbia, No. 111/2009.

immigration rights. According to the General Administrative Procedure Act, this principle means that:

- parties shall have the right to lodge an appeal against a decision adopted in the first instance;
- the law may only exceptionally prohibit the filing of an appeal in specific administrative matters, provided that the protection of rights and legal interests of the parties, i.e., the protection of legality, is otherwise ensured;
- where there are no second-instance authorities, an appeal against a decision adopted in the first instance may be lodged only in the cases specified under the law;
- parties shall have the right to file an appeal in the cases when the first-instance authority has failed to adopt a decision on the party's claim within the specified period of time (silence of the administration); and
- no appeal against a decision adopted in the second instance shall be allowed.[414]

450. According to the principle of two-tier proceeding, citizens have the right to request the review of an administrative act by a supervisory agency, and this review is also an essential precondition for filing an administrative lawsuit in court. Individual decisions or rulings of state administration authorities addressed to specific parties can be appealed and overruled through an internal timely recourse. If the decision was taken by a minister, the adjudication of the internal appeal belongs to the government. A consequence of this double administrative instance before going to court is that the subject matter of an administrative dispute is most frequently an administrative act decided in the second instance.

451. The Serbian system, similarly to the French system, in defining the extent of administrative suits, applies the *general clause principle in combination with negative enumeration*: judicial review proceedings may be instituted against all final administrative acts, except those the review of which has been expressly precluded by law.[415]

452. The general time period for filing an administrative appeal is fifteen days as of the day of delivery of the first instance resolution.[416] Other laws can set a different (shorter or longer) time period. If a potential appellant misses this time period, he/she is precluded from filing the appeal and the resolution becomes both non-appealable and final. The only thing left then to do, is to request a return (of the proceeding) to a previous state (*restitutio in integrum*), provided there is a justification for the failure to file an administrative appeal in the prescribed period of time[417] and then submit the appeal.

414. Article 12 of the General Administrative Procedure Act.
415. Dejan Vučetić, *Serbian Judicial Review of Administrative Acts and European Standards for Administrative Disputes*, 3 Facta Universitatis, Series: L. & Pol. 73–90 (2005).
416. Article 220 of the General Administrative Procedure Act.
417. Articles 93–98 of the General Administrative Procedure Act.

453. Administrative appeal is formally, physically handed in to the first instance authority, i.e., the one that rendered the challenged act. Even if a party would hand in the administrative appeal directly to the appellate authority, the latter would send it to the first instance authority.[418] Reason for doing this is the fact that the authority whose act is appealed has a role to play in the appellate proceeding as well. It has certain authorizations with regard to administrative appeal. In addition, the appellate authority shall deliver its resolution rendered on administrative appeal to the appellant through the first instance authority.[419] The aim of this provision, as well as of the previous one, is to facilitate the appellate proceeding for the appellant, because it is easier to communicate with the first instance authority, with which he/she had already communicated in the past and which might be closer to his/her place of residence, than with the appellate authority (especially in the case of administrative appeal to the head of the state administration authority, when its dislocated unit conducted the first instance proceeding).[420]

454. Two-instance misdemeanour proceedings are also provided. Pursuant to the Misdemeanour Act, an appeal may be lodged against first instance decisions. A judgment handed down in the misdemeanour proceedings shall become legally binding on the date of handing down the judgment by the Higher Misdemeanour Court and resolution of an administrative authority, on the date of handing down the judgment by the Misdemeanour Court of territorial jurisdiction. Moreover, Misdemeanour Act prescribes 'prohibition of reversal for the worse', i.e., that in the case an appeal has been lodged only in favour of the defendant, the judgment, in the part that is related to the imposed sanction, may not be amended to his/her detriment, nor, in the renewed proceedings, a judgment less favourable to the defendant may be handed down.[421]

§2. Refusal of the Right to Enter

455. Refusal of entry into Serbia to an alien may appear in at least three forms:

- the first one concerns aliens that are denied the right to enter Serbia at the border-cross points;
- the second one concerns aliens outside of Serbia whose applications for the right to enter into Serbia are denied by refusal to issuing a Serbian visa; and
- the third one relates refusal of entry into Serbia through decisions on international protection taken in the asylum procedure.

418. Article 220 of the General Administrative Procedure Act.
419. Article 220 of the General Administrative Procedure Act.
420. Vuk Cucić, *ibid.* at 52.
421. Article 87 of the Misdemeanour Act.

456. The Aliens Act explicitly states that there is no right of appeal against the decision to refuse one's application for visa or the decision to cancel a visa. Moreover, such a decision shall not require a statement of grounds.[422]

457. There are no direct regulations in the Serbian immigration law on the right on appeal in the case of refusal of entry at the border cross point. If the refusal on the border point was made by cancelling the visa, then the above-mentioned rule should be applied. The problem appears when an alien on the border is refused although possessing a visa and meeting all requirements for entry, and in spite of that is denied to enter on the ground of paragraph 8 of Article 11 of the Aliens Act. Namely, the Aliens Act extensively defines an unlawful entry into Serbia (Article 10) and reasons for denial of entry in Article 11. (*See* Part I, Chapter 3) While the majority of these reasons are related to administrative and other requirements for entry that are or should be clear to aliens when entering Serbia, there is paragraph 8 of Article 11 of the Aliens Act which, from the point of view of the right on appeal, seems to be controversial. Namely, there it is written that the border police may deny entry to an alien if 'there is reasonable doubt that he/she shall not use his/her stay for an intended purpose'. Such level of discretionary power of a border police officer may discourage aliens to lodge an appeal against the decision on denial of entry which in practice is not given in written form but is expressed orally. On the other hand, according to statements of responsible officers in the Border Directorate, the practice of lodging an appeal against denial of entry at the border crossing point is not usual and, in fact, does not exist. According to them, objections to such a procedure were not reported. Legal remedies are applicable against almost all decisions regarding aliens' movement and stay (asylum, temporary residence, permanent residence, etc.) but not against refusal of entry at the border cross point.

458. While a prohibition to appeal decisions on visa refusal seems to be justified, this is not a case with the tacit prohibition of legal remedies against the decision on refusal of entry at the border crossing point. Serbian Constitution and substantial legislation, especially the General Administrative Procedure Act, offer grounds for resolving this problem and for introducing a right on appeal in the case of denial of entry at the border. Although Serbian legislation is in the process of harmonization with EU law, for the time being there was no harmonization with the Schengen Borders Code which stipulates that persons refused entry shall have the right to appeal that should be exercised in accordance with national law.

459. This problem should be solved, perhaps, by appropriate interpretation of the law. In fact, interpreting by analogy, one could conclude that the prohibition of appeal for refusal of a visa is a legitimate act of the sovereign power that may be applied also in the case of remedies against refusal of entry at the border. If, however, one interprets this dilemma on the ground of *argumentum a contrario* and relies on the rule '*If not forbidden, it's permitted*' it is possible to conclude that the

422. Article 21 of the Aliens Act.

prohibition of appeal against refusal of entry on the border does not have solid foundations.

§3. Refusal of Application for Permanent Residence

460. In case of refusal of the application for permanent residence permit, appeal is allowed. Appeal against the decision of the Regional Border Police Directorate of the Ministry of Interior on rejection or refusal of an application for permanent residence shall be decided upon by the Government of Serbia. An appeal should be lodged within thirty days following the date of the first instance decision delivery. In the case of refusal, an alien may initiate an administrative dispute before the Administrative Court against the decision of the Government within thirty days following the date of the decision delivery.[423]

§4. Refusal of Application for Temporary Residence

461. Appeal against the decision of the Regional border police Directorate of the Ministry of Interior on refusal or rejection of an application for temporary residence is also allowed. Against such a decision an appeal may be filed to the central border police directorate within the Ministry of Interior, within fifteen days from the date of receipt of the decision. Against the decision on refusal or rejection of the appeal, the administrative dispute may be initiated before the competent judicial authority. The same conditions and time limits for appeal are applicable to appeals against decisions on refusal of application for extension of temporary residence, as well for cancelation of the temporary residence permit.[424]

§5. Refusal of Application for Asylum

462. As described in Part III, Chapter 3 on conditions for asylum, the first instance procedure, carried out by the Asylum Office, consists of five steps: (1) expression of intention to seek asylum and recording of data by the police; (2) registration of the asylum-seeker; (3) lodging an asylum application; (4) formal interview; and (5) decision making. The Asylum Act does not define any set period within which the Asylum Office should complete the first two steps of the asylum procedure. However, in accordance with the General Administrative Procedures Act, a maximum period of sixty days (two months) is applicable from the third step, lodging the asylum application, to the final step, the issuance of the decision of the Asylum Office. In practice, due to procedural delays, these last three steps often exceed the prescribed sixty days deadline.

---

423. *Responses of the Government of Serbia to the EU Questionnaire*, http:/www. responses_to_the_eu_commission_questionnaire2011.zip – ZIP archive, unpacked size 33.247.408 bytes (accessed 17 Oct. 2013).

424. *Ibid.*

463. An appeal against first-instance decisions of the Asylum Office may be lodged with the Asylum Commission, the second-instance body, within fifteen days of the receipt of the decision.[425] According to the General Administrative Procedures Act, the appeal has suspensive effect. The time limit for making a second-instance decision is sixty days from the day when the competent authority receives the appeal.

464. The Asylum Commission is comprised of nine members, each with a four-year term in office. It is ostensibly an independent governmental body although the Head of the Asylum Commission is also the Assistant to the Head of Border Police Directorate and the members of the Asylum Commission are mostly police officers. The Asylum Commission makes its decisions by majority vote.[426]

465. An asylum-seeker has the right to lodge an administrative appeal with the Administrative Court against the second-instance decision of the Asylum Commission. The Administrative Court generally conducts its review based on the merits of the case as well on errors of law. The Administrative Court rules on the appeals in three-member judicial panels. As a rule, an appeal filed with the Administrative Court shall not suspend the enforcement of the impugned administrative enactment.[427] The Court may, however, suspend the enforcement of a final administrative enactment on the motion of the claimant, until it rules on the administrative dispute in the event such enforcement would cause the claimant damage difficult to reverse, and the suspension is not in contravention of public interests and would not cause major or irreparable damage to the opposing party, i.e., interested party.[428] Exceptionally, the suspension of the enactment may be sought in an emergency, i.e., when an appeal without suspensive effect under the law has been lodged and the appeals procedure has not been completed. In such cases, the Administrative Court rules on the motions to suspend enforcement within five days from the day they are filed.[429]

§6. Recognition and Loss of Refugee Status under 1992 Refugees Act

466. Pursuant to the 1992 Refugees Act decisions in the first instance on the recognition and loss of refugee status under this Act are solved by the Commissioner for Migration and Refugees. Such a decision may be appealed within fifteen days

425. Article 35 of the Asylum Act.
426. Between 1 Jan. and 31 Dec. 2011, the second-instance Asylum Commission issued thirty-five decisions on appeals by asylum-seekers, and the third-instance Administrative Court issued eight decisions. No negative decision based on the application of the 'safe third country concept' was overturned. From Jan.to 17 Apr. 2012, the Asylum Commission issued ten decisions, and from January to the end of June 2012, the Administrative Court issued two decisions. No negative decisions were overturned. *See* Belgrade Centre for Human Rights, *Right to Asylum in the Republic of Serbia 2012* 29 (2013).
427. Article 2 of the Administrative Disputes Act.
428. *Ibid.*
429. Belgrade Centre for Human Rights, *Right to Asylum in the Republic of Serbia 2012* 29 (2013).

after the decision was made. The Minister for Diaspora decides on an appeal within fifteen days of receiving the appeal.[430]

§7. Refusal of the Application for Permit for Movement and Stopping in the Zone of a Border Crossing Point

467. Permit for movement and stopping of persons who perform activities on a permanent basis in the zone of a border crossing point is issued by the border police with a validity period of up to two years, which can be extended. Appeal against the decision on refusal, rejection, extension and withdrawing of this permit is allowed. It should be lodged within fifteen days from the date of receipt of the decision. An appeal against a decision on the time limit shall not have suspensive effect.[431]

§8. Working Permits Regulations

468. For remedies related to working permits and employment *see* Part VII, Chapter 5 and Part VIII, Chapter 4.

430. Article 13 of the 1992 Refugees Act.
431. Article 22 of the Aliens Act.

Chapter 2. Legal Remedies in Case of Expulsion and Detention

§1. Time Limit for Leaving Serbia

469. Appeal against the decision of the competent authority on the time limit within which an alien who unlawfully stays in Serbia should leave the country is allowed. Appeal against such decision should be filed within eight days from the date of receipt of the decision. The time limit for appeal is shorter given that the Aliens Act regulates that the time necessary for the alien to leave the territory of Serbia may not be longer than thirty days from the day of issuing the decision.[432] An appeal against a decision on the time limit shall not have suspensive effect.

§2. Ordering the Stay in the Immigration Detention Centre

470. A specific way to contest the first instance decision is applicable for appeal against the decision ordering the stay in the immigration detention centre. Active legitimation to lodge this appeal belongs to an alien who was ordered to stay in the immigration detention centre of the Ministry of Interior under close police surveillance, pursuant to a decision issued by the competent authority on the ground of Article 49 of the Aliens Act relating to conditions for aliens expulsion.[433] Appeal against this decision shall be decided upon by a competent district court. The procedure of resolving the appeals is subject to the provisions of Article 53 of the Police Act which regulates conditions of the alien's temporary detention. Appeal against the decision on ordering the stay in the detention centre shall not suspend execution of the decision.

§3. Travel Restriction Order

471. As said in the chapter on the expulsion of aliens, the competent authority may issue a decision by which travel restrictions are imposed upon an alien, requiring him/her to stay in a particular place, where such alien's identity is known, he/she has residence and means of subsistence, and cannot be forcibly removed immediately. An alien may, through the competent authority, lodge an appeal with the Ministry of Interior against such decision within eight days from the day of receipt of the decision. Appeal against the decision shall not suspend its execution.[434]

432. Article 43 of the Aliens Act.
433. Article 49 of the Aliens Act.
434. Article 54 of the Aliens Act.

Chapter 3. Procedural Safeguards

§1. Principles and Regulations

472. The General Administrative Procedure Act contains the most important procedural safeguards relevant for aliens' rights. Procedural safeguards relevant for these rights are also provided by other acts relevant to immigration (Aliens Act, Asylum Act, Misdemeanour Act, Police Act) and are used as subsidiary sources of law, as far as they are not in disaccord with the procedural safeguards guaranteed by the General Administrative Procedure Act.

I. General Administrative Procedure Act

A. Principles of Procedure

473. Procedural safeguards for aliens instituting proceedings before an administrative or judicial authority are listed in the procedure principles of the General Administrative Procedure Act:

- *Principle of Legality* means that the authorities acting in administrative matters shall adopt decisions pursuant to the law and other regulations. In administrative matters in which an authority is legally empowered to make discretionary decisions, the decision shall remain within the scope and the purpose for which the powers have been given.
- *Principle of Protection of Civil Rights and Protection of Public Interest* implies that authorities, when conducting a procedure and deciding in administrative matters, shall as much as possible facilitate the protection and exercise of the rights and legal interests of the parties to the procedure, ensuring that the exercise of their rights and legal interests is not detrimental to the rights and legal interests of other persons or in contravention of the legally established public interests. In case obligations are imposed on the parties and other participants in the procedure by virtue of law, the measures to be applied to them shall be the measures provided for under the relevant regulations that are more favourable for them if such measures are sufficient to achieve the purpose of the law.
- *Principle of Efficiency* means that the authorities conducting procedures and deciding in administrative matters shall ensure efficient, high-quality and complete exercise and protection of rights and legal interests of natural persons, legal persons or other parties.
- *Principle of Truth* implies that all facts and circumstances of relevance for adoption of a lawful and fair decision shall be accurately established in the procedure.
- *Principle of Conducting Hearings* means that before adopting a decision in the procedure, the parties must be allowed to make a statement concerning the facts and circumstances of relevance for decision-making. The decision may be adopted without a prior hearing of the parties only in the cases specified under the law.

- *Principle of Admission of Evidence* implies that the authorized officer shall at his/her own discretion determine which facts are to be admitted as evidence on the basis of a conscientious and careful assessment of each piece of evidence individually and the body of evidence as a whole, as well as on the basis of the outcome of the entire procedure.
- *Principle of Independent Decision-Making* means that the authority shall conduct the procedure and decide independently, within the powers defined by law.
- *Principle of Finality of Decisions* implies that a decision against which no appeal may be filed or no administrative procedure instituted (a final decision) and which grants certain rights or imposes certain obligations on a party may be annulled, cancelled or amended only in the cases specified under the law. If the party's claim is rejected in a final decision, a different decision may not be adopted in the same case, unless the facts of the case or its legal status have changed.
- *Principle of Cost-Effectiveness* means that the procedure shall be conducted without delay and at the lowest possible cost for the parties and other participants in the procedure, yet ensure that the facts which are essential for the adoption of a lawful and fair decision are accurately and completely established.
- *Principle of Assistance to the Parties* obliges authority conducting the procedure to ensure that the ignorance and illiteracy of the parties and other participants in the procedure do not prejudice the rights they enjoy under the law.[435]

B. Use of Language and Alphabet in the Procedure

474. Regarding the use of language and alphabet in the procedure, the General Administrative Procedure Act regulates that, if the procedure is not conducted in the language of the parties or other participants in the procedure, they shall be provided with the translation of the procedure into their language by an interpreter and shall be served summons and other documents in their own language and alphabet.[436]

C. Exemption from Payment of Costs of the Procedure

475. General Administrative Procedure Act regulates that foreign citizens shall be exempted from payment of costs when provided so in the relevant international agreement, and that – if there is no such agreement – the principle of reciprocity shall apply. Where there is doubt as to the existence of reciprocity, the authority responsible for foreign affairs shall provide the relevant clarification.[437]

435. Articles 5–15 of the General Administrative Procedure Act.
436. Article 16 of the General Administrative Procedure Act.
437. Article 110 of the General Administrative Procedure Act.

II. Asylum Act

476. The Asylum Act provides a number of procedural principles that are the backbone of procedural safeguards of the alien's rights:

- *The principle of providing information and legal aid ensures a*n alien who has expressed his/her intention to seek asylum in Serbia to be entitled to being informed about his/her rights and obligations in the course of the entire asylum procedure. An asylum seeker has the right to free legal aid and representation by UNHCR and NGOs whose objectives and activities are aimed at providing legal aid to refugees.[438] An asylum seeker shall have the right to contact authorized UNHCR staff at any stage of the asylum procedure.
- *The principle of providing free translation services* provided by Article 11 of the Asylum Act regulates that an asylum seeker who does not understand the official language of the procedure shall be provided with free services for the purpose of translation into the language of the country of origin or a language he/she can communicate in. An asylum seeker may engage an interpreter of his/her own choice and at his/her expense. The obligation of providing free translation services shall be applied also to the use of sign language and the availability of materials in the Braille alphabet and other accessible formats.[439]
- *The principle of personal delivery* means that any written official communication in the procedure should be delivered to an asylum seeker or his/her legal representative in person. A written official communication should be considered delivered when either of the above-mentioned persons had received it.[440]

III. Misdemeanour Act

477. The Misdemeanour Act contains a number of procedural safeguards that are relevant for the procedures implying alien's participation.

478. According to the principle of *aid to a party unlearned in the law*, the Act regulates that a court should see to it that ignorance or lack of learning of parties is not to the detriment of their respective rights.[441]

479. The Misdemeanour Act also provides *compensation for damage to an unfairly detained or punished person*. The person, who has been unfairly punished for a misdemeanour or has been detained without grounds, shall be entitled to compensation for damage that was thereby inflicted on him/her, as well as to other rights laid down by the law. At the request of this person the ministry in charge of justice

438. Article 10 of the Asylum Act.
439. Article 11 of the Asylum Act.
440. Article 13 of the Asylum Act.
441. Article 82 of the Misdemeanour Act.

affairs, shall conduct the proceedings for the purpose of reaching the agreement on existence, type, and amount of compensation.[442]

480. The Misdemeanour Act regulates reasons for *exemption of the obligation to reimburse costs of procedure*. In the decision by which it is decided on the costs, the court or the administrative authority may excuse the defendant from duty to fully or partly reimburse the costs of the misdemeanour proceedings, if their payment would put in question sustenance of the defendant or the persons he/she has the duty to sustain by the law.[443]

481. Pursuant to the Misdemeanour Act, costs of *translation into a language of national minorities*, incurred by applying the provisions of the Constitution and the law governing the official use of languages and alphabets, shall be borne by the court, or by the administrative authority that conducts the proceedings.[444] Although this regulation relates to national minorities it is in practice extended to any person who does not speak the Serbian language.

482. Examination of disabled persons through an interpreter is also provided. In the case that a defendant is deaf, questions shall be put to him/her in writing and, if he/she is mute, he/she shall be asked to answer in writing. If examination cannot be carried out in such a manner, the person who can communicate with the defendant shall be summoned as an interpreter.[445]

---

442. Article 89 of the Misdemeanour Act.
443. Article 135 of the Misdemeanour Act.
444. Article 136 of the Misdemeanour Act.
445. Article 180 of the Misdemeanour Act.

Part VII. Access to the Labour Market

Chapter 1. Overview of Applicable Legislation

483. Serbia is at the very beginning of establishing a modern system of employment of aliens. One could say that the legislation pertaining to alien's employment is one of the weaker points of Serbian immigration law. Namely, while the constitutional legislation as well the laws governing the alien's status and asylum and the state borders regime were harmonized with EU law, that is not the case with the legislation pertaining to the employment and work of aliens, their access to the labour market and conditions for self-employment. Until November 2014, Serbia still applied the 1978 Conditions for Foreign Citizens Employment Act,[446] which was passed in the former SFRY (although amended later several times).

484. This situation was substantially changed after adoption of the new Aliens Employment Act in November 2014.[447] This Act contains comprehensive and modern solutions in line with EU law. Therefore, this text took into account both legal documents and presented them in parallel – provisions contained in the earlier applicable Conditions of Aliens Employment Act as well those foreseen in the Aliens Employment Act on conditions under which aliens may be employed. New Aliens Employment Act demonstrates the direction in which Serbian immigration law will be further developed, and that is the reason why it deserves to be fully presented.

485. Objectives of the new legislation regarding employment of aliens were defined by the NES in preparation for Serbia's participation in the European Employment Services (EURES) network. According to the EC's Serbia 2013 Progress Report, Serbia has not relied on consistent labour market policies to address the low level of employment and high level of unemployment. Although spending on passive and active labour market policy measures in Serbia has been growing in the past couple of years, it is still low compared to the EU average, and is higher than in most other Western Balkan countries.[448] Such a situation is partly

---

446. *Zakon o uslovima za zasnivanje radnog odnosa sa stranim državljanima*, Official Gazette of the Socialist Federal Republic of Yugoslavia, Nos 11/1978, 64/1989, Official Gazette of the Federal Republic of Yugoslavia, Nos 42/1992, 24/1994, 28/1996 and Official Gazette of the Republic of Serbia, No. 101/2005.

447. *Zakon o zapošljavanju stranaca*, Official Gazette of the Republic of Serbia, No. 128/2014.

448. Vladimir Gligorov, Kosovka Ognjenović & Hermine Vidovic, *Assessment of the Labour Market in Serbia*, Research Reports 371 (The Vienna Institute for International Economic Studies May 2011).

due to the incomplete and obsolete employment legislation. It should be also said that until now the NES's vacancy database was incomplete, as there was no obligation on employers to register all vacancies centrally.[449] Apart from other aspects, these two problems are additional obstacles for the aliens to access the labour market.

486. The Constitution of Serbia contains a set of provisions relevant for labour, and they apply also to the status of aliens when employed and working in Serbia. Thus, the Constitution stipulates that every person shall have the right to work. The freedom of work, the free choice of profession and employment, and participation in management is also guaranteed. Everyone shall have equal access to jobs and functions. Employed persons may be dismissed against their will under conditions and in the manner established by the law and the collective agreement. Forced labour is explicitly prohibited.[450]

487. Employed persons are entitled to fair remuneration. The right to relief during temporary unemployment shall be guaranteed subject to conditions established by law.[451] Employed persons shall have the right to strike, in accordance with law.[452]

488. Employed persons are entitled to limited working hours, to a daily and weekly rest period, and to a paid holiday and leave of absence, in accordance with the law and/or collective agreement. Also, they are entitled to job safety, in accordance with law. Young people, women and disabled persons should enjoy special on-the-job protection, in accordance with law.[453]

489. Under an obligatory insurance scheme, in accordance with the law, the employed persons shall acquire for themselves the right to health care and other rights in the event of sickness, the rights in the event of pregnancy, childbirth, impairment or loss of work ability, unemployment, rights envisaged for the old age, and rights to other forms of social security, and for the members of their families – the right to health protection, the right to a family pension, and other social security rights. Social security rights for those citizens who are not covered by the obligatory social insurance scheme are regulated by law.[454]

490. Although some of the above listed rights are not fully accessible to the aliens, the basic fact remains that the right to employment is one of the general rights in Serbia and thus an alien with permanent or temporary residence has the

449. European Commission, Commission Staff Working Document: *Serbia 2013 Progress Report*. (Accompanying the document Communication from the Commission to the European Parliament and the Council), *Enlargement Strategy and Main Challenges 2013–2014*, SWD (2013) 412 final {COM(2013) 700 final (Brussels, 16 Oct. 2013).
450. Article 35 of the Constitution of Serbia.
451. Article 36 of the Constitution of Serbia.
452. Article 37 of the Constitution of Serbia.
453. Article 38 of the Constitution of Serbia.
454. Article 40 of the Constitution of Serbia.

right to work in private and public sector if he/she meets requirements stipulated by the law, general act or collective contract of a legal entity.

491. Besides the mentioned legislation, the main elements of policies concerning employment and work of aliens in the Republic of Serbia are defined in the following acts, strategies and documents:

- Labour Act.[455]
- Employment and Insurance in Case of Unemployment Act.[456]
- The Rules on Conditions and Manner of Issuing Work Permits to Foreign Citizens or Stateless Persons.[457]

Highly relevant are also:

- Aliens Act of the Republic of Serbia.[458]
- Migration management Act.[459]
- Diaspora and Serbs of the Region Act.[460]
- National Programme for Integration with the European Union.[461]
- Conditions for sending workers on temporary work abroad and their protection Act.[462]

455. *Zakon o radu*, Official Gazette of the Republic of Serbia, Nos 24/2005, 61/2005 and 54/2009.
456. *Zakon o zapošljavanju i osiguranju za slučaj nezaposlenosti*, Official Gazette of the Republic of Serbia, Nos 36/2009 and 88/2010.
457. *Pravilnik o uslovima i načinu izdavanja dozvole za rad strancu i licu bez državljanstva*, Official Gazette of the Republic of Serbia, No. 22/2010.
458. *Zakon o strancima*, Official Gazette of the Republic of Serbia, No. 97/2008.
459. *Zakon o upravljanju migracijama*, Official Gazette of The Republic of Serbia, No. 107/2012.
460. *Zakon o dijaspori i Srbima u regionu*, Official Gazette of the Republic of Serbia, No. 88/2009.
461. The Government of the Republic of Serbia, *Amended National Programme for Integration of the Republic of Serbia into the European Union* (December 2009). In para. 321 of this Programme has been written:

> The obligations that the Republic of Serbia has transposed to date through its membership of the Council of Europe and by ratification of the Revised European Social Charter (RESC) on 29 May 2009 and its entry into force on 1 November 2009, correspond in some elements to the obligations that the country will have by becoming an EU member state. It refers to the greatest extent to Article 19 of the Charter, which the Republic of Serbia adopted almost entirely (out of 12 numerated paragraphs, the first 10 were adopted), relating to the rights of migrant workers and their families to protection and help, and containing the provisions on prohibition of discrimination of migrant workers on the grounds of citizenship.

462. *Zakon o uslovima za upućivanje zaposlenih na privremeni rad u inostranstvo i njihovoj zaštiti*, Official Gazette of the Republic of Serbia, No. 91/2015.

Chapter 2. Conditions for Entitlement to Work in the Country as an Employed Person

§1. General Conditions

492. Provisions of the Labour Act are applicable to employees who are foreign nationals and stateless persons who work with employers in the territory of the Republic of Serbia, unless the law stipulates otherwise.[463] Aliens working in the territory of Serbia enjoy the same rights as the Serbian citizens, except for the rights explicitly acknowledged solely to the citizens of the Republic of Serbia. Owing to their importance, rights of aliens to health care and social security are especially emphasized. According to the Labour Act both direct and indirect discriminations are prohibited against persons seeking employment and employees in respect to their sex, birth, language, race, colour, age, pregnancy, health condition or disability, national origin, religion, marital status, family responsibilities, sexual orientation, political or other belief, social origin, property, membership in political organizations, unions or any other personal quality. In cases of discrimination, person seeking employment and employee may request compensation of damages before the competent court, pursuant to the law.[464]

493. Employment and Insurance in Case of Unemployment Act foresees that the NES issues the work permit to an alien or stateless person. Work permit is an approval for employment in regard to the Aliens Employment Act. Aliens with permanent residence in Serbia are equal to Serbian nationals in regard to employment. An alien with permanent residence personally files the request for work permit to the relevant branch of the NES.

§2. Aliens Employment Regime under 1978 Conditions for Foreign Citizens Employment Act

494. The 1978 Conditions for Foreign Citizens Employment Act foresees two conditions that an alien (and stateless person) has to fulfil in order to be employed:

- he/she should have permit for permanent or temporary residence (*see* Part II, Chapters 2 and 3); and
- he/she should have approval for employment (work permit).

495. An alien can be employed without approval for working (i.e., without work permit) under conditions foreseen by:

- the contract on business-technical cooperation;
- the contract on long-term production cooperation;

463. Article 2 of the Labour Act.
464. Article 18 of the Labour Act.

– the contract on technology transfer; and
– the contract on foreign investment.

In that case temporary residence is permitted until the expiry of the term of approved employment contract in the Republic of Serbia.

496. In accordance with the provisions of the 1978 Conditions for Foreign Citizens Employment Act work permits are issued by the NES. Exception of this rule is the case when the foreign national appears as founder or member of the company in the Republic of Serbia and wants to be employed in his own company. On the basis of the Registration Decision, a foreigner shall submit his application for the work permit (colloquially called 'business license') to the Border Police Directorate in the Ministry of Interior of the Republic of Serbia. 'Business license' is issued to a foreign national or stateless person who has the status of the entrepreneur or founder for the purpose of carrying out the business or company management, and it enables them to perform other tasks. This means that foreign nationals, as well as stateless persons who are entrepreneurs, founders or company members, do not get work permits in the NES, but they get the 'business license' in the Ministry of Interior of the Republic of Serbia. (*See* Part II, Chapter 2, §2).

497. According to the 1978 Conditions for Foreign Citizens Employment Act, foreign citizens and stateless persons may establish an employment if fulfilling general and special conditions. General conditions are defined under the Labour Act. According to these conditions, an employment relationship may be established with a person above the age of 15. Special conditions refer to the conditions stipulated by the collective agreement and/or general document referring to a specific job post. As already said, under this Law, general prohibition of discrimination is proclaimed in all respects, especially with regard to employment conditions and selection of candidates for a certain job, working conditions and all rights resulting from the employment, education, training and advanced training, promotion at work and termination of the employment contract.

498. Foreign citizens may be employed by an organization or employer. An organization or employer is obliged to submit details on the number, structure and duration of foreign citizens' employment to the NES (or employment services of autonomous provinces), pursuant to the regulations governing record keeping in the labour field.

499. Also, the 1978 Conditions for Foreign Citizens Employment Act provides for the possibility that an alien may work without employment contracts based on contract of temporary work. This agreement may be concluded for a period of up to three months in a calendar year.

§3. Aliens Employment Regime under the 2014 Aliens Employment Act

I. Basic Concept and Implementation Limits

500. The Aliens Employment Act regulates the conditions and procedures for the employment of foreigners in the Republic of Serbia and other issues of importance to the employment of foreigners in the Republic. According to this Act an alien employed in the Republic of Serbia has the same rights and obligations in terms of work, employment and self-employment that citizens of the Republic of Serbia have in accordance with the Act. An alien is considered unemployed in accordance with the regulations on employment and achieves the same rights as citizens of Serbia if the requirements are met in accordance with the law. An alien who is employed by the employer contrary to the provisions of this Act shall be entitled to remuneration due to them for the work performed in accordance with the rules of procedure, with taxes and contributions for social insurance for the entire period of work engagement, including for the period of illegal employment.[465]

501. The Aliens Employment Act uses legal notions and terminology close to those of European Union law. So, 'employment of aliens' in terms of this Act means the 'conclusion of the employment contract or other agreement by which an alien without employment, exercises the rights arising from the work in accordance with the law'. Self-employment of aliens, in terms of this Act, is considered 'an employment of an alien in a company or other form of business, in accordance with the law, in which the alien is the sole or controlling member'. Employer in terms of this Act should be deemed a domestic legal or natural person registered to perform activities in Serbia, as well as the organizational unit of a foreign employer legally registered in Serbia. As a 'foreign employer' is considered a foreign natural or legal person registered abroad. 'Sent person' in terms of this Act, is an alien who is employed by a foreign employer who temporarily performs activities in the territory of the Republic of Serbia, in accordance with the law or ratified international agreement.[466]

502. The Aliens Employment Act is not applicable to certain groups of aliens, which are defined by the Act. That means that for these persons work permits are not required although they do not have free access to the labour market. The following aliens are exempted from the implementation of the Aliens Employment Act:

- who are entitled to the privileges and immunities in accordance with ratified international agreements;
- who perform services on the basis of agreements with international organizations, agreements concluded between competent authorities or within international projects on professional technical assistance, education, training or research;

465. Article 4 of the Aliens Employment Act.
466. Article 2 of the Draft Aliens Employment Act.

- reporters for foreign media or correspondents accredited in Serbia;
- who perform religious service in the framework of institutionalized religious communities, and aliens who organize or head a humanitarian activity within registered organizations and religious communities;
- who perform voluntary work on the basis of the law regulating voluntary work;
- who on the basis of a contract concluded with authorities responsible for defence and interior affairs perform services needed for the defence and/or security of the State, and those who are in professional training in this field;
- who are members of crews of ships and aircrafts or conduct road or rail transport and are employed by a foreign employer;
- business visitors;
- who have the status of the artist or athlete, taking part in an artistic, cultural or sporting event or are members of organizational and technical staff preparing an artistic or sporting event;
- are members of rescue units that provide assistance in eliminating the consequences of accidents and natural disasters, as well as staff of humanitarian assistance;
- who alone or on behalf of the foreign employer reside in Serbia in order to perform the tasks of equipping and displaying equipment for trade fairs and exhibitions.

503. Conditions of employment of aliens under this Act do not apply to the employment of an alien whose stay in Serbia does not last longer than ninety days within six months from the date of first entry in Serbia, as well as to an alien who:

- is the owner, founder or representative of a legal entity, as well as a member of the entity or its organizational units registered for performing activities in Serbia, in accordance with the law, if not employed in the legal person;
- resides in Serbia in order to establish business contacts and attend business meetings or perform other business activities relating to the preparation of a foreign employer to establish a presence and begin to work in Serbia;
- is a lecturer or researcher who takes part in an organized professional meetings or research projects or work done in order to present or implement various scientific and technical achievements, as well as his supporting staff;
- is performing temporary educational, sporting, artistic, cultural, and other similar activities organized by authorized organizations, state bodies or bodies of territorial autonomy and local self-government, as well as his supporting staff;
- is sent to Serbia for executing works under a contract of purchase of goods, the acquisition or lease of machinery or equipment and its delivery, installation, assembly, repair or training to work on the machines or equipment, as well as other type of contract which are in the general interest of the State.

II. Free Access to the Labour Market for Nationals of Member States of the European Union

504. According to the Aliens Employment Act the right to free access to the labour market in Serbia – in regard to employment, self-employment and rights arising from unemployment – unless international agreements binding on Serbia provide otherwise, have:

- Nationals of Member States of the European Union.
- The family members of Nationals of EU Member States and can prove they have a temporary or permanent residence permit for family members in these countries. They have right to the free access to the labour market, under the condition that in the Republic of Serbia they have provided housing, health insurance and the means of subsistence which guarantee that they will be not the recipients of social assistance.

505. As family members of EU nationals are considered:

- spouses (marital or extramarital) of the EU countries nationals, in accordance with the law;
- direct descendants of nationals of EU or direct descendants of his/her marital or extramarital spouse under 21 years old;
- adopted children or stepchildren of the nationals of EU countries, his/her marital or extramarital spouse, under 21 years of age;
- above-mentioned direct descendants and adopted children or stepchildren older than 21 years who are unable to support themselves, if nationals of the EU countries (or his/her marital or extramarital spouse) are legally obliged to support them;
- direct ancestors of nationals of EU countries (and his/her marital or extramarital partner) if nationals of the EU countries (or his/her marital or extramarital spouse) are legally obliged to support them.[467]

506. Above listed persons have the right to free access to Serbian labour market also in the cases that:

- his/her employment is terminated during temporary inability to work due to illness or injury at work;
- they have lost a job without personal responsibility for that, given that their employment in Serbia lasted at least one year and under condition that they are registered as unemployed persons by the organization authorized for employment;
- they are involved in supplementary education and/or training.[468]

467. Article 5 of the Aliens Employment Act.
468. Article 6 of the Aliens Employment Act.

507. Nationals of EU countries are entitled to the free access to the labour market six months after termination of employment if:

- his/her employment terminated in the first twelve months without personal responsibility for that and if registered as unemployed by the NES;
- his/her terminated temporary employment lasted less than twelve months and if such person was registered as unemployed by the NES.[469]

III. Conditions of Aliens Employment

508. As previously stated, an alien shall establish an employment provided that he/she has obtained temporary or permanent residence and an appropriate work permit, in accordance with the Aliens Employment Act. Under the conditions of this Act an alien may be employed albeit without authorization for temporary or permanent residence if he/she has a residence registration in accordance with the Aliens Act and the appropriate application for work registered with the NES. (*See* Part II, Chapter 2). Evidences of eligibility for employment of the alien in accordance with this Act should be kept in the premises in which an alien works, in order to facilitate possible inspection or supervision of authorized bodies.

IV. Work Permit Types

509. The work permit, in terms of the Aliens Employment Act, is an act issued by an authorized body that constitutes the proof of legal ground of an alien's employment or self-employment in Serbia.

510. According to the Act, a work permit may be issued as:

- Personal work permit (*Lična radna dozvola*).
- Work permit (*Radna dozvola*).

For the same time period may be granted only one type of work permit.

V. Personal Work Permit

A. *Definition and Conditions*

511. The personal work permit is a document which is a prerequisite for the alien's employment by any employer in the territory of Serbia and it is issued only to persons designated by the law. The personal work permit for an alien to work in Serbia provides free employment, self-employment and rights arising from unemployment, in accordance with the Aliens Employment Act. Personal work permit is

469. *Ibid.*

issued for a period as long as the identity card issued to a foreigner who has a permanent residence or the period until the alien has a temporary stay, or until the person has the appropriate refugee status or status of persons from specific categories of aliens in Serbia.[470] (*See* below the definition of special category of aliens).

512. A personal work permit is issued at the request of an alien:

- if he/she is approved permanent residence;
- if he/she has the status of refugee, in accordance with the Asylum Act; this shall not apply to persons from the territory of the former Yugoslavia which were granted refugee status in accordance with the 1992 Refugees Act, to which this Act does not apply; and/or
- who belongs to a special category of aliens.

513. A personal work permit may be issued also in cases stipulated by international agreements binding Serbia, in accordance with that agreement.[471]

B. Personal Work Permit for Family Reunification

514. A personal work permit may be issued for the purpose of completing family reunification. It is granted on request of a close family member of an alien; however, the family member requesting the work permit should already have a permanent or temporary residence permit. The family member of an alien in the Republic of Serbia may submit the request for a working permit in the following cases:

- when such alien already has permanent residence;
- when such alien has a status of refugee under the Asylum Act; or
- if such alien belongs to a 'special category of aliens' (*See* below).

515. A personal work permit may be obtained also by the family member of citizens of Serbia or of an alien with Serbian origins as well of an alien who is linked with such persons until to third degree of consanguinity in the direct line, under condition that the person requesting a personal work permit fulfils the requirements regarding the minimum age for employment in accordance with labour regulations. As members of the 'close family' are considered marital or extramarital spouses of an alien who has a residence permit, minor children born in wedlock or out of wedlock, adopted children or underage minor stepchildren and other family members, in accordance with the law governing the residence of aliens.[472]

470. Article 12 of the Aliens Employment Act.
471. *Ibid.*
472. *Ibid.*

VI. Work Permit

A. Subtypes

516. According to the Aliens Employment Act a 'work permit' is a type of work permit (license) which includes the following subtypes:

– 'Work permit for employment' (*Radna dozvola za zapošljavanje)*;
– 'Work permit for the special cases of employment' *(Radna dozvola za posebne slučajeve zapošljavanja)*; and
– 'Work permit for self-employment' (*Radna dozvola za samozapošljavanje).*

An alien with any of the listed work permits in Serbia can perform only the activities (jobs) for which the permit was issued, or those who are functionally close to activities (jobs) for which the permit was issued.

B. Work Permit for Employment

517. Work permit for employment is an employment license on the basis of which the foreigner signs an employment contract or other agreement with a particular employer. In this case the employer is the one who requests the permit, and it is given only if there is no local citizen available who is registered unemployed with NES.

518. A work permit for employment may be issued at the request of the employer, in accordance with the state of the labour market, provided that the employer:

– before applying for a work permit for employment did not make redundancy programme, in accordance with applicable labour legislation;
– one month before applying for a work permit for employment did not find a citizen of Serbia who has free access to the labour market or an alien with a personal work permit, already registered by the National Service of Employment, having appropriate qualifications for the requested job;
– presents a proposal of the contract on employment or other contracts implying alien's working obligations, in accordance with the applicable labour law.[473]

519. A work permit for employment may be granted only to an alien who has a temporary residence permit and meets all employers' requirements relating to the knowledge and skills, qualifications, previous experience, etc. And, as said above, if there is no adequate candidate with a Serbian citizenship. A work permit for employment is issued for the planned period of employment, which means that the permit's validity cannot exceed the planned duration of temporary residence.

473. Article 16 of the Aliens Employment Act.

520. The employer who requested work permit for employment has a number of obligations. He/she should bear the cost of issuing these work permits and must not transfer these costs to an alien who obtained the permit. Besides, the employer at whose request a work permit for an alien's employment has been issued is obliged to register an alien with the Social Security Office, in accordance with the law. He/she is also obliged to notify to the National Employments Service if the alien fails to begin his/her work within fifteen days of the issuance of a work permit for employment. Lastly, the employer must not instruct the alien who obtained the work permit to work or send him/her to work for another employer.[474]

C. *Work Permit for the Special Cases of Employment*

521. Work permit for special cases of employment is issued at the request of the employer, in the following cases and for the following purposes:

- in the case of 'sent persons', i.e., employees sent to carry out particular working tasks;
- in the case of the employee's movement within the company;
- for independent professionals.[475]

1. Seasonal Work

522. A work permit for employment of an alien to perform seasonal work shall be issued at the request of the employer whose jobs are of seasonal nature (agriculture, forestry, construction or other activities that are characterized by a significant temporary increase in workload).[476]

2. Vocational Training of Aliens

523. Work permit for the purpose of vocational training, specialization, gaining qualifications or training shall be issued at the request of an employer who has a programme of professional development, specialization, gaining qualifications or training of an alien who has a temporary residence permit. The work permit is provided to employ an alien for a period not exceeding one year. When a training or specialization programme cannot be completed until the expiration of one year, the permit may be extended for up to one additional year, except in the field of medicine, when a work permit may be extended for the time necessary to obtain the qualification.[477]

---

474. Article 15 of the Aliens Employment Act.
475. Article 18 of the Aliens Employment Act.
476. Article 17 of the Aliens Employment Act.
477. Article 18 of the Aliens Employment Act.

3. Employees Sent to Carry Out Working Tasks in Serbia

524. A work permit for 'sent persons', i.e., employees sent to carry out working tasks, is issued at the request of the foreign employer to carry out work or performing services in the territory of Serbia. The condition for issuing such work permit is:

- that the foreign employer has obtained the temporary residence permit for the person who should perform particular working tasks;
- that the contract concluded between an employer who engages the 'sent person' providing services and his/her basic employer includes the place and time of the job;
- evidence that the 'sent person' was employed by the foreign employer for at least one year;
- that the foreign employer sending an alien to perform special working tasks encloses a document containing information on his/her accommodation in Serbia.

525. A work permit for 'sent persons' is issued for the period for which the contract was concluded between the employer for whom the services are performed and the foreign employer, but not longer than for one year. The work permit for the persons carrying out work or performing services under contracts for the procurement of goods, the acquisition or lease of machinery or equipment and its delivery, installation, assembly, repair or training to work on the machines or equipment, as well as other types of contracts that relate to a general State interest, is issued under the above-mentioned conditions for a period longer than ninety days or for the period required for the job.[478]

4. Workers' Movement within a Company

526. The work permit for workers' movement within a company registered abroad is issued at the request of the organizational unit or subsidiary company registered in Serbia in order to enable temporary relocation or moving the employee to work in the organizational unit or its subsidiary, provided that the alien in question is employed by the foreign employer for the key functions (business executives, managers or specialists in certain fields) at least one year and that they will perform the same tasks in Serbia.

527. The work permit for the mentioned purposes is issued for the period of a temporary stay of no longer than one year. In addition, the work permit is granted if conditions are fulfilled which are requested for the issuance of permits for 'sent persons', i.e., employees sent to carry out particular working tasks. (*See* above, paragraph 507)

478. Article 20 of the Aliens Employment Act.

5. 'Independent Professional'

528. A work permit for an alien, who is an independent professional or a foreign natural person–entrepreneur registered for activities abroad, who on the basis of direct contracts with local employers and end users perform tasks in the territory of Serbia shall be issued at the request of the service user. This work permit shall be issued under conditions that such independent professional:

- possesses a temporary residence permit;
- has obtained an appropriate contract with the local employer or end users provided that such contract includes a deadline for the job;
- has appropriate academic degrees and / or professional qualifications and relevant work experience.

The work permit shall be issued for the period required for the job, but shall not exceed one year.[479]

6. Foreign Pupils and Students

529. A work permit for foreign pupils and students (under 26 years of age) is issued at the request of the employer or of the youth or student unions, provided that their work is performed for more than ten hours per week or forty hours per month. When such works are performed within the period of academic and curricular activities, they must not exceed twenty hours per week and eighty hours per month.[480]

7. Daily Work of Aliens-Migrants

530. The work permit for the daily work of an alien migrant, i.e., the foreigner who is employed in the territory of Serbia and returns every day or at least once a week to the country where he/she resides, is issued at the request of the employer employing such alien. The temporary residence permit for the mentioned person is requested for the whole duration of his/her stay in Serbia.

D. Work Permit for Self-employment

530.1. *See* Part VII, Chapter 2, §2.

479. Article 22 of the Aliens Employment Act.
480. Article 17 of the Aliens Employment Act.

531. According to the Aliens Employment Act, the work permit for self-employment is issued at the request of a foreigner who has a temporary residence permit in the Republic.

532. When asking to be issued a work permit for self-employment, with the application the alien should enclose:

- A statement of the type, duration and scope of working/business activities he/she is planning to engage in.
- Evidence that he/she has the appropriate qualifications to perform planned activities.
- Pre-contract or agreement evidencing ownership or lease of office space in which he/she plans to perform activities.
- Evidence that he/she possesses appropriate equipment to perform the planned activities.
- A statement of the number and structure of people whom he/she plans to hire, especially citizens of Serbia, people who have free access to the labour market and foreigners with a personal work permit.

533. The work permit for self-employment shall be issued for a period as long as the temporary residence permit, with the maximum of one year but with the possibility of extension, provided that the alien shall prove that he/she continues to perform the same work under the same conditions under which the permit was issued.

534. An alien who receives a work permit for self-employment is obliged to begin conducting activities within ninety days of obtaining the license.[481]

§4. Access to the Labour Market Limitations

I. Limitations Introduced by Particular Laws

535. The Aliens Employment Act did not contain any general provisions setting forth different treatment, on the ground of citizenship, of Serbian nationals and aliens regarding employment; however, it was mandatory for the alien seeking employment to have already been issued a temporary or permanent residence permit. On the other hand, the Rules on Conditions and Manner of Issuance of a Work Permit to an Alien adopted in 2005 and later amended,[482] allows the branch office of the NES to refuse a request for issuing a work permit to an alien if records in the branch office contain unemployed citizens of the Republic of Serbia who fulfil conditions required for performing of activities stated in the request for issuing a work permit to an alien.[483]

481. Article 23 of the Aliens Employment Act.

482. *Pravilnik o uslovima i načinu izdavanja dozvole za rad strancu i licu bez državljanstva*, Official Gazette of the Republic of Serbia, No. 22/2010.

483. Article 5 of the Rules on Conditions and Manner of Issuance of a Work Permit to an Alien.

536. Special conditions for employment of aliens for certain jobs are prescribed by particular laws or regulations related to the organization and job description as defined by the employer. Thus, the NES carries out a preliminary selection of persons, taking into account the conditions defined by the employer, the specificity of the job – the required type and level of education, occupation, work experience and other knowledge and skills (e.g., computer skills, foreign languages, driver's license), which candidates should obtain.

537. Limitations for employing aliens in the public sector[484] can be found in the provisions of the Civil Servants Act (*Zakon o javnim službenicima*) which applies to employees in state authorities, courts, public prosecutor' offices, the State Attorney, services of the National Assembly, services of the President of the Republic and the Government, Constitutional Court and services of the authority whose members are elected by the National Assembly. State authorities include ministries, special organizations, administrative offices within ministries, and professional services of administrative districts. Aliens, in fact, are excluded from access to mentioned jobs given that the condition for employing in public administration is that the person must be the citizen of the Republic of Serbia.[485]

538. Some of the limitations which the aliens are facing when wanting to access the labour market and find employment are related to specific requirements by which the aliens must have knowledge of the Serbian language, or membership in Serbian professional organizations and chambers. Thus, provisions of the Health Care Act stipulate that a foreign health worker can independently provide health protection (individual work) in a medical institution, private practice or can with another employer, by means of this Act, perform certain duties of health service, if he/she has completed internship and passed the professional exam and if is registered in the Serbian Chamber of Physicians' directory.[486] In case of physicians and health workers, for instance, it is required that they have gained or renewed the so-called approval for independent work.[487] Independent work in case of physicians

484. 'Public sector' is not a legal category in the legal system of the Republic of Serbia. Whereas the term 'public sector' actually means public governance in the broadest sense, public administration or public governance in the legal system of Serbia primarily refer to the professional part of the state administration, as well as the local self-government which includes provincial, city and municipal authorities of a public nature. Consequently, the area of employment relations in the public sector of the Republic of Serbia is regulated by the Civil Servants Act (*Zakon o državnim službenicima*), Official Gazette of the Republic of Serbia, Nos 79/2005, 81/2005, 83/2005, 64/2007, 67/2007, 116/2008 and 104/2009 and the Labour Relations in the State Authorities Act (*Zakon o radnim odnosima u državnim organima*), Official Gazette of the Republic of Serbia, Nos 48/1991, 66/1991, 44/1998, 49/1999, 34/2001 and 39/2002.

485. According to the Art. 45 of the Civil Servants Act, a person who is legally an adult, has the nationality of the Republic of Serbia, has prescribed professional qualifications and fulfils other requirements prescribed by law, other legislation or the Regulation on internal organization and description of job positions may be employed as a civil servant, if his or her employment relationship was not earlier terminated due to grave breach of obligation from the employment relationship and if he or she was not convicted by prison sentence of at least six months. Besides, an university degree and at least nine years of working experience is needed for the work in the appointed position.

486. Article 168 of the Health Care Act.

487. *Ibid.*

and health workers, within the meaning of this Law, means that the individual is providing health care without direct supervision of another health worker. An alien who performs activities related to health care in Serbia should, in addition, know the Serbian language as well as another language in official use, in accordance with the regulations on the official use of languages in Serbia.

539. Similar limitations exist regarding foreign nationals working as attorney-at-law. According to the Legal Profession Act (*Zakon o advokaturi*), a foreign citizen, listed in the directory of lawyers – foreign nationals of the Bar Association of Serbia is limited to giving oral and written legal advice and opinions regarding the application of law of his home country and international law. Also, an attorney-at-law listed in the directory of lawyers – foreign nationals is not entitled to:

- elect and be elected as a member of bodies and holders of positions in the Bar Association of Serbia or in the bar association in whose directory of the attorneys – foreign nationals he/she is enrolled;
- hire law trainees to perform in accordance with the Legal Profession Act;
- be appointed as a temporary agent, tax agent or counsel, or to provide legal aid in accordance with applicable regulations, or to act as agent of a party that is exempt from payment of court costs, or be the mediator.[488]

540. The Tourism Act (*Zakon o turizmu*) prescribes that a tourist guide and a tourist escort must have Serbian citizenship and domicile in the territory of Serbia.[489]

II. The Quota System

541. The Conditions for Foreign Citizens Employment Act does not provide any limitation regarding the number of aliens that are employed or seeking working permit in Serbia. However, the Aliens Employment Act establishes quotas that are defined through several criteria, such as: territory (district), labour market demands, etc.

542. According to the Aliens Employment Act, the Government may by special decision limit the number of aliens who are issued work permits in the case of disturbances on the labour market, in line with the migration policy and the status and trends on the labour market. The quotas are determined on the recommendation of the ministry responsible for employment with the prior opinion of the Social Economic Council of the Republic and the NES.[490]

488. Article 25 of the Legal Profession Act.
489. Article 94 of the Tourism Act, Official Gazette of the Republic of Serbia, Nos 36/2009 and 88/2010.
490. Article 24 of the Aliens Employment Act.

543. Quota does not apply to an alien, or an employer who intends to employ an alien, applying for:

- personal work permit, other than a personal work permit, which is issued at the request of a special category of aliens;
- a work permit for training, specialization or gaining qualifications;
- employment in jobs in the fields of culture, sports, science and other activities if such work is related to personality, personal knowledge and personal experience of the alien;
- a work permit for movement within the company;
- a work permit for persons sent to perform work under the contract on procurement of goods, the acquisition or lease of machinery or equipment and its delivery, installation, assembly, repair or training to work on the machines or equipment, as well as other type of contract that expresses a general social interest, for a period longer than ninety days within six months from the date of first entry into the Republic of Serbia;
- a work permit for daily migrant worker;
- persons engaged in teaching in schools in the language and script of national minorities.

544. The quota system is not applicable to aliens who have free access to the labour market. That regards nationals of Member States of the EEA and the Swiss Confederation who have free access to the labour market as well as the members of their families who are not nationals of these states but have permission for temporary or permanent residence with regard to members of their families in those states.[491]

545. Regarding quotas, Serbia's main problem is that there are no precise data on about labour force supply and demand. Due to the discrepancy between qualifications and the labour market needs, there is a permanent false surplus/deficiency in occupations. There are three types of problem: the labour market looks for the profiles that do not exist; the required profiles exist but without appropriate competences; the required profiles exist but people do not want to work within the given occupation (because of more profitable 'grey economy', bad working conditions, low wages, etc.). Therefore, Serbia has to create a compatible system of education to meet labour market demands. Then there is a need for collecting data on real surplus and deficient occupations, and for making projections on the future labour demands. Demographic projections have also been taken into consideration in the process of making annual immigration quota.[492]

491. *Ibid.*
492. Tanja Pavlov, Towards *New Policy of Employment of Foreigners in Serbia*, Mutual Learning Programme, Peer Review on 'Renewed Procedures for Employing Migrant Workers with the Emphasis on Favouring Highly-Qualified Labour', 10, paper submitted by GHK in consortium with CERGE-EI, Estonia (11–12 Jun. 2009).

§5. ADMINISTRATIVE RULES AND PROCEDURES

I. Basic Procedure Rules

546. A foreign citizen with permanent residency in the Republic of Serbia is to submit an application for a work permit to the NES. As stated before, the only exception is the so-called business license granted to a foreign national who is a founder or member of a company in Serbia and wants to be employed in his own company – in such case the application for work permit should be submitted to the Border Directorate of the Ministry of Interior.

547. Foreign citizens with permanent residence permits in the Republic of Serbia are issued work permits with the validity period corresponding to that of the permanent residence permit. Equally, foreign citizens with temporary residence permits in the Republic of Serbia are issued work permits for a period that may not exceed the temporary residence permit validity period.

548. An alien who is employed must have his/her Workbook which is issued under the same conditions as to the citizen of the Republic of Serbia and in accordance with the Regulations on the Workbook.[493]

549. The necessary documents for obtaining the work permit for an alien with permanent residence are: (a) application form (available at the NES), and (b) certified copy of the approval for permanent residence in the Republic of Serbia or a photocopy of the personal ID.

550. Aliens with temporary stay permits can obtain a work permit on the ground of employer's request. The employer files the request with the relevant branch of the NES (the form is available at the NES according to the place of the employer's registered head office) and encloses the certificate on the alien's temporary residence permit along with photocopy or his/her personal ID. Such request should be accompanied by employer's written explanation of the need for the employment of that person and a validated diploma as a proof of the level of education, or other document showing that the alien meets the requirements for the activities and duties related to the requested work permit.

551. The head of the NES branch decides on issuing a working permit within thirty days from the day the application was submitted.

552. In order to register himself/herself with the NES unemployment register, a foreign citizen is required to provide the following documents:

- Residence permit.
- ID card for aliens.

493. *Pravilnik o radnoj knjižici*, Official Gazette of the Republic of Serbia, No. 17/1997.

– Workbook (verified by the municipal administration).
– recognized foreign education degree/diploma.

II. Extension of Work Permits

553. The employment relationship may be extended to a foreign citizen if his/her temporary residence is extended and if he/she is granted a new permission for the establishment of a labour relation. An application for extension of the work permit is submitted in person or by mail to the NES branch. The average time for obtaining the work permit is two days. The work permit can be renewed without obstacles and the procedure is identical with the first application. Extended work permits are issued with a validity of three to twelve months and are renewable.

III. Cessation of Validity of Work Permit

554. According to the Conditions for Employment of Aliens Act, the work permit validity is terminated when:

– the alien's stay in the country expires;
– the work permit is annulled;
– alien's stay is cancelled; and
– alien's contract expires.

555. The Aliens Employment Act specifies that the alien's work permit expires in the following cases:

– by the expiration of the period for which it was issued;
– by abnegation;
– by the termination of the employment contract or other agreement on terms of work performance;
– if the alien loses his/her entrepreneur/employer or his/her legal entity ceases to exist before the expiry of the work permit for self-employment;
– if the alien's entitlement to permanent residence or his/her temporary residence have expired;
– for reasons of maintaining public order or security of the Republic of Serbia and its citizens;
– if the alien is granted citizenship of Serbia;
– in case of death;
– if the alien has resided outside Serbia for more than six consecutive months.[494]

494. Article 30 of the Aliens Employment Act.

IV. Cancelation of Work Permits

556. According to the Aliens Employment Act, a work permit may be cancelled if:

- an alien performs work for which no work permit was granted or if he/she works for another employer;
- the work permit was issued on the ground of false or falsified information, i.e., forged documents;
- an alien who is issued a work permit fails to commence the work in the time limits provided by this Act (fifteen days);
- an alien who is issued a permit for self-employment does not start to perform activities within ninety days of receiving the permit;
- the NES should cancel ex officio any work permit after reporting of circumstances requiring cancelation of work permit.[495]

V. Records

557. The NES keeps special records on work permits issued to foreign citizens who were granted permanent or temporary residence. According to the Employment and Unemployment Insurance Act, the NES should maintain separate registries on:

- Foreign citizens and stateless persons.
- Persons with inactive unemployment rights.
- Persons with temporary incapacity to work pursuant to regulations governing health insurance.[496]

§6. Conditions for Special Categories of Workers

558. As said before, according to the Aliens Employment Act a personal work permit is issued to refugees if they had got such status in accordance with the Asylum Act, (excluding persons from the former Yugoslavia to whom the refugee status was granted under the 1992 Refugees Act) and to the 'special category of aliens'. Under the Aliens Employment Act, a special category of aliens who may be issued a personal work permit includes:

- asylum seekers;
- persons whom temporary protection has been granted;
- persons whom subsidiary protection has been granted;
- victims of human trafficking.

495. *Ibid.*
496. Article 83 of the Employment and Unemployment Insurance Act.

559. The personal work permit may be issued to asylum seekers one year after applying for asylum, if the decision on his/her request of asylum has not been postponed because of his/her responsibility. The work permit in such cases is issued for a period of six months with the possibility of extension, as long as the status of asylum seekers is in force.

560. A person who has been granted temporary protection shall be issued the personal work permit with validity equal to the duration of the status of person with temporary protection.

561. A person who has been granted subsidiary protection a personal work permit shall be issued with a validity equal to the duration of the status of persons with subsidiary protection.[497]

562. To the victim of trafficking a personal work permit shall be issued for the duration of the residence permit.

497. Article 13 of the Aliens Employment Act.

Chapter 3. Sanctions against Illegal Participation in the Labour Market

§1. General Remarks

563. Serbian penal legislation does not recognize the criminal offence of illegal participation in the labour market, i.e., employment and work that are founded against provisions of current applicable immigration and labour law. In Chapter XVI 'Criminal offences against labour rights', the Serbian Criminal Code foresees a few offences that are somewhat relevant for the aliens' status in the field of employment and work; however, they do not criminalize directly offences of illegal participation in the labour market. These offences are '*Violation of Labour Rights and Social Security Rights*' (Article 163), '*Violation of the Right to Employment and the Rights during Unemployment*' (Article 164), '*Unlicensed Practice of a Profession*' (Article 353), as well as the security measure of '*Prohibition to Practice a Profession, Activity or Duty*' (Article 85). Prohibition of all kinds of illicit work, including such work where a legal person or a sole proprietor employs an alien or a stateless person contrary to provisions of the Conditions for Foreign Citizens Employment Act and Labour Act is set forth in these acts – a range of misdemeanour sanctions are stipulated for both, the employers and aliens. The most elaborated sanctions against illegal employment and similar offences one can find in the Aliens Employment Act.

§2. Sanctions against Employers

564. The Aliens Employment Act prescribes a fine of RSD 800,000–1,000,000 (EUR 5,500–9,000) that shall be imposed on a legal person if it:

- Employs a foreign citizen in violation of Article 9 of this Act, i.e., if such person employs an alien without a legally obtained work permit and residence permit.
- Employs a foreign citizen in violation of Articles 14–17 of this Act, i.e., if such person employs a foreign citizen without labour contract and fails to take from the foreign citizen a written declaration accepting the jurisdiction of the Serbian judiciary in case of disputes with the company or the employer on matters arising from the labour.

For the above listed offences the responsible person in the organization or employer shall be fined from RSD 20,000 to 150,000 (EUR 150 to 1,300).[498]

565. The Labour Act does not stipulate in a direct way the offences of illegal employment and work but it does foresee sanctions for employers for a number of misdemeanour offences that are relevant or implicitly connected to the illegal participation in the labour market. An employer (in the capacity of a legal person) shall

498. Article 34 of the Aliens Employment Act.

be fined in the amount of RSD 800,000–1,000,000 (EUR 7,000–9,000) for the following misdemeanour offences:

- if he/she violates prohibition of discrimination pursuant to this Act (Articles 18–21). Besides, if this offence inflicts material damage to an employee or other natural person, a protective measure of prohibition to pursue business may be pronounced to such employer;
- if he/she fails to conclude a labour contract or other contract, pursuant to this Law (Article 33 and Articles 197–202);
- if he/she fails to furnish a copy of the mandatory social insurance policy to an employee (Article 35);
- if he/she fails to pay the salary or minimum wage (Articles 104 and 111);
- if he/she fails to pay the salary in money, except in case referred to in Article 45 of this law (Article 110);
- if he/she fails to pass a programme of redundancy problem management (Article 153);
- if he/she cancels the labour contract contrary to provisions of this law (Articles 179–181 and Articles 187 and 188);
- if he/she fails to pay all outstanding salary, compensation of salary and other emoluments (Article 186);
- if he/she fails to comply with decision of a labour inspector pursuant to provisions of this Law (Article 271);
- if he/she prevents a labour inspector to conduct supervision or prevents such supervision in other ways.[499]

566. The Aliens Employment Act stipulates that a fine of RSD 800,000–1,000,000 (EUR 7,000–9,000) shall be imposed on a legal person if such, legal person:

- has hired an alien in contravention of this Act, i.e., if it has hired an alien without a work and/or residence permit;
- has failed to keep proof of eligibility for employment of an alien in the professional field in which he/she works;
- has hired an alien for jobs for which no work permit was obtained (Article 13, paragraph 2);
- has given false or forged information relevant for granting a work and/or residence permit (Article 14 paragraph 1);
- has transferred the financial burden of issuing work permits to the alien;
- has failed to register an alien to the Social Security Office, in accordance with the law or to notify to the National Employments Service if the alien has failed to begin his/her work within the prescribed time limit after the work permit for employment was issued;
- has referred an alien who has received a work permit to another employer in violation of Article 15 of the Act;

499. Article 273 of the Labour Act.

- has hired an alien in violation of provisions of Articles 17–24 of this Act related to the work permit for the 'special cases of employment';
- has given false or forged information to obtain a work permit for the 'special cases of employment' established by Articles 17–24 of this Act;
- has hired foreign pupils and students (under 26 years of age) for a period longer than the duration of employment laid down in Article 23 of this Act;
- has failed to report to competent authorities an alien who does not have permission to work;
- has given false or forged information for the application of work;
- has not submitted a request for an extension of the work permit within the prescribed time limit;
- has failed to comply with the provisions related to the cessation of the work permit.[500]

567. A fine of RSD 500,000–1,000,000 (EUR 4,200–9,000) shall be imposed on a legal person, or the organization in charge of employment services if they:

- do not allow employment and self-employment to an unemployed foreigner exercising the rights specified in Article 4 of this Act stipulating equal legal status of foreign nationals and Serbian citizens related to work;
- issue multiple types of licenses for the same time period in contravention of Article 9 of this Act;
- issue a work permit contrary to the provisions of Articles 26 and 27 of this Act related to quotas limiting the number of work permits granted to aliens;
- do not respect provisions of Articles 29–35 related to rules of procedure in issuing work permits or conduct contrary to the provisions of this Law.

A fine of RSD 20,000–150,000 for above listed offences shall be imposed on the responsible person in the organization charged with employment services.

§3. Sanctions against Workers

568. According to the Aliens Employment Act, a fine of RSD 20,000–150,000 (EUR 150–1,300) will be imposed on an alien for the misdemeanour offence if he/she:

- is employed contrary to the provisions of this Act, i.e., without appropriate residence permit (if required);
- has given false or forged information referred to in Article 11 of this Act, (related to requirements for refugee status and 'special cases of employment' and family reunification);
- is performing work for which a work permit has not been granted;

500. Article 34 of the Aliens Employment Act.

- has given false or forged information in violation of Articles 18–25 of this Act, related to the work permit for the 'special cases of employment';
- has failed to comply with the provisions of Article 34 of this Act related to cessation of validity of the work permit.[501]

501. *Ibid.*

Chapter 4. Legal Remedies and Procedural Safeguards

569. Appeals against refusals to issue a work permit and against other measures such as the cancellations of work permits and refusal of issuing a work permit to an alien and offering instead to the employer a Serbian citizen listed in the records of the NES branch, are addressed to the NES as the first instance body. Appeals are examined by the authority designated by the statute of the Republic or provincial employment service, i.e., the Director General of the NES.

570. As said before, the work permits for foreign citizens are issued by the NES. In the case of a negative decision, applicants may appeal the relevant decision within fifteen days of the delivery of such decision. The appeal against such decision should be addressed to the to the Director General of the NES within fifteen days from the day the decision was delivered, and the Director General is to decide on such an appeal within thirty days from the day the appeal was received.[502]

571. Rules on the Conditions of Realisation of Rights and Obligations of Individuals Seeking Employment (*Pravilnik o uslovima i načinu ostvarivanja prava i obaveza lica koja traže zaposlenje*) provides that in case a branch of the NES has in its records a person who is a citizen of the Republic of Serbia and who equally meets the criteria established by the employer as an alien with temporary stay, the branch may refuse the request for issuing the work permit to the alien and offer the employer the person from the record of the NES branch. Equally as for the work permit refusal, the foreign applicant in such case can appeal the decision of the NES within fifteen days period from the date he/she has received the decision. The appeal should be submitted to the body foreseen by the Statutes of the NES, which has to decide upon the complaint within thirty days.[503]

572. In the second instance, appeals are examined in administrative procedure, defined by the General Administrative Procedure Act, which means that the safeguards described under legal remedies available in the field of residence rights of aliens apply to the matter of access to labour market as well. In accordance with the General Administrative Procedure Act, the appeal to the competent Administrative Court does have a suspensive effect. On the other hand, appeal to the Supreme Court of Cassation against an Administrative Court decision does not have a suspensive effect. Possibilities of extraordinary legal remedies, which are available for the parties after the judicial decision becomes final, are available in very limited circumstances. (*See* Part VI, Chapter 1 and Chapter 4).

502. Article 26 of the Aliens Employment Act.
503. Article 48 of the Rules on the Conditions of Realisation of Rights and Obligations of Individuals Seeking Employment.

Part VIII. Access to Self-employed Activities

Chapter 1. Overview of Applicable Legislation

573. Serbian applicable legislation contains relatively poor sources on self-employment of aliens. As said before, the Conditions for Foreign Citizens Employment Act being not aligned with EU legislation, (as well as with the SAA, especially with Article 58 thereof), does not foresee possibilities of granting personal work permits for self-employment, compared to those existing in the laws in force in the European Union. As previously stated, the Conditions for Foreign Citizens Employment Act provides possibility for aliens to get the so-called business license that is a work permit issued by the Ministry of Interior contrary to the general rule that work permits are issued by the NES. The 'Business license' is issued to a foreign national or stateless person who has the status of the entrepreneur or founder for the purpose of carrying out the business or company management, and it enables them to perform other tasks.

574. On the other hand, the Aliens Employment Act which is harmonized with EU Directives regarding employment contains a definition of alien's self-employment. Self-employment of foreigners, in terms of this Act, means 'the employment of an alien in a company or other form of business, in accordance with the law, in which the alien is the sole or controlling member'.[504]

575. The Labour Act does not define the term self-employed worker, however, it prescribes that, pursuant to the law, any natural person may independently perform any business activity as an entrepreneur. The Labour Act considers self-employment as an activity performed by an individual for himself/herself outside of employment relations, which is different from business owners or and it is not applicable to entrepreneurs who conduct business activities independently or with their household members (spouse, children and parents) who can work at the shop or some other form of business entity without being employed.[505]

504. Article 2 of the Aliens Employment Act.
505. Article 203 of the Labour Act.

576. The Employment and Unemployment Insurance Act defines self-employment as an activity undertaken by a single unemployed person or an association of unemployed persons to establish a sole proprietor shop, cooperative, agricultural estate or other form of entrepreneurship, as well as the establishment of a company if the founder is employed in that company. Self-employed person, i.e., person who receives income from self-employed activity, shall be liable to pay contributions for compulsory social insurance and income tax.[506]

577. The Companies Act (*Zakon o privrednim društvima*)[507] stipulates that an entrepreneur, within the meaning of this Law, is a natural person who is registered and who performs all activities allowed by the law in the form of occupation for the purpose of gaining profit, including arts and old crafts and cottage industry activities. For registration of an entrepreneur in the Register of Entrepreneurs kept within the Register of Business Entities, it is necessary to submit a registration application form, a copy of identity card and a proof of fee payment.[508]

506. Article 51 of the Employment and Unemployment Insurance Act.
507. *Zakon o privrednim društvima*, Official Gazette of the Republic of Serbia, Nos 36/2011 and 99/2011.
508. Article 48 of the Companies Act.

Chapter 2. Condition for Entitlement to Work in the Country as Self-employed

§1. General Conditions

578. Conditions for self-employment of aliens in Serbia are regulated mostly within the same sources of law as employment of aliens in general. The Serbian legislation does not contain any differences or discriminatory provisions in respect of the rights of foreign natural and legal persons to establish companies and branches of foreign legal persons in the Republic of Serbia in comparison to the rights and obligations of Serbian natural and legal persons as founders. The only difference in the establishment of companies relates to the required proof of identity of the founders (for resident natural persons photocopies of identity cards should be enclosed, whilst for foreign natural persons photocopies of passports and for foreign legal persons an extract from the register they are registered with shall be enclosed). Accordingly, there are no specific requirements in terms of general conditions, language, and citizenship of the owner prescribed by the Companies Act, which may affect the right of establishment of self-employing companies in Serbia.

579. According to the Draft of the Aliens Employment Act, the work permit for self-employment is issued at the request of a foreigner who has a temporary residence permit in the Republic of Serbia.

580. Rules on the Conditions of Realisation of Rights and Obligations of Individuals Seeking Employment provides that 'the right to self-employment, an unemployed person may achieve if independently or associating with other unemployed persons sets up companies, cooperatives, shops, farm or other form of entrepreneurship.' Such persons may exercise the right to:

- one-time cash payment of unemployment compensation, in accordance with the law;
- subsidies for self-employment, in accordance with the Rules on the Manner and the Procedure for Exercising the Right to Subsidies for Self-employment;
- further education and training;
- support of the Business centre, according to the Law.[509]

§2. Administrative Rules and Procedures

581. A foreign national may be founder or member of the company in the Republic of Serbia and has the right to be employed in his own company. On the basis of the Registration Decision, an alien submits the application for 'business license' to the Border Police Directorate in the Ministry of Interior of the Republic

509. *Pravilnik o načinu i postupku za ostvarivanje prava na subvenciju za samozapošljavanje*, Official Gazette of the Republic of Serbia, No. 7/2004.

of Serbia. That document is issued to a foreign national or stateless person who has the status of the entrepreneur or founder for the purpose of carrying out, carrying out the business or company management and it enables them to perform other tasks. This means that foreign nationals, as well as stateless persons who are entrepreneurs, founders or company members, do not get work permits in the NES; they get a 'business license' in the Ministry of Interior of the Republic of Serbia

582. For registration of an entrepreneurial workshop, a foreign national should submit: registration application form, a copy of the travel document (passport), the certificate of notification of the alien's stay in the Republic of Serbia and the prescribed fee. After registering the entrepreneurial workshop, a foreign national shall submit the request for granting temporary residence to the competent authority in the Republic of Serbia, unless he/she has already been granted a temporary stay on some other basis, or if he/she has permission for permanent residence in the Republic of Serbia.

583. According to the Aliens Employment Act, in the procedure of issuing work permits for self-employment, with the application, an alien should also enclose:

- A statement of the type, duration and scope of working/business activities he/she is planning to deal with.
- Evidence that he/she has the appropriate qualifications to perform planned activities.
- Pre-contract or agreement evidencing ownership or lease of office space in which it is planned to perform activities.
- Evidence that he/she possesses appropriate equipment for planned activities.
- A statement of the number and structure of people who they plan to hire, especially citizens of Serbia, people who have free access to the labour market and foreigners with a personal work permit.

584. The work permit for self-employment is issued for a period equal to the one for which the temporary residence permit had been issued, with the maximum of one year with the possibility of extension, provided that the alien prove that he/she continues to perform the same work under the conditions under which the permit was issued. An alien who receives a work permit for self-employment is obliged to begin conducting activities within ninety days upon of obtaining the license.[510]

510. Article 23 of the Aliens Employment Act.

Chapter 3. Sanctions against Illegal Exercise of Self-employment

585. Sanctions against illegal self-employment are mostly the same which are applicable to violation of law on employment of aliens in general.

586. Explicit sanctions against self-employed aliens one can find in the Aliens Employment Act which prescribes a fine of RSD 50,000–500,000 (EUR 400–4,000) for a violation of provisions of this Act related to the work without prior solving the residence status and/or obtaining the work permit (if applicable). The Labour Act imposes a fine of RSD 20,000–150,000 (EUR 150–1,300) for a self-employed person if such person violates prohibition of discrimination pursuant to the Labour Act (Articles 18–21).

587. A protective measure of prohibition to pursue business may be pronounced to an alien (as well as to the Serbian citizen) if by violating prohibition of discrimination provisions of the Labour Act he/she inflicts material damage to an employee or other natural person. Such measure is not necessarily accompanied by cancellation of the residence or work permit. The mentioned offences are related to:

- Article 18 of the Labour Act (prohibition of both direct and indirect discriminations against persons seeking employment and employees in respect to their sex, origin, language, race, colour of skin, age, pregnancy, health status or disability, nationality, religion, marital status, familial commitments, sexual orientation, political or other belief, social background, financial status, membership in political organizations, trade unions or any other personal quality.
- Article 19 of the Labour Act (prohibition of direct discrimination that puts a person seeking employment or employee in a less favourable situation than other persons in the same or similar situation, as well as prohibition of indirect discrimination which, pursuant to this Act, is recognized, in case an apparently neutral provision, criterion or practice puts or would put a person seeking employment or employee in a less favourable situation than other persons, due to a certain quality, status, belief or position of such person).
- Article 20 of the Labour Act (prohibition of discrimination in relation to: employment conditions and selection of candidates for a certain job; working conditions and all rights resulting from the labour relationship; education, training and advanced training; promotion at work; termination of the labour contract.
- Article 21 of the Labour Act (prohibition of harassment, i.e., violation of dignity of a person seeking employment or employee, causing fear or breeding adverse, humiliating or insulting environment and sexual harassment which, pursuant to this Act, is any verbal, non-verbal or physical behaviour aimed at or representing violation of dignity of a person seeking employment or employee in the area of sexual life, causing fear or breeding adverse, humiliating or insulting environment.[511]

511. Articles 18–21 of the Labour Act.

Chapter 4. Legal Remedies and Procedural Safeguards

588. There are no specific legal remedies and procedural safeguards relating to the legal status of self-employed aliens that are different for those regarding employment of aliens in general. (*See* Part V, Chapters 1–4 and Part VII).

Selected Bibliography

§1. Books and Articles

Albert, M. *Prima Facie Determination of Refugee Status: An Overview and Its Legal Foundation*. Working Paper Series No. 55, Refugee Studies Centre, Oxford Department of International Development, University of Oxford, 2010.

Azarov, Y. *From the History of Russian Belgrade*. 28 December 2009, available at: http://russkiymir.ru/en/publications/139488/ (accessed 7 August 2016).

Bakonyi, A. et al. *Serbia as a Safe Third Country: A Wrong Presumption, Report based on the Hungarian Helsinki Committee's field mission to Serbia* (2011).

Bondarev, N. *Russia and Russians in Serbian History*. Part 3, 20 July 2009, available at: http://russkiymir.ru/en/publications/139497/ (accessed 7 August 2016).

Cucić, V. *Administrative Appeal In Serbian Law*. Transylvanian Review of Administrative Sciences, No. 32 E, Cluj-Napoca (2011).

Dimitrijević, D. *Regulisanje državljanstva na prostoru bivše SFR Jugoslavije*. Medjunarodni problemi, Vol. LX, No. 2-3, Belgrade (2008).

Dragojlović, D. 'Migrations of the Serbs in the Middle Ages'. In *Migrations in Balkan History*, edited by Ivan Ninić. Serbian Academy of Sciences and Arts, 1989.

Fine, J.V.A. *The Late Medieval Balkans: A Critical Survey from the Late Twelfth Century to the Ottoman Conquest*. U. Michigan Press, 1994.

Gaćeša, N. *Agrarna refarma i kalonizacija u Jugoslaviji 1945–1948* (Agrarian Reform and Colonization in Yugoslavia 1945–1948. Matica Srpska, Novi Sad 1984).

Gillade, K. *Readmission Agreements Concluded by the EU*. Masterproef van de opleiding 'Master in de rechten', Universiteit Gent, Academiejaar 2010–2011, Gent, 2011.

Gligorov, V., Ognjenović, K. & H. Vidovic. *Assessment of the Labour Market in Serbia*. Research Reports 371, The Vienna Institute for International Economic Studies May 2011.

Grečić, V., Vida Bakondy 'Changing the Strategies: Current Migration Policy and Discourses in Serbia'. In *Good Luck! Migration Today*, Vienna, Belgrade, Zagreb, Istanbul, The Initiative Minderheiten, in Vienna: Cooperation with Academy of Fine Arts Vienna, 2010, 160–170.

Grečić, V. 'Managing Population Movements: The Challenge for Diplomacy in Southeast Europe', *Whitehead Journal of Diplomacy and International* Relations 9 (2010): 127–143.

Selected Bibliography

Grečić, V. *La communaute emigree serbe aux Etats-Unis*, in: *Une communaute dans un contexte de guerre: la serbe en Occident*. 179–199, Chapitre 6, L' Harmattan, Paris (2003).

Grečić, V. *Eine grenzuberschreitende Liebe zur Heimat. Die Geschichte der weltweiten serbischen Migration*. in: *Als Serbe warst du plotzlich nichts mehr wert, Serben und Serbinnen in der Schweiz*, 173–182. Dejan Mikić & Erika Sommer (eds), Orell Fussli Verlag (2003).

Grečić, V. *Former Yugoslavia*. In *The Politics of East-West Migration*, edited by Ardittis, S. Solon Macmillan Press & Martin's Press, 1994.

Grečić, V., Russell King (ed.) *Mass Migration from Former Eastern Europe and the USSR: A Challenge for the 'West'?*. In *The Geography of New European Migrations*. Belhaven, 1993.

Grečić, V. 'Economic Impact of Expatriates and Migrants on the Sending Countries: Case-study of Serbia'. *Südosteuropa* 57, H.4 (2009): 452–471.

Group 484. *Challenges of Forced Migration in Serbia, A Second Look at the Issue of Asylum and Readmission*. Group 484, 2013.

Group 484. *Underage Asylum-seekers in Serbia: At the Verge of Dignity*. 2011.

Huddleston, T. (Migration Policy Group). *Serbia: A MIPEX Assessment*. Grupa 484, Belgrade, December 2012.

Kogovšek Šalamon, N. *Slovenia*. Migration Law. Suppl. 2 Wolters Kluwer Law & Business, 2011.

Kostić, M. & A. Mihajlović. *Counteracting and Preventing Human Trafficking in the Republic of Serbia*. Facta Universitatis, Series: Law and Politics Vol. 10, No. 2, Nis, 2012.

Krstić, I. *Protecting the Rights of Migrants in the Republic of Serbia*. Belgrade: Organization for Migration – Mission to Serbia, Belgrade, 2012.

Manke, M. *Towards Developing a Policy on Labour Migration in the Republic of Serbia*. A White Paper, International Organization for Migration, Belgrade, December 2010.

Minić, J. et al. *A Joint European Vision: Free Movement for Goods and People in Kosovo and Serbia, Policy Paper, European Movement in Serbia Belgrade and Kosovar Institute for Policy Research and Development* Priština. 2005.

Norwegian Refugee Council (NRC). *Serbia: Integration Stalled*. The Internal Displacement Monitoring Centre, 2013.

Pavlov, T. 'Towards New Policy of Employment of Foreigners in Serbia, Mutual Learning Programme'. Peer Review on *Renewed Procedures for Employing Migrant Workers with the Emphasis on Favouring Highly-Qualified Labour*, 10, A paper submitted by GHK in consortium with CERGE-EI, Estonia, 11–12 June 2009.

Pavlowitch, Stevan K. *Serbia: The History Behind the Name*. C. Hurst & Co. Publishers, 2002.

Pejin-Stokić, Lj. & V. Grečić. *Social Impact of Emigration and Rural-Urban Migration in Central and Eastern Europe*. Final Country Report – Serbia, Brussels: The European Commission, DG Employment, Social Affairs and Inclusion and GVG, 2012,. available at: http://ec.europa.eu/social/BlobServlet?docId=8824&langId=en.

Protić, M. St. Migrations Resulting from Peasant Upheavals in Serbia During the 19th Century. In *Migrations in Balkan History,* edited by Ivan Ninić. Serbian Academy of Sciences and Arts, 1989.

Rakić, D. (ed.). *Challenges of Forced Migration in Serbia: Position of Refugees, Internally Displased Persons, Returnees and Asylum Seekers.* 11, Group 484, 2011.

Samardžić, R. *Migrations in Serbian History.* In *Migrations in Balkan History,* edited by Ivan Ninić. Belgrade: Serbian Academy of Sciences and Arts, 1989.

Todić, D. *Izbeglice iz Hrvatske i Slovenije u Jugoslaviji (Refugees from Croatia and Slovenia in Yugoslavia).* 18–24, 4/92, Forum - čovek i pravo, Beograd (1992).

Todić, D. *Neke karakteristike jugoslovenskog zakonodavstva o izbeglicama u svetlu odredaba međunarodnog prava o izbeglicama* (*Some characteristics of the Yugoslav legislation on refugees in the light of the international refugee law*) 83–93, 1-2/93, Jugoslovenska revija za međunarodno pravo, Beograd (1993).

Todić, D. *Zakon o izbeglicama Republike Srbije u svetlosti odredaba o izbeglicama sadržanim u saveznom zakonodavstvu i međunarodnim instrumentima* (Law on Refugees of the Republic of Serbia in the light of provisions contained in the federal legislation and international law), 131–151, 1/93, Arhiv za pravne i društvene nauke, Beograd (1993).

Todić, D. *Non-refoulement kao princip međunarodnog prava* (*Non-refoulement as a principle of international law*), 196–169, 1/96, Jugoslovenska revija za međunarodno pravo, Beograd (1996).

Tylec, E. *Serbian Asylum System in the Wake of EU Accession – Challenges and Opportunities*. Belgrade: Belgrade Centre for Human Rights, 2013.

Vekarić, V. *Uporedna analiza nadležnosti, organizacije i izbora sudija vrhovnih i kasacionih sudova u odabranim evropskim zemljama (Comparative Analysis* of *Supreme Courts Competences, Organization and Judges Selection in Selected European Countries*), UNDP, Belgrade: Ministry of Justice of Serbia, 2007.

Vučetić, D. *Serbian Judicial Review of Administrative Acts and European Standards for Administrative Disputes.* Facta Universitatis, Series Law and Politics, Vol. 3, No. Nis (2005).

§2. National Legislation

Act Amending the Citizenship Act of the Republic of Serbia (*Zakon o izmenama i dopunama Zakona o državljanstvu Republike Srbije*), Official Gazette of the Republic of Serbia, No. 90/2007.

Act Amending the Conditions for Foreign Citizens Employment Act (*Zakon o izmenama i dopunama Zakona o uslovima za zasnivanje radnog odnosa sa stranim drzavljanima*), Official Gazette of the Federal Republic of Yugoslavia, No. 42/1992.

Act Amending the Refugees Act (*Zakon o izmeni i dopuni Zakona o izbeglicama*), Official Gazette of the Republic of Serbia, No. 45/2002.

Foundations of the Education System Act (*Zakon o osnovama sistema obrazovanja i vaspitanja*), Official Gazette of the Republic of Serbia, No. 72/2009.

Selected Bibliography

Administrative Disputes Act (*Zakon o upravnim sporovima*), Official Gazette of the Federal Republic of Yugoslavia, No. 46/96.

Administrative Taxes Act (*Zakon o administrativnim taksama*), Official Gazette the Republic of Serbia, No. 70/2011.

Aliens Act (*Zakon o strancima*), Official Gazette of the Republic of Serbia,No. 97/2008.

Asylum Act (*Zakon o azilu*), Official Gazette of the Republic of Serbia, No. 109/ 2007.

Asylum Act (FRY) (*Zakon o azilu*), Official gazette of the Serbia and Montenegro, No. 12/2005.

Citizenship Act of the Republic of Serbia (*Zakon o državljanstvu Republike Srbije*), Official Gazette of the Republic of Serbia, No. 135/2004.

Civil Procedure Code (*Zakon o gradjanskom postupku*), Official Gazette of the Republic of Serbia, No. 72/2011.

Conditions for Foreign Citizens Employment Act (*Zakon o uslovima za zasnivanje radnog odnosa sa stranim drzavljanima*), Official Journal of the Socialist Federal Republic of Yugoslavia, No. 11/1978.

Constitution of the Republic of Serbia (*Ustav Republike Srbije*), Official Gazette of the Republic of Serbia, No. 98/2006.

Criminal Code of the Republic of Serbia (*Krivični Zakonik Republike Srbije*), Official Gazette of the Republic of Serbia, No. 85/2005.

Criminal Procedure Code (*Zakonik o krivičnom postupku*), Official Gazette of the Republic of Serbia, No. 46/2006.

Crossing the State Border and Movement in the Border Area Act (*Zakon o prelaženju državne granice i kretanju u graničnom pojasu*), Official Journal of the Socialist Federal Republic of Yugoslavia, No. 34/1979.

Decree on Control of Border Crossing the Administrative Line to the Autonomous Province of Kosovo and Metohija (*Uredba o kontroli prelaska administrativne linije prema Autonomnoj pokrajini Kosovo i Metohija*), Official Gazette of the Republic of Serbia, No. 98/2011.

Decree on Establishing a List of Safe Countries of Origin and Safe Third Countries (*Odluka o utvrdjivanju liste sigurnih zemalja porekla i sigurnih trećih država*), Official Gazette of the Republic of Serbia, No. 67/2009.

Decree on More Specific Conditions and Procedure for Issuing Visas at the Border Crossing Point (*Uredba o bližim uslovima i načinu izdavanja vize na graničnom prelazu*), Official Gazette of the Republic of Serbia, No. 59/2009.

Decree on More Specific Conditions and Procedure for Issuing Visas at the Border Crossing Point (*Uredba o bližim uslovima i načinu izdavanja vize na graničnom prelazu*), Official Gazette of the Republic of Serbia, No. 59/2009.

Decree on More Specific Conditions for Refusal of Entry of Foreigners into the Republic of Serbia (*Uredba o bližim uslovima za odbijanje ulaska stranca u Republiku Srbiju*), Official Gazette of the Republic of Serbia, No. 75/2009.

Diaspora and Serbs of the Region Act (*Zakon o dijaspori i Srbima u regionu*), Official Gazette of the Republic of Serbia, No. 88/2009.

Discrimination Prohibition Act (*Zakon o zabrani diskriminacije*), Official Gazette of the Republic of Serbia, No. 22/2009.

Employment and Insurance Against Unemployment Act (*Zakon o zapošljavanju i osiguranju za slučaj nezaposlenosti*), Official Gazette of the Republic of Serbia, No. 36/2009.

Family Act (*Porodični zakon*), Official Gazette of the Republic of Serbia, No. 18/ 2005.

Financial Support to Families with Children Act (*Zakon o finansijskoj podršci porodici sa decom*), Official Gazette of the Republic of Serbia, No. 16/2002.

General Administrative Procedure Act (*Zakon o opštem upravnom postupku)*, Official Gazette of the Republic of Serbia, No. 111/2009.

Health Insurance Act *(Zakon o zdravstvenom osiguranju)*, Official Gazette of the Republic of Serbia, No. 107/2005.

Instruction on the Conditions for Granting Temporary Residence to Foreign Nationals Victims of Human Trafficking (*Uputstvo o proceduri odobrenja privremenog boravka stranim državljanima žrtvama trgovine ljudima*) Ministry of Interior, No. 03/1 br. 26-1658/04, 20 September, 2004.

Migration Management Act (*Zakon o upravljanju migracijama)*, Official Gazette of the Republic of Serbia, No. 107/2012.

Misdemeanour Act (*Zakon o prekršajima*), Official Gazette of Republic of Serbia, No. 101/05.

Movement and Stay of Foreigners Act (*Zakon o kretanju i boravistu stranaca*), Official Journal of the Socialist Federal Republic of Yugoslavia, No. 56/1980.

Ombudsman Act (*Zakon o zaštitniku gradjana)*, Official Gazette of the Republic of Serbia, No. 79/2005.

Permanent and Temporary Residence of Citizens Act (*Zakon o prebivalištu i boravištu gradjana),* Official Gazette of the Socialist Republic of Serbia, No. 42/ 1977.

Permanent and Temporary Residence of Citizens Act (*Zakon o prebivalištu i boravištu gradjana)*, Official Gazette of the Republic of Serbia No. 87/2011.

Police Act (*Zakon o policiji)*, Official Gazette of the Republic of Serbia, No. 101/ 2005.

Protection of the State Border Act (*Zakon o zastiti državne granice)*, Official Gazette of the Republic of Serbia, No. 97/2008.

Refugees Act (*Zakon o izbeglicama)*, Official Gazette of the Republic of Serbia, No. 18/1992.

Rules on Conditions for Accommodation and Provision of Basic Living Conditions in the Asylum Centre (*Pravilnik o uslovima smeštaja i obezbedjivanju osnovnih životnih uslova u Centru za azil*), Official Gazette of the Republic of Serbia, No. 31/2008.

Rules on More Specific Conditions, Request Form and Manner of Extending the Visa Validity Period (*Pravilnik o bližim uslovima, obrascu zahteva i načinu produžavanja roka važenja vize*), Official Gazette of the Republic of Serbia, No. 59/2009.

Rules on the Manner of Registering the Domicile, Residence and Change of Address and Deregistration of Foreigner from their Residence (*Pravilnik o načinu prijavljivanja boravišta, prebivališta i promene adrese i odjave prebivališta stranca*), Official Gazette of the Republic of Serbia, No. 59/2009.

Rules on Visas (*Pravilnik o vizama*), Official Gazette of the Republic of Serbia, No. 27/2010.

Rules on Medical Examinations of Asylum Seekers during the Admission to the Asylum Centre (*Pravilnik o lekarskim pregledima trazilaca azila za vreme boravka u Centru za azil*), Official Gazette of the Republic of Serbia, No. 93/2008.

Rules on Meeting the Requirements for Permitting the Temporary Residence to Foreigner for the Purpose of Family Reunification (*Pravilnik o ispunjenosti uslova za odobravanje privremenog boravka stranca radi spajanja porodice*), Official Gazette of the Republic of Serbia, No. 59/2009.

Rules on the Manner and the Procedure for Exercising the Right to Subsidies for Self-employment (*Pravilnik o načinu i postupku za ostvarivanje prava na subvenciju za samozapošljavanje*), Official Gazette of the Republic of Serbia, No. 7/2004.

Rules on Meeting the Requirements for Permitting the Temporary Residence to Foreigner for the Purpose of School Education, Studying or Specialisation, Scientific and Research Work, Practical Training, Participation in International Exchange Programmes for School and University Students and/or Other Scientific and Education Activities (*Pravilnik o ispunjenosti uslova za odobravanje privremenog boravka stranca radi školovanja, studiranja ili specijalizacije, naučno-istraživačkog rada, praktične obuke, učestvovanja u programima međunarodne razmene učenika ili studenata, odnosno drugim naučno-obrazovnim aktivnostima*), Official Gazette of the Republic of Serbia, No. 59/2009.

Rules on the Requirements for Aliens Temporary Residence Permit Regarding the Health Insurance (*Pravilnik o ispunjenosti uslova za odobrenje privremenog boravka stranca u pogledu zdravstvenog osiguranja*), Official Gazette of the Republic of Serbia, No. 59/2009.

Rules on Social Assistance for Asylum Seekers or Persons Who Have Been Granted Asylum (*Pravilnik o socijalnoj pomoći traziocima azila i osobama kojima je odobren azil*), Official Gazette of the Republic of Serbia, No. 44/2008.

Rules on the Manner of Entering the Compulsory Residence into the Travel Document and the Layout of Form of the Temporary Identity Card (*Pravilnik o načinu unošenja obaveznog boravka u putnu ispravu i izgledu obrasca privremene lične karte*), Official Gazette of the Republic of Serbia, No. 66/2009.

Rules on the Manner of Record Keeping and Contents of Registry of Persons Accommodated at the Asylum Centre (*Pravilnik o načinu vođenja i sadržini evidencija o licima smeštenim u Centru za azil*), Official Gazette of the Republic of Serbia, No. 31/2008.

Social Protection Act (*Zakon o socijalnoj zaštiti*), Official Gazette of the Republic of Serbia, No. 24/2011.

Travel Documents Act (*Zakon o putnim ispravama*), Official Gazette of the Republic of Serbia, No. 90/2007.

Travel Documents of Yugoslav Citizens Act (*Zakon o putnim ispravama jugoslovenskih državljana)*, Official Gazette of the Republic of Serbia, No. 18/92.

Yugoslav Citizenship Act (*Zakon o jugoslovenskom državljanstvu*), Official Gazette of the Federal Republic of Yugoslavia, No. 33/1996.

§3. EU LAW

Council Directive 2004/114/EC of 13 December 2004 on The Conditions of Admission of Third-Country Nationals for the Purposes of Studies, Pupil Exchange, Unremunerated Training or Voluntary Service, Official Journal of the European Union L 375 of 23.12.2004.

Council Directive 2005/71/EC of 12 October 2005 on A Specific Procedure for Admitting Third-Country Nationals for the Purposes of Scientific Research, Official Journal of the European Union L 289/15 of 3.11.2005.

Council Directive 2001/55/EC of 20 July 2001 on Minimum Standards for Giving Temporary Protection in the Event of a Mass Influx of Displaced Persons and on Measures Promoting a Balance of Efforts between Member States in Receiving Such Persons and Bearing the Consequences Thereof, Official Journal of the European Communities L 212/12 of 7.8.2001.

Council Directive 2004/83/EC of 29 April 2004 on Minimum Standards for the Qualification and Status of Third Country Nationals or Stateless Persons as Refugees or as Persons Who Otherwise Need International Protection and the Content of the Protection Granted, Official Journal of the European Union L 304/12 of 30.9.2004.

Council Directive 2009/50/EC of 25 May 2009 on The Conditions of Entry and Residence of Third-Country Nationals for the Purposes of Highly Qualified Employment, Official Journal of the European Union L 155/17.

Council Regulation (EC) No. 539/2001 of 15 March 2001 Listing the Third Countries Whose Nationals Must Be in Possession of Visas when Crossing the External Borders and Those Whose Nationals Are Exempt from That Requirement, Official Journal of the European Communities L 81/1, Brussels, of 21.3.2001.

Council Regulation (EC) No. 1244/2009 of 30 November 2009 Amending Regulation (EC) No. 539/2001 Listing the Third Countries Whose Nationals Must Be in Possession of Visas when Crossing the External Borders and Those Whose Nationals Are Exempt from That Requirement, Official Journal of the European Communities L 336 18.12.2009.

Council of Europe Convention on the Recognition of Qualifications concerning Higher Education in the European Region, CETS No. 165, Lisbon, 11.4.1997.

Directive 2011/95/EU of the European Parliament and of the Council on Standards for the Qualification of Third-Country Nationals or Stateless Persons as Beneficiaries of International Protection, for a Uniform Status for Refugees or for Persons Eligible for Subsidiary Protection, and for the Content of the Protection Granted of 13 December 2011, Official Journal of the European Union L 337/9 of 20.12.2011.

Directive 2008/115/EC of the European Parliament and of the Council of 16 December 2008 on Common Standards and Procedures in Member States for Returning Illegally Staying Third-Country Nationals [2008], Official Journal of the European Union, L 348/98 (Return Directive).

Guidelines for Integrated Border Management in the Western Balkans, Updated Version, January 2007, Document of the European Commission (EC).

Responses of the Government of Serbia to the EU Questionnaire, Belgrade, 12.9.2012.

Serbia 2013 Progress Report, Commission Staff Working Document SWD(2013) 412 final in: Enlargement Strategy and Main Challenges 2013–2014, Communication from the Commission to the European Parliament and the Council COM (2013) 700 final, Brussels, 16.10.2013.

§4. Case Law

Federal Constitutional Court of the Federal Republic of Yugoslavia, Decision No. I.U.253/2002 of 29 June 2002.

Constitutional Court of the Republic of Serbia, Decision No. I.Uo-812/2012 of 24 April 2013.

§5. Reports

Administrative Records on Work Permits Issued to Foreigners and Foreigners Registered as Unemployed. National Employment Service. Ministry of Economy and Regional Development. Unpublished Paper, Belgrade (2010).

Belgrade Centre for Human Rights (BCHR), *Asylum in Republic of Serbia: Report for the Period January–June 2013*, Belgrade (2013).

Belgrade Centre for Human Rights (BCHR), *Right to Asylum in the Republic of Serbia 2012*, Belgrade (2013).

Belgrade Centre for Human Rights (BCHR), *Status of Asylum Seekers in Serbia*, Belgrade (2012).

European Commission, Commission Staff Working Document: *Serbia 2013 Progress Report* (Accompanying the document, Communication From the Commission to the European Parliament and the Council), *Enlargement Strategy and Main Challenges 2013–2014*, SWD(2013) 412 final COM(2013) 700 final, Brussels (2013).

Statistical Office of the Republic of Serbia (RSO), various documents, available at: http://media.popis2011.stat.rs/2013/publikacije/Saopstenje29novembarKnjiga1_engl.pdf (accessed on 12 November 2013).

United Nations High Commissioner for Refugees (UNHCR), *Serbia As A Country Of Asylum, Observations on the Situation of Asylum-Seekers and Beneficiaries of International Protection in Serbia*, UNHCR, Belgrade (2012).

Vlada Republike Srbije, *Migracioni profil Republike Srbije za 2012.godinu* (*Government of the Republic of Serbia, Migration Profile of the Republic of Serbia for 2012*), Belgrade (2013).

Vlada Republike Srbije, *Migracioni profil Republike Srbije za 2010.godinu* (*Government of the Republic of Serbia, Migration Profile of the Republic of Serbia for 2010)*, Belgrade (2011).

Index

The numbers here refer to paragraph numbers.

Index

Index

Index

Made in the USA
Monee, IL
18 October 2026

66037574R10129